Divine Grace and Emerging Creation

Divine Grace and Emerging Creation

Wesleyan Forays in Science and Theology of Creation

EDITED BY

THOMAS JAY OORD

PICKWICK *Publications* · Eugene, Oregon

DIVINE GRACE AND EMERGING CREATION
Wesleyan Forays in Science and Theology of Creation

Copyright © 2009 Wipf and Stock Publishers. All rights reserved. Except for brief quotations in critical publications or reviews, no part of this book may be reproduced in any manner without prior written permission from the publisher. Write: Permissions, Wipf and Stock Publishers, 199 W. 8th Ave., Suite 3, Eugene, OR 97401.

Pickwick Publications
A Division of Wipf and Stock Publishers
199 W. 8th Ave., Suite 3
Eugene, OR 97401

www.wipfandstock.com

ISBN 13: 978-1-60608-287-4

Cataloging-in-Publication data:

Divine grace and emerging creation : Wesleyan forays into science and theology of creation / edited by Thomas Jay Oord.

xiv + 230 p. ; 23 cm. —Includes index.

ISBN 13: 978-1-60608-287-4

1. Wesley, John, 1703–1791—Theology. 2. Christianity and Science. I. Oord, Thomas Jay. II. Title.

BL241 .D57 2009

Manufactured in the U.S.A.

To Randy L. Maddox

Contents

Introduction
Introducing Wesleyan Theology and Science
Thomas Jay Oord | ix

1 **John Wesley's Precedent for Theological Engagement with the Natural Sciences**
Randy L. Maddox | 1

2 **John Wesley's Vision of Science in the Service of Christ**
John W. Haas Jr. | 37

3 **Degrees of Certainty in John Wesley's Natural Philosophy**
Laura Bartels Felleman | 58

4 **Mystery and Humility in John Wesley's Narrative Ecology**
Marc Otto and Michael Lodahl | 81

5 **Sighs, Signs, and Significance: Natural Science and a Hermeneutics of Nature**
Jürgen Moltmann | 106

6 **The Consonance of Wesleyan Theology and Modern Science**
Timothy Crutcher | 122

7 **How the Discoveries of Science and Archaeology Shift Interpretations of Genesis**
Robert D. Branson | 138

8 **Rooting Evolution in Grace**
Rebecca J. Flietstra | 156

9 **On Giving Intelligent Design Theorists What They Say They Want**
   W. Christopher Stewart | 170

10 **Attachment, Spiritual Formation, and Wesleyan Communities**
   Sarah DeBoard Marion and Warren S. Brown | 198

Contributors | 213

Index | 215

Introduction

Introducing Wesleyan Theology and Science

Thomas Jay Oord

John Wesley was a theologian deeply interested in science. He kept abreast of the scientific developments of his day by reading the works of leading scientists and philosophers. He often reprinted scientific work in an edited version and strongly recommended that his pastors learn the theories of science. Scientific theories, research, and methods influenced the way John Wesley thought about God, creatures, and the world. Science shaped his understanding of ethics, epistemology, ecclesiology, ecology, and aesthetics.

Developments in science after Wesley's death have played an important role for why Wesley's theology is less influential today that it otherwise might be. Wesley knew little or nothing about the theory of evolution, for instance, and evolutionary theory plays a significant role in a variety of scientific disciplines today. Science of mind, cosmology, and the social sciences are significantly different today than in Wesley's time.

In some instances, however, scientists and philosophers of science are returning to the questions and answers of Wesley's day.[1] The view of logical positivism—that truth must be logically necessary or empirically

---

1. A strong argument for the relevance of Wesley's theology for understanding science, ecology, and the God-creature relationship is Michael Lodahl, *God of Nature and of Grace: Reading the World in A Wesleyan Way* (Nashville: Kingswood, 2004).

verified by our five senses—has been largely discredited as a comprehensive epistemology for science. The view that science can provide indubitable evidence for sure and certain statements about the world is now largely discredited. Scientists are returning to the more humble approach of considering science a means for discovering partial truths. This more tentative orientation returns to the view that science relies fundamentally on inductive and hypothesis-based methods. Scientists today—especially in the social sciences and those proposing metaphysical schemes—are more likely to appeal to creaturely freedom, values, and even love as important factors for scientific explanations.[2]

These developments in contemporary science mean that Wesley's approach to science can be an important resource again. In fact, some today believe that Wesley's reflections on nature, science, and theology and the ongoing reflection in Wesleyan communities provide important grounds for exploring and making progress in answering the biggest questions we now face.[3] Many essays in this book support this view.

One of the more important contributions of the Wesleyan tradition is its emphasis upon the synergy of human and divine action. This synergism suggests that both divine and creaturely action contributes

---

2. My own interest has especially emphasized the importance of science, theology, and love. See Thomas Jay Oord, *A Turn to Love: The Love, Science, and Theology Symbiosis* (Grand Rapids, MI: Brazos, 2009) and *Science of Love: The Wisdom of Well-Being* (Philadelphia: Templeton, 2004).

3. Although significant diversity exists within the Wesleyan tradition today, the following are some of its orienting theological beliefs: 1) God's primary attribute is love, or as Charles Wesley put it in a hymn: "God's name and nature is love"; 2) God is triune: the loving Father has been revealed in Jesus Christ through the power of the Holy Spirit; 3) God acts first in any particular moment to offer salvation, and humans freely respond to God; this notion is today called "prevenient grace"; 4) Jesus' life, death, and resurrection make possible a fruitful relationship with God; 5) God does not predestine some to heaven and others to hell: All have the opportunity to experience eternal life; 6) Christians should consult the Bible, Christian tradition, reason, and contemporary experience when thinking and acting (i.e., the Wesleyan quadrilateral); 7) Scripture's primary purpose is to teach the way of salvation: one may or may not affirm its statements about scientific, historical, or cultural matters; 8) the Church and its practices are crucial to Christian understanding, living, and compassion toward others and self; 9) spiritual transformation begins in this life: Christians are not merely waiting for joy and happiness in the afterlife; 10) personal religious experience, not merely rational consent to cardinal doctrines, characterizes flourishing Christians; 11) Christians are sanctified as they love God, others, and themselves; 12) God values and seeks to redeem all creation, not just humans; 13) everything that exists reflects, to some degree, the glory of God.

to the fullest truth about existence. Divine-creature synergism suggests that both the creatures and the Creator play a role in the epistemological and ontological questions pursued in science-and-theology research.

Wesleyans typically call the divine aspect of this relation "prevenient grace." This grace is God's loving, empowering, inspiring, and freedom-giving presence provided to creatures. Creatures rely upon God's initiating action, in each moment, for creaturely existence and self-determination. The Wesleyan view of prevenient grace fits well with a variety of kenosis theories, and some scholars in the science-and-theology discussion find a kenotic model especially helpful for their research.[4]

The creaturely side of the Creator-creature relation emphasizes the genuine life and response of creatures to God. To argue that creatures have a genuine causal role in the coming to be of existence provides grounds for affirming scientific pursuit of truth. This dual emphasis upon both divine and creaturely action in each moment of existence provides a means to overcome what Wesleyan and distinguished theoretical chemist, Charles Coulson, called the "God of the gaps" problem. There are no events or things that can be fully explained by natural causes alone, because every event or thing exists because of divine and creaturely causal action.

A second Wesleyan contribution to methodological questions of science-and-theology research is especially relevant for discussions of creation in Christian communities. This contribution is the typical Wesleyan view that the purpose and function of the Bible is soteriological. Although Wesleyans consider scripture to be supremely authoritative, such authority is limited to matters of salvation. Most Wesleyans do not consider the Bible authoritative on scientific matters. "The Scriptures were never intended to instruct us in philosophy, or astronomy," Wesley says on this matter, "and therefore, on those subjects, expressions are not always to be taken in the literal sense."[5] Wesley

---

4. See, for instance, the collection of essays in John Polkinghorne, ed., *The Work of Love: Creation as Kenosis* (Grand Rapids, MI: Eerdmans, 2001); Philip Clayton, *Adventures in the Spirit: God, World, Divine Action* (Minneapolis: Fortress, 2008); and Nancey Murphy and George Ellis, *On the Moral Nature of the Universe: Theology Cosmology and Ethics* (Minneapolis: Fortress, 1996).

5. John Wesley, *A Survey of the Wisdom of God in Creation: A Compendium of Natural Philosophy*, 4th ed. (London: J. Paramore Upper-Moorfields, 1784).

would likely have agreed with the classic line in Roman Catholicism: "The Bible tells us how to go to heaven, not how the heavens go." And he would likely have approved of my own biologically-oriented suggestion that the Bible tells us how to find abundant life, not the details of how life became abundant.

The essays in this book can be roughly divided into three sections, although the conceptual overlap among the essays is substantial enough that this delineation is very rough. Randy L. Maddox offers the initial essay. Maddox provides a wide-ranging examination of Wesley's thought on science, and he offers suggestions for how contemporary science-and-theology research might benefit from Wesleyan insights. John W. Haas, Jr. follows with an essay exploring some of the same issues, but Haas's background as professor of chemistry influences how he frames those issues. Laura Bartels Felleman offers a historical essay that focuses upon Wesley's understanding of reason and knowledge for science and theology in comparison to others in his day. Marc Otto and Michael Lodahl explore Wesley's work, *A Survey of the Wisdom of God in Creation*, with the purpose of offering insights into how Wesley understood the God-world relationship.

The more methodologically-oriented essays in the book include Jürgen Moltmann's essay on natural science and the hermeneutics of nature. Although not a Wesleyan theologian in name, Moltmann's theology is consonant with contemporary Wesleyan theology. Many Wesleyan scholars have drawn upon Moltmann for their own constructive work. Timothy Crutcher argues in his contribution that contemporary scientific method and Wesleyan theological method are very similar. Both allow for empirical experience to challenge (or not) our construals of reality, but both also demand some *a priori* construal to function at all. Robert D. Branson addresses the important issues of biblical interpretation in light of contemporary science. Branson emphasizes the point mentioned earlier that Wesleyans see the Bible—especially the opening chapters of Genesis—as helpful for theology and less helpful if regarded as scientific statements.

The final section of this book addresses contemporary scientific issues and concerns more directly than most essays in the previous sections. Rebecca J. Flietstra suggests that theory of evolution is actually good news—not bad news—for Wesleyan theologians who seek to root nature in God's grace. She sees evolution as an opportunity for constructive theology. W. Christopher Stewart addresses the important discussion of Intelligent Design theory and what it means for both theologians and scientists. Stewart cautions Wesleyans to be wary of some claims and implications of the Intelligent Design movement and its ideas. The book concludes with an exploration by neuroscientists Warren S. Brown and Sarah D. Marion of attachment theory and spiritual formation in Wesleyan communities.

The essays in this book, with one exception, were originally presented at the forty-third annual meeting of the Wesleyan Theological Society. The meeting, "Sighs, Signs, and Significance: Pentecostal and Wesleyan Explorations of Science and Creation," was held jointly with the Society for Pentecostal Studies at Duke University Divinity School on March 13–15, 2008. Plenary speakers, respondents, and panelists included Barry Callen, Terry Cross, Heather Curtis, Ellen Davis, Harold Koenig, Diane Leclerec, Michael Lodahl, Randy L. Maddox, Steven K. McCormick, James K. A. Smith, Wolfgang Vondey, and Frederick L. Ware. We were especially pleased that Jürgen Moltmann agreed to travel from Germany to deliver the conference keynote address and provide substance for the plenary panel discussion. I offer thanks to these people and to the essayists in this book for their work.

I was privileged to co-chair the Duke meeting with Society for Pentecostal Studies vice-president elect, Amos Yong. Amos and I had a great time planning the event together, we enjoyed each other's company at the meeting, and we have worked well together as we each pursued publishing volumes after the joint meeting. The volume of Pentecostal essays Amos edited stands as a companion to this book. I offer my thanks to Amos, because he did at least as much as I if not more to make these ventures so worthwhile.

A number of people made the joint Wesleyan Theological Society/Society for Pentecostal Studies meeting at Duke University a great success. Our campus hosts, Stephen Gunter, Gregory Jones, and Randy Maddox, were most helpful. Society secretaries David Roebuck and Sam Powell proved invaluable. I also thank the Wesleyan Theological Society members who presented papers at the conference or attended.

Thanks is also due the John Templeton Foundation for the grant that underwrote part of the conference expenses as well as subsidized the editorial cost for this volume. I especially thank Drew Rick-Miller and Paul Wason for their help in various aspects of the project. I am grateful for the vision of the Templeton foundation to support research exploring the connections between science and theology.

I also appreciate those from my own university who have supported the work on this book. My assistant, Jill Jones, provided help in many ways. My colleague and friend, Jay Akkerman, served as graphic artist and offered general support. And my school dean and friend, Mark Maddix, has always been supportive my academic endeavors. My president, David Alexander, and my academic dean, Samuel Dunn, have also been encouraging. I thank each of them.

Thanks to Charlie Collier and the editorial team at Pickwick Publications for their guidance. Diane Farley at Pickwick has been very helpful in working through the details of the publication process.

Finally, I dedicate this book to my friend and leading Wesleyan scholar, Randy L. Maddox. Randy's erudition and general wisdom have proved helpful in many ways over the years. I thank Randy for his inspiring scholarship and for his encouraging friendship.

1

John Wesley's Precedent for Theological Engagement with the Natural Sciences

Randy L. Maddox

Reflection on the implications of the study of nature for Christian teaching spans the history of the church. This reflection increasingly took on the tone of debate with the transitions marking the "modern" age in Western culture. However, this age also fostered periodic efforts to reframe the interchange between science and religious faith into constructive *dialogue*, seeking to deepen understanding of their differences and heighten appreciation for their areas of resonance. The last two decades have witnessed a vigorous effort at such "science and religion dialogue."[1]

While the current dialogue has yielded many insights, it has been hampered by the tendency to construe "religion" too abstractly. At the most extreme, religion is viewed as a human trait that is assumed to

1. For typological surveys of the dialogue, see John F. Haught, *Science and Religion: From Conflict to Conversation* (Mahwah, NJ: Paulist, 1996); Niels Henrik Gregersen & J. Wentzel van Huyssteen, eds., *Rethinking Theology and Science: Six Models for the Current Dialogue* (Grand Rapids: Eerdmans, 1998); Ted Peters, "Science and Theology: Toward Consonance," in *Science and Theology*, edited by T. Peters (Boulder, CO: Westview, 1998) 11–39; and Christopher Southgate et al., *God, Humanity, and the Cosmos: A Textbook in Science and Religion*, 2nd ed. (New York: Continuum, 2005). For an extensive bibliography see: http://www.meta-library.net/mdxbib/index-frame.html.

be expressed in all religious traditions. In reality, as the other religious traditions have protested, this supposed generic trait typically reflected convictions of the religions of the Middle East (Judaism, Christianity, and Islam). As such, the most helpful recent studies have begun to pay attention to how the focus of concern about current scientific claims and practices may differ *between* major world religions.

But the problematic impact of abstraction finds expression as well *within* major religions. In particular, the range of variance in evaluating scientific claims and practices can be as wide between alternative theological camps within Christianity as it is between Christians and other religious or secular stances. If we hope to increase mutual understanding and cooperation among Christians in their engagement with the natural sciences, we need to pay more attention to the relevant characteristic and/or distinctive convictions and concerns of the major theological traditions within the Christian church. My purpose in this essay is to start a conversation about this topic within the Wesleyan tradition. I attempt this by probing John Wesley's engagement with the study of nature in his day, watching for the convictions and concerns that emerge, and suggesting their relevance for our own setting.

Historical Perspective for Engaging Wesley's Precedent

Few would question that John Wesley might provide an instructive precedent for reflections on spiritual formation practices at the outset of the twenty-first century. Turning to Wesley for insights about constructive theological engagement with the natural sciences in our day is a much less obvious proposal. To understand why this is the case, and yet why a small—but growing—number of scholars are embracing the latter project, it will be helpful to begin with some historical perspective.

Early Influential Dismissals

The proposal that one might want to consider Wesley when looking for insights about constructive theological engagement with the natural sciences would have astonished Sir Leslie Stephen, author of a two-volume *History of English Thought in the Eighteenth Century* published in 1876. Writing nearly a century after Wesley's death, Stephen assured his readers that "we already find in Wesley the aversion to scientific reasoning which has become characteristic [in Stephen's day] of orthodox theologians."[2] Andrew Dickson White echoed this evaluation twenty years later in his (in)famous *History of the Warfare of Science with Theology in Christendom*, citing Wesley several times as an influential proponent of beliefs that stifled the emergence of modern science.[3] For both writers, the leading indictment against Wesley was his openness to demonic causes of affliction and the possibility of witches, closely intertwined with his corollary providential accounts of events like earthquakes and his expectation of miraculous healing. Also highlighted by White was Wesley's ascription to the Genesis account of creation, where animals are portrayed as naturally domesticated to humans and all death results from human sin, assumptions that conflict directly with the Darwinian model of evolution.[4]

The most significant problem with these influential earlier dismissals of Wesley's precedent for engaging the natural sciences is that they rely mainly on secondary sources and passing comments in Wesley's *Sermons* and *Journal*. As a result, they provide little sense of the scope of Wesley's engagement with the natural sciences—or "natural philosophy" as it was pursued in his day. In 1763, Wesley published for the benefit of his Methodist preachers and people *A Survey of the Wisdom of God in Creation; or, A Compendium of Natural Philosophy*, a two-volume work distilling his reading of several book-length works as well as extracts from the *Philosophical Transactions* of the Royal Society and other journals. By its third edition in 1777, this *Survey* had grown into a five-volume collection. To increase its availability to his followers, Wesley serialized excerpts from the *Survey* in his monthly *Arminian Magazine*, beginning in 1781. In addition to this broad ranging work, Wesley also published *The Desideratum; or, Electricity Made Plain and Useful* (1760) and a number of independent short pieces on topics in natural philosophy in the *Arminian Magazine*. This breadth of material surely qualifies Wesley for consideration as a precedent for theological engagement with science topics, particularly among the various branches of his ecclesial offspring.

---

2. Leslie Stephen, *History of English Thought in the Eighteenth Century* (London: Smith, Elder, 1876) 2:412.

3. Andrew Dickson White, *History of the Warfare of Science with Theology in Christendom*, 2 vols. (New York: D. Appleton, 1896) esp. 1:128, 148, 340, 361–63, 2:125–26.

4. Cf. ibid., 1:29–30, 220, 289.

Problematic Idealized Appeals

One must be aware of Wesley's broader work to understand the earliest *positive* appeals to his precedent in engaging the natural sciences, which were contemporaneous with White's dismissal—and equally problematic. In 1893, William Harrison Mills gave a lecture titled "John Wesley an Evolutionist" at the Chit-Chat Club in San Francisco. The lecture was circulated as a booklet and a summary was published in *Popular Science Monthly* the following year.[5] Sparked by Mills, James W. Lee enlightened readers of the *Southern Magazine* the same year that "the founder of Methodism wrote out the whole theory of evolution and the origin of species ... eighty-four years before Mr. Darwin published his celebrated work upon the same subject."[6] The main difference between Darwin and Wesley, according to Lee, concerned causation—what Darwin attributed to natural selection and survival of the fittest, Wesley attributed to the will of God.

Both Mills and Lee assumed their contention would be surprising, even to Methodists, because so few were familiar with Wesley's *Survey of the Wisdom of God*. They based their argument on extracts from the *Survey*, particularly from volume 4, which offers a sketch of the "gradual progression of beings" that climaxes:

> By what degrees does nature raise herself up to man? How will she rectify this head, that is always inclined towards the earth? How change these paws into flexible arms? What method will she make use of to transform these crooked feet into supple and skillful hands? Or how will she widen and extend this contracted stomach? In what manner will she place the breasts, and give them a roundness suitable to them? The ape is this rough draught of man; this rude sketch and imperfect representation; which, nevertheless, bears a resemblance to him and is the last creature that serves to display the admirable progression of the works of God![7]

---

5. William Harrison Mills, *John Wesley an Evolutionist* (San Francisco: Chit-Chat Club, 1893); summarized in "John Wesley an Evolutionist," *Popular Science Monthly* 46 (1894–95) 284–85.

6. See James W. Lee, "A Methodist Evolutionist," *Southern Magazine* (Louisville) 4 (1894) 348–54; here, 348.

7. See John Wesley, *A Survey of the Wisdom of God in the Creation, or A Compendium of Natural Philosophy*, 4th ed. (London: Paramore, 1784) 4:102. Unless noted otherwise, all references will be to this last edition published under Wesley's direction. Mills quotes this passage in *John Wesley*, 18; Lee in "Methodist Evolutionist," 350.

The problem with the appeals of Mills and Lee to this passage is not that it is from Wesley's abridgement of a book by Charles Bonnet (for Wesley *is* endorsing Bonnet), but that they were blind to the setting of the original quote. Wesley was embracing here the philosophical model of the "chain of being" that remained popular in the eighteenth century.[8] A central claim of this model is that creation demonstrates the perfection of its Creator by its organization into an exhaustively populated series of progressively more complex beings—from the simplest elements to the highest spiritual beings. Importantly, precisely because it was meant to demonstrate an immutable God, this chain of beings was considered static! The progressive description of beings as "higher" or "next" did not indicate their temporal succession. They were assumed to have come into being at the same instant, each as a unique creation of God, and the possibility of change or extinction of any species of being was specifically rejected. They were simply being *described* sequentially. Thus, Wesley was hardly offering a prescient version of Darwin's theory of evolution.

The claims of Mills and Lee were shaped more by the emerging fundamentalist/modernist tensions of their time than by contextual study of Wesley. This continued to be the case for a series of popular essays in the 1920s that invoked Wesley as a forerunner for accepting evolution in the midst of the controversy peaking in the Scopes trial (1926).[9] If there was anything new in efforts of this period, it was a tendency to broaden the argument, presenting Wesley as a pioneer of scientific empiricism in general (in the mode of Francis Bacon and John Locke) and of empirical theology in particular.[10] One champion put it

---

8. The standard study of this model is Arthur O. Lovejoy, *The Great Chain of Being: A Study of the History of an Idea* (Cambridge, MA: Harvard University Press, 1961).

9. Francis M. Larkin, "Evolution," *California Christian Advocate* 61 (6 April 1922) 4; Karl Stoolz, "John Wesley and Evolution," *Christian Century* 40 (1923) 663; Frank Wilbur Collier, *Back to Wesley* (New York: Methodist Book Concern, 1924) 34–49; Charles W. Hargitt, "John Wesley—Evolutionist," *Zion's Herald* 103 (1925) 1061, 1088; and Frank Louis Barber, "Wesley, an Evolutionist," *Canadian Journal of Religious Thought* 4 (1927) 28–33.

10. See in particular Frank Louis Barber, *The Philosophy of John Wesley* (Toronto: Methodist Book & Publishing House, 1923); Charles W. Hargitt, "John Wesley and Science: A Challenge from the Eighteenth Century," *Methodist Review* 110 (1927) 383–93; William C. S. Pellowe, "Wesley's Use of Science," *Methodist Review* 112 (1927) 394–403; and Frank Wilbur Collier, *John Wesley Among the Scientists* (New York: Abingdon, 1928). Each included the suggestion that Wesley was open to evolution in some form.

this way: "Back to Wesley is forward into the spirit of what is best in the twentieth century."[11] In striking contrast to Stephen and White, another insisted

> While not a few among Wesley's contemporary clergy were noisily engaged in anathematizing such scientists as Newton, Kepler, La Voisier, Boyle and Priestly, . . . this man, busiest of all his cult, found time to acquaint himself with scientific progress and cordially accepted it . . . [which is] a splendid lesson and admonition to intolerant and benighted successors of the twentieth century.[12]

Emerging Contextual Studies

The lesson actually dawning on Wesley's successors by mid-twentieth century was that both the earlier dismissals and the sweeping panegyrics lacked balance and nuance.[13] They were not sufficiently aware of the specific options in the engagement of theology and natural science or of the various factors influencing choices between these options—in Wesley's time or in their own. Accordingly, they "read" Wesley anachronistically as exemplifying current positions that they either rejected or championed.[14]

An essential resource in guarding against such misreading is careful historical-contextual study of Wesley's writings on science topics. The first serious effort in this regard was published in 1953 by Robert Schofield, professor of the history of science at Harvard University.[15] While clear that Wesley could not be considered a "scientist" by even eighteenth-century standards, Schofield judged that he had broader

---

11. Collier, *Back to Wesley*, 5. Collier was a professor of philosophy, trained in Boston Personalism and teaching at American University in Washington DC.

12. Hargitt, "John Wesley and Science," 393. For a somewhat more reserved encomium, see Pellowe, "Wesley's Use of Science," 403.

13. An early expression of emerging caution are the chapters on science and evolution in William C. S. Pellowe, *John Wesley: Master in Religion* (Nashville: MECS Publishing House, 1939) 97–121.

14. This point is developed well, with focus on the readings championing Wesley, in Laura Bartels Felleman, "John Wesley's *Survey of the Wisdom of God in Creation*: A Methodological Inquiry," *Perspectives on Science and Christian Faith* 58 (2006) 1–6.

15. Robert E. Schofield, "John Wesley and Science in 18th Century England," *Isis* 44 (1953) 331–40.

and more enduring interest in scientific studies than most of his university-educated peers. Wesley's experimentation with and writing on electricity was given particular notice. Most significantly, allowing that there were better specialized treatments of each subject area covered in Wesley's *Survey of the Wisdom of God*, Schofield suggested that there was likely no better single survey treatment for general readers.[16] In evaluating Wesley's influence, Schofield posited that the *Survey* likely increased openness to study of nature among Wesley's followers. He also discounted the supposed impact of Wesley's "superstitious" views about witches and miracles on later developments. In their place, Schofield suggested that the biases of Wesley that ran most counter to elements that account for the advance of modern science were his negative attitudes toward mathematics and hypothetical theories.[17]

While helpful, Schofield's essay antedated the flourishing of study of the history of science over the last few decades and particularly of investigations into Christian interactions with science.[18] This makes it all the more regrettable that his essay remained the only serious historical study for forty years. Fortunately, this situation is beginning to change. In the early 1990s, John English provided the first rigorous account of Wesley's academic training in the various fields of the study of nature in his day, as well as a nuanced evaluation of Wesley's fluctuating sympathies in the current debates over Isaac Newton's cosmology.[19] Shortly thereafter, John Haas published three general essays that draw on some of the recent scholarship to contextualize Wesley's basic interest in science topics.[20]

16. Cf. ibid., 337–38.

17. Ibid., 338.

18. Two recent works that can provide a sense of these developments are Peter J. Bowler and Iwan Rhys Morus, *Making Modern Science: A Historical Survey* (Chicago: University of Chicago Press, 2005); David C. Lindberg & Ronald L. Numbers, eds., *When Science and Christianity Meet* (Chicago: University of Chicago Press, 2003).

19. See John Cammel English, "John Wesley's Scientific Education," *Methodist History* 30.1 (1991) 42–51; and English, "John Wesley and Isaac Newton's 'System of the World,'" *Proceedings of the Wesley Historical Society* 48 (1991) 69–86.

20. John W. Haas Jr., "John Wesley's Views on Science and Christianity: An Examination of the Charge of Antiscience," *Church History* 63 (1994) 378–92; Haas, "Eighteenth Century Evangelical Responses to Science: John Wesley's Enduring Legacy," *Science and Christian Belief* 6 (1994) 83–102; and Haas, "John Wesley's Vision of Science in the Service of Christ," *Perspectives on Science and Christian Faith* 47 (1995) 234–43. See Haas's essay in the present book.

This flurry of studies capping the twentieth century deepened our awareness of how much work remains on the historical front, studying Wesley's writings on science topics in relation to their original context. Given Wesley's reliance on multiple sources (often without citation) for his publications, a pressing foundational task is identification of his sources and consideration of how he selectively adopts and adapts them. In the first dissertation ever focused on Wesley's *Survey*, Laura Bartels Felleman has recently demonstrated with select samples the insight that can emerge from such study.[21] This type of textual work is farthest along in the specific area of Wesley's publications on medicine (which includes the *Desideratum* on electricity).[22] The project of providing a critical edition of the full *Survey of the Wisdom of God*, identifying all sources and the changes through various editions, is just getting underway.[23]

As adequate critical text is provided, it becomes possible to explore more deeply the contextual dynamics and characteristic concerns of Wesley's engagement with his sources. Here again, the most developed studies to-date focus on Wesley's ventures in medicine.[24] But enough of a broader sense is emerging to highlight a few items, in hopes of stimulating both additional historical studies of the range of Wesley's engagement with science topics and hermeneutically-sensitive reflections on the insights that might be drawn from his precedent.

---

21. Laura Bartels Felleman, "The Evidence of Things Not Seen: John Wesley's Use of Natural Philosophy" (PhD diss., Drew University, 2004).

22. See particularly James G. Donat, "The Rev. John Wesley's Extractions from Dr. Tissot: A Methodist *Imprimatur*," *History of Science* 39 (2001) 285–98; and Donat, "Empirical Medicine in the 18th Century: The Rev. John Wesley's Search for Remedies that Work," *Methodist History* 44 (2006) 216–26. Donat is editor of the future volume (17) which collects John Wesley's medical writings in *The Works of John Wesley*, edited by Frank Baker and Richard Heitzenrater (Nashville: Abingdon, 1984). Note: hereafter this collection is referred to simply as *Works*.

23. This project is being supported by the Center for Studies in the Wesleyan Tradition at Duke University, under my direction.

24. See Deborah Madden, *"A Cheap, Safe and Natural Medicine": Religion, Medicine and Culture in John Wesley's "Primitive Physic"* (Atlanta: Rodopi, 2007); Randy L. Maddox, "John Wesley on Holistic Health and Healing," *Methodist History* 46 (2007) 4–33; and Randy L. Maddox, "Reclaiming the Eccentric Parent: Methodist Reception of John Wesley's Interest in Medicine," in *"Inward and Outward Health": John Wesley's Holistic Concept of Medical Science, the Environment, and Holy Living*, edited by Deborah Madden (London: Epworth, 2008) 15–50.

Character of the "Science" that Wesley Engaged

We need to begin with some comments on the character of the "science" that Wesley engaged. I have put scare quotes around the word, because Wesley inhabited a transitional period prior to the solidifying of many aspects commonly associated with science today. Three points deserve to be highlighted in this regard.

First, Wesley's century was a period of major transition in the self-understanding of academic study of nature about its goals and methods. This is important to emphasize, because an earlier generation of historiography (e.g., Herbert Butterfield, *The Origins of Modern Science*[25]) presented the "scientific revolution" as taking place rapidly across seventeenth-century Europe. Historiographers suggested that "science" was understood in England by the outset of the eighteenth century among leading practitioners like Isaac Newton as a mode of inquiry that was: 1) independent from religious or philosophical constraints, thus equally at home in all cultures and times; 2) aimed at elucidating how the processes of nature work, so that these processes could be used for human betterment; and 3) grounded in a hypothetico-deductive methodology, wedding the certainty of mathematics with the objectivity of rigorous empirical verification of hypotheses. If this model was firmly in place by Wesley's day, any divergence evident in his writings from these emphases is easily read as resistance to or rejection of science (as by Stephen and White).

But scholars of the history of science over the last two decades have demonstrated that the various emphases just listed for the "modern" understanding of science remained *contested* among leading practitioners through most of the eighteenth century, particularly in England.[26] (As an aside, I would add that a major stream of the philosophy of science and sociology of science over the last two decades has also challenged both the adequacy and desirability of this "modern" account of science *for our day*.[27]) This recent scholarship encourages us to take seriously

---

25. Herbert Butterfield, *The Origins of Modern Science* (London: Bell, 1949).

26. See Andrew Cunningham and Perry Williams, "De-centering the 'Big Picture': *The Origins of Modern Science* and the Modern Origins of Science," *British Journal for the History of Science* 26 (1993) 407–32; and, more generally, Bowler and Morus, *Making Modern Science*.

27. A good place to begin exploring these debates is A. F. Chalmers, *What is this Thing Called Science?* 3rd ed. (Indianapolis: Hackett, 1999); and James Robert Brown,

that folk like Isaac Newton labeled their studies of nature not "science" but "natural philosophy" (e.g., Newton's *Philosophiae Naturalis Principia Mathematica*, 1697).[28] They stress that this latter name reflects important continuities with an earlier understanding of the academic study of nature.

Some background is necessary to appreciate this earlier understanding. Influenced by Aristotle's distinction between *epistēmē* and *technē*—which passed over into Latin as *scientia* and *ars* (art)—medieval educational practices stressed the difference between pursuing *understanding* of reality (*scientia*) and acquiring *practical knowledge* or know-how (*ars*). One implication was that vocational skills pursued on their own, usually by the lower or servant classes (the *illiberales ars*, or arts of the non-free), were not part of a university education. But the distinction also found expression in university education. The base of this education was training in the seven *liberal* arts (i.e., necessary skills for free men): grammar, rhetoric, dialectic, arithmetic, geometry, astronomy, and music. These sets of practical knowledge provided the foundation for students to approach the capstone study of the nature of reality itself (*scientia*)—in philosophy and theology. By the eighteenth century, philosophy had developed sub-divisions of logic, metaphysics, moral philosophy, and natural philosophy. The specific focus of the latter was on *understanding* the natural world (it was often also called "physics," echoing the Greek word for nature: *physis*).

Against this backdrop we can illuminate the assumptions of natural philosophy about its task and methods as it entered the eighteenth century.[29] Consider the specific case of studying the heavens. As a *scientia*, natural philosophy traditionally focused on questions like of what the heavens are made; what moves the sun, moon, and planets; and whether the universe is finite or infinite. By contrast, astronomy, as an *art* (integrally connected to mathematics), was concerned with tracking lights in the sky, developing formalized descriptions and predictions

---

Who Rules in Science: An Opinionated Guide to the Wars (Cambridge, MA: Harvard University Press, 2001).

28. Cf. Andrew Cunningham, "How the *Principia* got its Name," *History of Science* 29 (1991) 377–92.

29. This summary draws on several sources; one of the most recent is Peter Dear, *The Intelligibility of Nature: How Science Makes Sense of the World* (Chicago: University of Chicago Press, 2006) 1–14.

of their movements, offering reliable calendars, and other such practical tasks. It had been rare for astronomers to ask what the heavenly bodies were made of or why they moved, while natural philosophers had devoted little attention to mathematics or the practical use of their explanations of reality.[30]

Challenges to these disciplinary distinctions began to emerge in the late seventeenth century. On one front, Francis Bacon injected the suggestion, which gained increasing hold, that the value of *any* study of nature was proportionate to the technological benefits it provided for human control and exploitation of the natural world. On another front, Newton's *Principia Mathematica* began to elevate the centrality of mathematics to accounts of the nature of the universe. By the turn to the nineteenth century, these and other threads had woven together the distinct agendas of *scientia* and *ars* in the study of nature. This reality was signaled by the fading of the label "natural philosophy," with "science" in its modern sense taking its place.

The key point, for our purposes, is that this transition stretched *through* the eighteenth century in England, resulting in numerous works with mixtures of the relevant emphases. Few works in this period embody consistently the assumptions of "modern science" outlined earlier, including Wesley's *Survey*. The fact that in this "compendium of natural philosophy" Wesley discounted the role of mathematics, for example, is evidence less of his intentional resistance to a recognized commitment of "science" than of his location in this transitional period.

Second, Wesley's transitional century was marked by prolonged debate among competing models of physics and cosmology, with particular focus on the perceived limitations of Newton's proposals. This is important to emphasize, because a common evidence cited by critics to show that Wesley was anti-science was his hesitance about endorsing Newton. Recent surveys of eighteenth-century science in England make clear that a number of Newton's professional peers shared this hesitance, and for understandable reasons.[31] Everyone recognized that, with its

---

30. Cf. Peter Dear, "The Mathematical Principles of Natural Philosophy: Toward a Heuristic Narrative for the Scientific Revolution," *Configurations* 6 (1998) 173–93.

31. Good surveys of these debates are available in Peter Hanns Reill, "The Legacy of the 'Scientific Revolution': Science and the Enlightenment," in *The Cambridge History of Science, Volume 4: The Eighteenth Century*, edited by Roy Porter (New York: Cambridge, 2003) 23–43; John Gascoigne, "Ideas of Nature: Natural Philosophy," in

mathematical advances (particularly calculus), Newton's *Principia* provided a much more accurate *description* of the movement of the planets, comets, and tides. But this was a task traditionally assigned to the *art* of astronomy, not the *explanatory* goal of *natural philosophy*, which Newton claimed in the full title of his work. Thus, Newton's *Principia* was often greeted at first with stunned incomprehension, even at his own University of Cambridge.[32]

A little background may help in understanding this reaction. Through most of the medieval period, the reigning physics was that of Aristotle, which accounted for all natural motion by "final causes" that were integral to every type of being. Thus planets moved in their orbits, because they were realizing their *entelechy* (the "desire to fulfill one's nature"). By the latter medieval period, many were dissatisfied with the subtle pan-psychic suggestions of this explanation, spawning alternative *mechanical* accounts of motion in the heavens. The starting premise of these accounts was that entelechy was limited to living beings; physical matter was inert, and was moved solely by the application of external force. But how was this force applied? Here a divergence emerged within mechanical accounts of cosmic motion, framed by the question of whether space was a void. Accepting that space was a void made it difficult to account for application of force at a distance, such as the influence of the moon on the earth's ocean tides. So most insisted that space was entirely filled by matter of varying size, including sizes not visible to human observation. René Descartes developed the most sophisticated mechanical account in this vein, ascribing planetary motion to the carrying force of vortices in this cosmic soup. If one instead accepted that space *was* a void, they typically either attributed motion to direct causation by God or echoed earlier hermetic suggestions about "resonance" across distance between certain elements.

Newton stepped into the middle of these ongoing debates. Aligning with the mechanists, he rejected entelechy, agreeing that matter was inert. Yet he eventually spurned Descartes's hypothesis of forms of matter too small for empirical detection, leaving him with space as a void. While he was willing to speak about God intervening occasionally to adjust the motion of planets and other cosmic bodies, Newton

---

ibid., 285–304; and William B. Ashworth, "Christianity and the Mechanistic Universe," in Lindberg and Numbers, *When Science and Christianity Meet*, 61–84.

32. Gascoigne, "Ideas of Nature," 289.

believed that the regularity and interdependence of this motion indicated instead the presence of an abiding natural law. He named this law of mutual influence of bodies upon one another "gravity." But he immediately conceded that he could not yet explain how gravity conveyed its impact across the void of space. To many of his peers, Newton's "gravity" seemed like another unacceptable appeal to hermetic influences. Others concluded simply that he had failed to do what natural philosophers were supposed to do—provide an account of *how* the movements of bodies take place.

In hindsight, Newton ventured a promising suggestion about how gravity worked in the "General Scholium" he added to the second edition (1713) of *Principia*. At the end of this short piece he referred to an "electric and elastic spirit" that appears to pervade and lay hid in all gross bodies, noting that there was not yet sufficient experimental input to provide an account of its impact.[33] It would take a century for further experimentation to result in James Maxwell's account of the dynamics of electromagnetic fields and the correlation of these with gravitational fields. Only at this point was the project of Newton's *Principia* as a "natural philosophy" fully achieved. This is a good example of Imre Lakatos's point that significant revisions in major "research programs" take time, because of the need to work through a range of supporting hypothesis and evidences (and often the need to create relevant experimental instrumentation).[34] It is anachronistic to fault those who do not endorse a significant proposed revision of a field of knowledge early in the process simply because of the eventual success of the proposal. This point has been made effectively against those who criticize the church for not adopting Galileo's cosmology immediately when a number of his relevant "scientific" peers still harbored significant questions.[35] The same would apply through much of the eighteenth century in regard to Newton's physics and cosmology.

---

33. See *Philosophiae naturalis principia mathematica*, 2nd ed. (Cambridge, 1713) 484; in first English translation, *The Mathematical Principles of Natural Philosophy* (London: Benjamin Motte, 1729) 2:393.

34. See Imre Lakatos, *Philosophical Papers. Volume 1: The Methodology of Scientific Research Programmes* (New York: Cambridge University Press, 1980). There is a helpful introduction to Lakatos in Chalmers, *What Is . . . Science?*, chapter 9.

35. Cf. David C. Lindberg, "Galileo, the Church, and the Cosmos," in Lindberg and Numbers, *When Science and Christianity Meet*, 33–60.

The key point, for our purposes, is not just to suggest that there was some legitimate room for Wesley to be hesitant in endorsing Newton. His awareness of the ongoing disagreement between competing models, and of Newton's precedent for not advancing *explanatory* accounts until there was compelling evidence, also helps explain the restriction Wesley adopted in his edited collation of works in natural philosophy:

> It will be easily observed that I endeavor throughout not to *account for* things, but only to *describe* them. I undertake barely to set down what appears in nature, not the cause of those appearances. The facts lie within the reach of our senses and understanding, the causes are more remote. That things are so, we know with certainty; but why they are so, we know not. In many cases we cannot know; and the more we enquire, the more we are perplexed and entangled.[36]

Obviously, this restricted goal falls short of the full agenda of natural philosophy. But Wesley's *Survey* was not intended to *advance* this discipline. It had the more limited goal of providing for his readers a survey of the most interesting and instructive aspects of nature as highlighted in recent work in natural philosophy.

Third, in Wesley's transitional setting "natural philosophy" retained an overarching theological concern. If we wanted to take the time, we could consider counter-evidence to all three of the major emphases of "modern science" that Butterfield and others suggested were in place by the outset of the eighteenth century in England. Newton's strong contrast between his adherence to experimental induction and the reliance of Descartes and others upon unwarranted metaphysical hypotheses is just one example that a self-conscious integrated hypothetico-deductive methodology was far from shared. Likewise, Newton's deferral of an account of *how* gravity conveyed its effect fits poorly with the second emphasis listed above. But the suggestion of earlier historiography with which recent scholars have taken the most exception is the sharp separation of "scientific" investigation from religious or theological considerations.

These scholars have argued that, in keeping with its medieval roots, natural philosophy at the outset of the eighteenth century retained an

---

36. Wesley, Preface, §5, *Survey*, 1:vi–vii; also in *The Works of John Wesley*, 14 vols., edited by Thomas Jackson (London: Wesleyan Methodist Book Room, 1872) 14:301. Note: hereafter this collection is referred to as *Works* (Jackson).

overarching theological goal.[37] Its subject-matter was nature, but it approached nature as the "book of God's works." Moreover, it assumed that part of its task was to elucidate the attributes of God that could be demonstrated from God's works. Newton can again serve as our example. The "General Scholium" that he added as the capstone to *Principia* was devoted mainly to insisting that "this most beautiful system of the sun, planets, and comets could only proceed from the counsel and dominion of an intelligent and powerful being," and then elucidating the attributes of this being which we can deduce from "his most wise and excellent contrivances of things." He concluded these reflections with an explicit affirmation that such discourse about God, drawn from consideration of nature, "does certainly belong to natural philosophy."[38]

To be sure, there were occasional figures like Thomas Hobbes who adopted purely materialistic accounts of nature. But these remained rare in England into the last quarter of the eighteenth century.[39] Thus, Wesley was echoing the methodological assumption of most of his sources when he described the goal of his compendium of natural philosophy as "not barely to entertain an idle barren curiosity, but to display *the invisible things of God*, his power, wisdom, and goodness."[40] If Wesley went beyond his sources, it was in his characteristic hope that the collection would also "warm our hearts, and fill our mouths with wonder, love, and praise!"[41]

---

37. This point was pressed initially by Andrew Cunningham in "Getting the Game Right: Some Plain Words on the Identity and Invention of Science," *Studies in the History and Philosophy of Science* 19 (1988) 365–89; and developed in other studies cited above. The sharpest critic of Cunningham has been Edward Grant—cf. "God, Science, and Natural Philosophy in the Late Middle Ages," in *Between Demonstration and Imagination*, eds. L. Nauta & A. Vanderjagt (Leiden: Brill, 1999) 243–67; and "God and Natural Philosophy: The Late Middle Ages and Sir Isaac Newton," *Early Science and Medicine* 5 (2000) 279–98. Most have come to agree in general with Cunningham, as evidenced by Peter Dear, "Religion, Science, and Natural Philosophy: Thoughts on Cunningham's Thesis," *Studies in the History and Philosophy of Science* 32 (2001) 377–86; and Peter Harrison, "'Science' and 'Religion': Constructing the Boundaries," *Journal of Religion* 86 (2006) 81–106.

38. Newton, *Mathematical Principles of Natural Philosophy* 2:388–92.

39. See Jeremy Gregory, "Christianity and Culture: Religion, the Arts, and the Sciences in England, 1660–1800," in *Culture and Society in Britain, 1660–1800*, edited by Jeremy Black (Manchester: Manchester University Press, 1997) 102–23.

40. Wesley, Preface, §1, *Survey*, 1:iii–iv; in *Works* (Jackson), 14:300.

41. Ibid., §7, 1:viii; in *Works* (Jackson), 14:302.

Characteristics of Wesley's Theological Engagement with "Science"

The more that careful historical study highlights the differences between the "science" that Wesley engaged and science as dominant today, the more that one might doubt the relevance of Wesley's precedent for current theological engagement with the natural sciences. But I would suggest that this difference is one of the things that make dialogue with Wesley valuable. If engaged with empathy, the dialogue can increase our awareness of the range of options available for relating theology and the natural sciences. It can also increase sensitivity to the contextuality of *current* reigning scientific models. One assumption shared by both the dismissals of Wesley's precedent and the idealized appeals to him as a forerunner at the turn to the twentieth century was confidence in the superiority of their own *modern* view; Wesley was worth considering only to the degree that he agreed with that view. Like David Ford, I appreciate how our "postmodern" situation has encouraged us to challenge modernity's undue superiority complex, allowing us to recognize in a new way what is of value in premodernity, in modernity, and in postmodernity.[42]

In this spirit, I want to highlight five characteristics of Wesley's theological engagement with "science" (or the study of nature), which have been selected in part because of their resonance with strands in the science and religion dialogue of the past two decades. I would stress that I am not hereby trying to rehabilitate Wesley, or show him a prescient precursor of current positions. My goal is more like the hermeneutic quest of "merging horizons" between different contexts, in order to facilitate exchange of insights. I would also note that my list is far from exhaustive, being intended more as proposals for continuing research and dialogue.

Committed to a Modest Natural Theology

It was just noted that natural philosophy retained a theological dimension in Wesley's day, devoting some attention to implications that could be drawn from study of the material world about the existence and nature of spiritual beings, including the Ultimate Being or God. This

---

42. David F. Ford, *The Shape of Living* (Grand Rapids, MI: Baker, 1997) 21.

attention intersected with another subsection of philosophy in the medieval curriculum known as "natural theology." The latter was devoted to knowledge about God that could be demonstrated by rational reflection on 1) the human soul; 2) human moral insight, or "natural law"; and 3) the natural world. Thus, natural theology drew the culminating reflections of natural philosophy into a larger conversation about what could *theoretically* be known about God apart from special revelation. I stress the theoretical nature of this knowledge, because natural theology was part of the Christian curriculum, and its wisest practitioners were aware that they were reflecting on the "book of nature" through lenses shaped to some degree by the "book of scripture." Their concern was less to elicit faith from non-believers than to confirm and enrich nascent faith.[43]

To be sure, not all voices were so wise. There was plenty of fodder to fuel the suspicion of Protestant reformers about the triumph of unregenerate reason over revelation in the enterprise of natural theology. This is not to say that the reformers set the enterprise fully aside. At the very least, they retained some emphasis on universally demonstrable "natural law" as a basis for civil society.[44] John Calvin went further, affirming that study of nature was a beneficial supplement to study of scripture for those who had the opportunity.[45] But the general Protestant emphasis was on the sufficiency of God's revelation in scripture, rendering theological appeal to the "book of nature" clearly subordinate and surely not essential for basic Christian life.

This is a point where the "Anglican" approach to theological reflection diverged from more staunchly Protestant approaches.[46] The roots

43. Nicholas Wolterstorff develops this point in "The Migration of the Theistic Arguments: From Natural Theology to Evidentialist Apologetics," in *Rationality, Religious Belief, and Moral Commitment*, edited by R. Audi and W. Wainwright (Ithaca: Cornell University Press, 1986) 38–81. See also John Hedley Brooke, "Natural Theology," in *The History of Science and Religion in the Western Tradition*, edited by Gary Ferngren (New York: Garland, 2000) 58–64.

44. For this emphasis in the Lutheran setting, see Sachiko Kusukawa, *The Transformation of Natural Philosophy: The Case of Philip Melanchton* (New York: Cambridge, 1995).

45. Cf. Susan Elizabeth Schreiner, *The Theater of His Glory: Nature and the Natural Order in the Thought of John Calvin* (Durham, NC: Labyrinth, 1991).

46. The term "Anglican" is increasingly restricted by scholars to naming a set of emphasis firmly in place only by the beginning of the eighteenth century in England; cf. John Walsh & Stephen Taylor, "Introduction: the Church and Anglicanism in the 'long'

of this difference go back to Richard Hooker, who argued that while scripture is sufficient for the basic knowledge of salvation, all Christians should be encouraged to seek the fullness of understanding and felicity, which is derived from *conjoined* study of scripture and nature.[47] This emphasis underlies the significant interest in natural theology that emerged in England in the middle of the seventeen century and carried through Wesley's life into the nineteenth century.[48] While strongest in Anglican circles, the interest was evident as well among moderate dissenting writers like Richard Baxter.[49] Wesley drew upon works in natural theology from both circles for his theological reflections interspersed through *Survey of the Wisdom of God*.

But this brings us to an important question. Why did Wesley designate the *Survey* as a work in natural philosophy instead of natural theology? Part of the answer may have been his recognition that the scope of natural theology was traditionally broader than natural philosophy (including reflections on natural law and the human soul, which play little part in the *Survey*.) But a more important reason was surely his recognition of the difference in amount of attention given to nature itself in the works he consulted of each genre. Works in natural philosophy devoted the majority of their time to describing the natural world, usually gathering their explicit theological reflections in a short section at the end (like Newton's "General Scholium"). By contrast, efforts in natural theology—like William Derham's *Physico-Theology* and *Astro-Theology*[50]—were organized around and dominated by theological reflection, interspersing brief appeals to the natural world as spring boards

---

Eighteenth Century," in *The Church of England, c. 1689–c. 1833*, edited by Walsh et al. (New York: Cambridge University Press, 1993) 1–64.

47. Richard G. Olson, "Science and Religion in England, 1590–1740," in *Science and Religion, 1450–1900* (Westport, CT: Greenwood, 2004) 84–91.

48. In addition to Olson, "Science and Religion in England"; see David M. Knight, "The Rise and Fall of Natural Theology," in *Natural Science Books in English 1600–1900* (New York: Praeger, 1972) 47–62.

49. See Dewey D. Wallace Jr., "Natural Theology Among the Dissenters: Richard Baxter and His Circle," in *American Society of Church History Papers for 1992 Meeting* (Portland: Theological Research Exchange Network, 1993) 1–38.

50. William Derham, *Physico-Theology; or, A Demonstration of the Being and Attributes of God from His Works of Creation* (London: William Innys, 1713); and *Astro-Theology; or, A Demonstration of the Being and Attributes of God, from a Survey of the Heavens* (London: William Innys, 1715).

for or evidence backing their theological claims. On this spectrum, Wesley's *Survey* lines up much closer to the "natural philosophy" pole.

The work that Wesley chose to frame and provide the largest portion of text for the first edition of *Survey* was a classic example of natural philosophy, published in Latin by Johann Franz Buddeus while a professor of philosophy at the University of Halle.[51] The bulk of this textbook is devoted to surveying the natural world—beginning with the human body; moving to other animals; then to plants, fossils, and the physical elements of earth, fire, and water; before turning toward the heavens, considering air, meteors, and cosmology. Wesley retained each of these sections in *Survey*; though he omits a subsequent section devoted to debates in physics[52] (remember his limitation to "describing," not "accounting for"). His abridgements within the various sections are infrequent, and sometimes amusing—such as the deletion of descriptions of human reproductive organs.[53] More striking are the additions. Wesley incorporated into *Survey* entire new chapters describing birds, fish, and reptiles, as well as numerous scattered additional examples of natural species and phenomena. Apparently judging that the Buddeus text did not provide *enough* description of the wonders of God's creation, Wesley scoured a number of books and journals to supplement. If I might suggest an analogy—just as Wesley exhorted his people to immerse themselves in the whole of scripture, not rest content with a few proof texts; he was inviting them to contemplate broadly the "book of nature" (natural philosophy), not render it simply a source for select evidences of divine design (natural theology).

Of course, Wesley *did* believe that the natural world bore evidence of God's wisdom and design. So there is a theological component in his *Survey*. But several things should be noted about this component. To begin with, Wesley omits the final section of Buddeus's text, which was devoted to metaphysical description and debates about spirits, angels, and God.[54] In its place Wesley intersperses through the *Survey* occasional theological interludes that provide more limited reflection upon the wisdom and goodness of God as manifest in the aspect of

51. Johann Franz Buddeus, *Elementa Philosophiae Theoretica* (Halle: Glauche-Hallensis, 1706).

52. Ibid., 253–323.

53. Compare ibid., 70–72, to *Survey*, 1:96.

54. See ibid., 326–92.

the natural world just described. While a few of these reflections are original to Wesley, he draws most from other writers, including leading exemplars of natural theology like William Derham, Thomas Morgan, Bernard Nieuwentyt, and John Ray.[55]

Given his dependence on so many works of natural theology, the question recurs of why Wesley did not call the *Survey* a natural theology. One other reason for his hesitance, I would suggest, is awareness of a difference in tone. Prominent works of "natural theology" in Wesley's day were sliding from the more modest classical stance of seeking to *confirm belief*, into the more ambitious Enlightenment stance of *evidentialist apologetics*.[56] The latter is a stance which assumes that the path to reliable knowledge requires first setting aside all belief, then accepting as truth only those claims for which there is undeniable or objectively compelling evidence. On this model, the prime task of natural theology becomes demonstrating God's *existence*, not merely reflecting upon evidence of God's wisdom and character; and the standard to be attained becomes *certainty*, not merely reasonable consonance. This model could also encourage more strident rhetoric. John Ray's *Wisdom of God Manifested in the Works of Creation* can serve as an example. Peppered through this work are comments that anyone who does not recognize that the world was produced by divine reason and art must be "stupid as the basest beasts," "stupid as the dirt one walks on," "forsaken of reason," and "sottish."[57]

Wesley clearly recognized this shift in some of his sources, and he was *not* ready to follow. But this fact has not been broadly appreciated, because there has been little attention paid to Wesley's selective appropriation of his sources.[58] As a beginning example, while Wesley incorporated into his *Survey* at least four extracts from Ray's *Wisdom*

---

55. In addition to Derham's *Physico-Theology* and *Astro-Theology*, see Thomas Morgan, *Physico-Theology* (London: T. Cox, 1741); Bernard Nieuwentyt, *The Religious Philosopher; or, The Right Use of Contemplating the Works of the Creator* (London: Senex & Taylor, 1718); and John Ray, *The Wisdom of God Manifested in the Works of Creation*, 4th ed., enlarged (London: Samuel Smith, 1704—the last edition published during his life).

56. On this distinction, see again Wolterstorff, "Migration of Theistic Arguments."

57. Cf. Ray, *Wisdom of God*, 39, 47, 122–23, 249, 389.

58. Felleman, "Evidence of Things not Seen," 90–92, makes a beginning in this direction.

of God, he chose none with the type of strident apologetic agenda just noted.[59]

William Derham's *Astro-Theology* can serve as a more extensive example. The setting for this work is the claim in Psalm 19 that the heavens declare God's glory. Derham declared his purpose as showing:

> That the observation of the Psalmist is agreeable to experience, is manifest from the deductions which *all* nations have made from God's works, particularly from those of the heavens; namely, that *there is* a God; and that such as have pretended to atheism and have deduced God's works from chance, etc. are singular and *monstrous* in their opinions.[60]

This tone recurs frequently in Derham's volume, such as in the section where he describes briefly the sun and moon, then queries "should there be any found among rational beings so stupid, so vile, so infatuated with their vices as to deny these works to be God's and ascribe them to a *necessity of nature*, or indeed a mere *nothing*, namely *chance*!"[61] Derham goes on to admit that there are indeed a few such depraved individuals in our midst. Derham seeks to correct them by collecting proofs of the existence of God through appeal to the heavens from early Greek and Roman writers—to show that this knowledge is *not* dependent upon special revelation.[62]

Turning to the comparison: Wesley incorporates a section of *Astro-Theology* in his *Survey* that comprises nearly a third of Derham's original text, though significantly abridged.[63] None of the selections just summarized, with their strong apologetic tone, were within the section chosen. More importantly, Wesley edits out the few places in the section chosen that echo this tone. For example, after reflecting on the proportion of distances of heavenly bodies from one another, Derham asks "can we, without great violence to reason, imagine this to be any other than the work of God?" Wesley omits this question, leaving a paragraph

---

59. See *Survey*, 1:308–12, which incorporates Ray, *Wisdom of God*, 134–42, 145–49; and *Survey*, 2:136–40, which incorporates Ray, *Wisdom of God*, 22–31, 61–63.

60. Derham, *Astro-Theology*, 2–3 (*emphasis* added to highlight Enlightenment tone).

61. Ibid., 196–97 (*emphasis* in original).

62. Cf. ibid., 201–9.

63. *Survey*, 3:308–12 is an abridgement of *Astro-Theology*, 50–131 (which has very small pages).

that simply admires God's evident concern for order and life.[64] Likewise, when Derham invokes the annual motion of planets as a "clear manifestation of the [existence of the] great Creator," Wesley revises it to a "clear manifestation of the Creator's wisdom."[65] Finally, Wesley deletes Derham's rhetorical flourish about the stupidity of those who cannot see evidence of God in the regularity of motion in the heavens.[66]

When read alongside works like Ray's *Wisdom of God* and Derham's *Astro-Theology*, the theological reflections that Wesley incorporates into *Survey* can only be described as *modest* in their tone and agenda. While these reflections can speak of nature *displaying* God's wisdom or providential care, they rarely verge on portraying this knowledge as so evident that no rational person could reject it. The general tone is captured well in Wesley's conclusion, which he drew from Matthew Hale's "Account of a Steward." Here Wesley invites the reader to affirm to God:

> I have not looked upon thy works inconsiderately, and passed them over as ordinary things. But I have studiously and diligently searched into them.... And this observation did not rest in the bare perusal of the works themselves, or in the searching out, so far as that could be done, their immediate natural causes. But I traced their being, dependence, and government unto thee, the First Cause of all. And by this tracing of things to their original, I was led to a demonstrative conviction that there is a God, who is the great cause both of their being and motions; yea, that there is but one God; that he is most powerful, most wise, knowing all things, governing all things, supporting all things. Upon these convictions, I was strengthened in the belief of thy holy Word, which had so great a congruity with these truths. And upon these convictions, I did learn the more to honour, reverence, and admire thee; and to worship, serve, and obey thee; ... to love and adore thee, as the fountain of all being and good.[67]

Note how this summary values consideration of the "book of God's works" not as the *foundation* for belief in God or God's various at-

---

64. Compare *Survey*, 3:308 to *Astro-Theology*, 59.

65. Compare *Survey*, 3:310 to *Astro-Theology*, 84.

66. Compare *Survey*, 3:311 to *Astro-Theology*, 99–100.

67. *Survey*, 5:225–27; drawn from Matthew Hale, *Contemplations, Moral and Divine* (London: Shrowsbury & Leigh, 1677) 427–31.

tributes, but as a means of *strengthening* the faith, reverence, and love awakened by God's word, a means of building nascent convictions into demonstrative convictions. This resonates with classical natural theology at its best, much more than with the ambitious evidentialist apologetics of many of Wesley's peers.

This is an important point to recognize in light of Michael Buckley's argument that the ambitious apologetic approach paved the way for modern atheism by virtue of the mechanistic theism that it made central to much Christian teaching by the early nineteenth century. A God who is first and foremost the architect and supreme contriver behind nature's orderly processes is not only subject to being disproved at any moment by alternative accounts for those processes, but also directly blameworthy for any perceived deficiencies in the processes.[68] Moreover, by focusing on the apparent design in nature as the foundation for belief in this God, the evidentialist approach placed a religious burden on the sciences, which they could not bear.[69]

John Hedley Brooke, Professor of Science and Religion at Oxford University, has recently argued that Wesley's *Survey* remains of theological interest today precisely because its modest claims are less prone to the dangers Buckley highlights in more evidentialist natural theologies.[70] I would concur. More to the point, I would suggest that—to the degree that we have imbibed this characteristic commitment—Wesley's present heirs will find themselves resonating in the renewed debates over natural theology more with modest approaches like that of John Polkinghorne than with the evidentialist agenda of the Intelligent Design camp.[71]

---

68. See Michael J. Buckley, *At the Origins of Modern Atheism* (New Haven, CT: Yale University Press, 1987), esp. 338.

69. Cf. John Hedley Brooke, *Science and Religion: Some Historical Perspectives.* (New York: Cambridge University Press, 1991) 195.

70. Cf. John Hedley Brooke, "Science and Dissent: Some Historiographical Issues," in *Science and Dissent in England, 1688–1945*, edited by Paul Wood (Burlington, VT: Ashgate, 2004) 19–37; here, p. 21.

71. See in this regard John Polkinghorne, "Where is Natural Theology Today?" *Science and Christian Belief* 18 (2006) 169–79, esp. 171–72. Concerning the Intelligent Design camp, see William Dembski, "Introduction," in *Mere Creation: Science, Faith & Intelligent Design*, edited by W. Dembski (Downers Grove, IL: InterVarsity, 1998) 13–30, esp. 15, 17, 26–27.

Calling for Epistemic Humility in Both Theology and Science

The modest tone of the theological reflections in *Survey* is not just an evangelistic strategy. It reflects an epistemological conviction that Wesley imbibed with his initial academic training, which deepened and broadened over time. In response to growing awareness of the lack of absolute certainty in most human knowing, seventeenth-century theologians like William Chillingsworth, John Tillotson, and Edward Stillingfleet began to argue that absolute certainty was not necessary. In its place, they advocated a "common sense" approach of asking only for conviction beyond a reasonable doubt. This allowed them to affirm theological claims as reasonable that were not amenable to strict deductive logic.[72]

Wesley was introduced to this stance in his Oxford years, and he embraced its implications over time. He repeatedly found convictions that he thought to be certain called into question, by his own experience and by dialogue with the experience and reasoning of others. Ultimately, this convinced Wesley that *all* human understandings of our experience, tradition, and scripture itself are "opinions." They are *interpretations* of their subject matter. While that subject matter may exist as objective fact, our interpretations of it remain *fallible*, and should remain open to the possibility of further confirmation or modification.[73] Wesley's mature sense of this human reality is captured in his 1750 sermon, "Catholic Spirit," where he insists

> Although every man necessarily believes that every particular opinion which he holds is true (for to believe any opinion is not true, is the same thing as not to hold it); yet can no man be assured that all his own opinions, taken together, are true. Nay, every thinking man is assured they are not, seeing *humanum est errare et nescire*: "To be ignorant of many things, and to mistake in some, is the necessary condition of humanity."[74]

He then balanced and elaborated this point by noting that

---

72. See Henry G. Van Leeuwen, *The Problem of Certainty in English Thought: 1630-90* (The Hague: Martinus Nijhoff, 1970).

73. For more on this see Randy L. Maddox, "Opinion, Religion, and 'Catholic Spirit': John Wesley on Theological Integrity," *Asbury Theological Journal* 47.1 (1992) 63–87; and Maddox, "The Enriching Role of Experience," in *Wesley and the Quadrilateral*, edited by W. S. Gunter (Nashville: Abingdon, 1997) 107–27.

74. Sermon 39, "Catholic Spirit," §1.4, *Works* 2:84.

> A catholic spirit is not speculative latitudinarianism. It is not an indifference to all opinions.... A man of a truly catholic spirit has not now his religion to seek. He is fixed as the sun in his judgment concerning the main branches of Christian doctrine. ... [While] he is always ready to hear and weigh whatsoever can be offered against his principles.[75]

In Wesley's emerging Enlightenment setting, most folk welcomed such recognition of the fallibility of theological claims, with its implication of modesty and openness to further dialogue. Where Wesley ran into opposition was when he suggested that scientific claims were in the same epistemological camp—they too were ultimately human "opinions" that remained fallible or less than absolutely certain. This assumption on Wesley's part was clear in the *Survey* from its first edition in 1763, because scattered through this and later editions are accounts of disagreements over both specific issues like the size of the moon and broader issues like cosmological models. In these accounts, Wesley typically refused to choose sides, commenting instead on the limits of human knowledge. His reserve triggered a letter from a writer calling himself "Philosophaster," published in late 1764 in the *London Magazine*, which invoked "clear facts" to dismiss several alternative positions in these debates and lampooned Wesley's caution.[76] Wesley's published response worked through the debated topics again, underlining the continuing disagreements among current authors, and concluded by admonishing the writer

> Permit me, sir, to give you one piece of advice. Be not so *positive*, especially with regard to things which are neither easy nor necessary to be determined. I ground this advice on my own experience. When I was young I was *sure* of everything. In a few years, having been mistaken a thousand times, I was not half so sure of most things as before. At present I am hardly sure of any thing, but what God has revealed to man.[77]

Wesley included his letter in subsequent editions of *Survey*, followed by extracts from writers like Robert Boyle who similarly emphasized the

---

75. Ibid., §3.1, *Works* 2:92–93.

76. Philosophaster, "To Mr. John Wesley," *London Magazine* 34 (1764) 570–73.

77. Letter to the Editor of the *London Magazine* (January 1, 1765), *London Magazine* 35 (1765) 26–29, quote on 28. Philosophaster's reply to Wesley was published in *London Magazine* 35 (1765) 128–30.

disagreements among and limitations of reigning accounts of nature. Wesley prefaced the extracts with the insistence that "I do not *deny*, but only *doubt* the present system of astronomy."[78]

It is important to add that Wesley's hesitance to claim certainty about a particular cosmological model was not provisional. He was not just waiting until conclusive evidence was found. Rather, his epistemic humility was rooted in the theological conviction that "God hath so done his works that we may admire and adore, but we cannot search them out to perfection."[79] And it was reinforced by his philosophical conviction of the fallibility of our understanding of what God has revealed—whether in the book of scripture or the book of nature.

Wesley's mature broad-ranging epistemic humility was out of step with the push of the Enlightenment for certainty and particularly with the emerging modern approach to science.[80] But it resonates with a two-sided call for epistemic humility in the current science-and-religion dialogue. One side of this call is addressed to theology, with scientists and theologians desiring a "humility theology" that operates on the assumption there is more to know about God and about the natural world than is now known or ever will be known.[81] The other side of the call challenges the hubris of "scientism," which seeks to account for all reality—including religion and ethics—on purely naturalist grounds.[82] I believe that Wesley's precedent would encourage his present heirs to support both of these sides, and perhaps press the second side a little further.

Most critiques of scientism focus on admonishing science to "stick to its field," but say less about the importance of epistemic humility even within its proper field. Wesley was clearly no precursor of the radical skepticism of Paul Feyerabend, but his stress on epistemic

---

78. Wesley's letter is found in *Survey* 3:321–28, quote on 327. The extracts occupy 3:328–55, with Wesley's opening observation on p. 328.

79. Wesley, Preface, §5, *Survey*, 1:vii; in *Works* (Jackson) 14:301. This is the concluding line of his explication of the restricted goal of *Survey* quoted earlier. See also Sermon 69, "The Imperfection of Human Knowledge," 1.5–13, *Works* 2:571–77.

80. Cf. Stephen Toulmin, *Cosmopolis: The Hidden Agenda of Modernity* (New York: Free Press, 1990).

81. See Robert L. Herrmann, ed., *God, Science & Humility: Ten Scientists Consider Humility Theology* (Philadelphia: Templeton Foundation Press, 2000).

82. See Mikael Stenmark, *Scientism: Science, Ethics, and Religion* (Burlington, VT: Ashgate, 2001).

finitude strikes some resonance with the emphasis on the contextuality of scientific paradigms introduced into recent philosophy of science by Thomas Kuhn. In my view, the strongest resonance with the balance in Wesley's comments on "Catholic Spirit" among current philosophies of science is to be found in Imre Lakatos's model of progressive research programs.[83]

Convinced of the Importance of "Honoring the Dialogue"

I mentioned above that dialogue with the experience and reasoning of others made Wesley aware of the fallibility of his "opinions" or interpretations of matters under consideration. I now want to stress that over time he found in dialogue the most helpful way to *test* opinions, seeking those which are most adequate. For theological opinions, this involved overlapping dialogues: Wesley modeled testing them in an ongoing dialogue between scripture, tradition, experience of life and the world, and reason; all read in dialogue with other interpreters. When confronted with an apparent conflict between scripture and experience, for example, his way forward proved to be not simply debating which was more authoritative but engaging in the difficult (and often lengthy) reconsideration of his *interpretations* of *both* of these—and of tradition—often prodded by alternatives defended by others, until an interpretation emerged that *did justice to all*.[84]

A fairly well-known example of this ongoing process was Wesley's changing stance on women preachers.[85] I want to sketch an instance where Wesley's dialogue with the "science" of his day—the carefully reflective experience of the natural world—helped him to revise a traditional theological viewpoint, moving to a stance that could do better justice to scripture.

While scripture speaks of God's ultimate salvific goal as the "new heavens and earth" (i.e., transformation of everything in the universe),

---

83. A good introduction to these alternatives can be found in Chalmers, *What Is ... Science?*

84. In this description I am trying to provide a bit more dynamic and dialogical account of what is often termed the "Wesleyan Quadrilateral."

85. See Paul Wesley Chilcote, *John Wesley and the Women Preachers of Early Methodism* (Metuchen, NJ: Scarecrow, 1991).

a variety of influences led Christians through the first millennium to assume increasingly that our final state is "heaven above." The latter was seen as a realm where human spirits dwelling in ethereal bodies join eternally with all other spiritual beings—a category that did not include animals!—in continuous worship of the Ultimate Spiritual Being.[86] By contrast, they assumed that the physical universe, which we abandon at death, would eventually be annihilated. Wesley imbibed this understanding of our final state in his upbringing, and through much of his ministry it was presented as obvious and unproblematic. A good example is the preface to his first volume of *Sermons*:

> I am a spirit come from God and returning to God; just hovering over the great gulf, till a few moments hence I am no more seen—I drop into an unchangeable eternity! I want to know one thing, the way to heaven—how to land safe on that happy shore. God himself has condescended to teach the way; for this very end he came from heaven.[87]

In the last decade of his life, however, Wesley reclaimed the biblical imagery of God's cosmic renewal, shifting his focus from "heaven above" to the future new creation.[88] After a tentative defense of animals having "souls" in 1775, he issued a bold affirmation of final salvation for animals in the 1781 sermon "The General Deliverance."[89] While not without precedent, this sermon was unusual for its time, and it is often cited as a pioneer effort in reaffirming the doctrine of animal salvation in the Western church. Broadening the scope even further, Wesley's 1785 sermon on "The New Creation" refused to limit God's redemptive purposes to sentient beings, insisting that the very elements of our current universe will be present in the new creation, though they will be dramatically improved over current conditions.[90]

---

86. For a good history of the ascendancy of this model, see Colleen McDannell and Bernhard Lang, *Heaven: A History* (New Haven, CT: Yale University Press, 1988).

87. *Sermons* (1746), Preface, §5, *Works* 1:105.

88. For more details on this transition, see Randy L. Maddox, "Nurturing the New Creation: Reflections on a Wesleyan Trajectory," in *Wesleyan Perspectives on the New Creation*, edited by M. Douglas Meeks (Nashville: Kingswood Books, 2004) 21–52; here, 43–49.

89. Sermon 60, "The General Deliverance," *Works* 2:437–50.

90. Sermon 64, "The New Creation," *Works* 2:500–10.

What contributed to Wesley's reclaiming of the biblical theme of the cosmic scope of redemption? One factor was clearly a concern about animal suffering and theodicy. Wesley shared the sentiments of his friend George Cheyne:

> It is utterly incredible that any creature . . . should come into this state of being and suffering for no other purpose than we see them attain here. . . . There must be some infinitely beautiful, wise, and good scene remaining for all sentient and intelligent beings, the discovery of which will ravish and astonish us one day.[91]

Wesley's proposal about this scene would likely have astonished even Cheyne! Wesley had long doubted the adequacy of a theodicy that justified God's goodness in permitting the possibility of the fall by contending that God would restore things to their pre-fallen condition. In his view, a truly loving God would only permit the present evil in the world if an *even better* outcome might be achieved by allowing this possibility than without it. Thus, he insisted that in our resurrected state God would shower humanity with greater capacities and blessings than Adam and Eve ever enjoyed.[92] In "General Deliverance" Wesley extended this proposal to the lower animals, suggesting that as compensation for the evil they experienced in this life God would bestow greater abilities on them in the new creation, including perhaps even the ability to relate to God as humans do now.[93]

While this proposal may strike us as fanciful, and ill-fitting to scripture, I want to stress that Wesley was brought to it through his deeper engagement with leading works in natural philosophy that utilized the model of the "chain of beings" to organize their study. Recall that this model arranges the various "beings" in a hierarchal progression of relative excellence of abilities. For example, fish were higher in the chain than plants, dogs higher than fish, humans higher than dogs, and celestial beings higher than humans. Moreover, a central assumption of the model was that the only type of cosmos fitting for a Perfect Being to produce was one in which every conceivable niche was occupied by

---

91. George Cheyne, *An Essay on Regimen* (London: Rivington, 1740) 86–87.

92. See Sermon 59, "God's Love to Fallen Man," *Works* 2:423–35; and Sermon 63, "The General Spread of the Gospel," §27, *Works* 2:499.

93. See Sermon 60, "General Deliverance," §3.6–7, *Works* 2:448.

its appropriate type of being. The work of natural philosophers became identifying and placing each creature in its appropriate niche.

Lest we dismiss it too quickly, I would note that Clarence Glacken has argued that the modern ecological ideas of the unity of nature and the balance and harmony of nature trace their roots to this model of the chain of beings.[94] Glacken particularly highlights the role of John Ray and Charles Bonnet in adapting the model to frame surveys of the burgeoning knowledge of the natural world in the eighteenth century. Wesley was familiar with Ray's *Wisdom of God* from the early 1730s. He encountered the writings of Charles Bonnet, a prominent Swiss naturalist, in the early 1770s.[95] It was through Bonnet that Wesley gained deeper appreciation for the implications of the chain of beings. Indeed, he came to value the model so highly that he incorporated an abridgement of Bonnet's 2-volume overview of the chain of beings into *Survey* in 1777.[96]

Wesley almost certainly took the suggestion of animals gaining greater powers in the next life from Bonnet, who proposed that the entire chain of beings would be moved up a notch at the end of this age.[97] A more significant notion that Wesley clearly embraced from Bonnet concerns our human connection with the rest of the chain. He retained in his abridgment of Bonnet a response to the suggestion that it would be better if humans were angels, which counsels:

> Confess your error and acknowledge that every being is endued with a perfection suited to the ends of its creation. It would cease to answer that end the very moment it ceased to be what it is. By changing its nature it would change its place and that which it occupied in the universal hierarchy ought still to be the residence of a being resembling it, otherwise harmony would be

---

94. Clarence J. Glacken, *Traces on the Rhodian Shore: Nature and Culture in Western Thought from Ancient Times to the End of the Eighteenth Century* (Berkeley: University of California Press, 1967) esp. 379.

95. Vol. 2 of Charles Bonnet, *La Palingénésie philosophique; or Idées sur l'état passé et sur l'état futur des etres vivans*, 2nd ed. (Munster: Philip Henry Perrenon, 1770), is among the books of Wesley's library that have survived, in the collection at Wesley's house, London. This volume is signed by Wesley and dated as obtained in 1772.

96. Charles Bonnet, *The Contemplation of Nature*, 2 vols. (London: Longman & Becket, 1766); cf. *Survey*, 4:60–333.

97. Bonnet makes this proposal in *Palingénésie philosophique*, Parts 1–5 (1:187–97) and 14 (2:62–84).

destroyed. In the assemblage of all the orders of *relative* perfections consists the *absolute* perfection of this whole, concerning which God said "that it was good."[98]

If this is taken seriously, there can be no eschatological ideal that limits salvation to humanity (even in the subtle form of stressing that humans are "microcosms" of the whole cosmos). It would be a thwarting of God's creative will and a deprivation of all concerned!

I am convinced that Wesley's pondering of this point as he read and abridged Bonnet in the mid-1770s played a significant role in his strong reclaiming of cosmic redemption shortly thereafter. As an Anglican theologian, raised with deep appreciation for the *conjoined* witness of the book of scripture and the book of nature, Wesley was open to welcoming an insight from the science of his day that brought back into focus a biblical (and early Christian) theme that had been obscured. He would surely encourage his twenty-first century progeny to exercise a similar openness in their theological reflection.

Concerned to Push for Appropriate Consonance

I hasten to add that Wesley would immediately reject any suggestion that the challenge to existing interpretations moves only one direction—from science to theology. While he did not consider it his role to advance explanatory accounts in natural philosophy, he was more than ready to encourage reconsideration of accounts that appeared to conflict with central theological convictions or broadly-shared understandings of scripture.

An appropriate case in point is Wesley's response to David Hartley's *Observations on Man*, published in 1749.[99] Hartley was a physician and known to Wesley through their mutual friend, John Byrom. Hartley also knew Charles Wesley, and presented him a signed copy of *Observations* shortly after it was published.[100] Hartley's study is an early work in physical psychology, which presents all of the operations

---

98. Wesley, *Survey*, 4:62.

99. David Hartley, *Observations on Man: His Frame, His Duty, and His Expectations*, 2 vols. (London: Charles Hitch & Stephen Austen, 1749).

100. The copy is now part of the holdings of the Methodist Archives in the John Rylands University Library (shelf number MAW CW66-67). It bears the inscription "To the Rev. Charles Wesley from the author. June 26, 1753" as well as Charles's signature.

of the soul—all thoughts, volitions, feelings, etc.—as dependent upon vibrations of fibers in the brain (at least, as long as the soul remains connected to the body). Significantly, Hartley commented in the preface that he had slowly and reluctantly reached the conclusion that this integral association entailed a thorough determinism of all human experience and behavior.[101]

Wesley waited to respond publicly to Hartley's study, but eventually made it a main target of *Thoughts upon Necessity* (1774) and an abridged version, "A Thought on Necessity" (1780).[102] In his response it is clear that this instance of dialogue with natural philosophy had not led Wesley to revise his theological emphasis on authentic liberty in human willing. Rather, he stressed his judgment that a thorough determinist account of human behavior undercuts both human moral accountability and the justice of God in condemning or rewarding human actions. These were central theological convictions that he could not easily set aside or credibly interpret in a way compatible with determinism. Yet, Wesley allowed that Hartley's emphasis on the physical dimension of human consciousness and volition contained "a great deal of truth."[103] Wesley's obvious desire was to affirm the full participation of our physical dimension in inclining humans to various states and actions, while maintaining some modest ability to resist or refuse automatic enactment of these inclinations.[104] His ultimate solution in response to Hartley was to insist that God, as sovereign, surely had the power to interrupt the causal chain.[105]

This solution is patently inadequate. It simply substitutes a supernatural account of human behavior for a natural account. Wesley would have been better served by further elaboration of his notion of "liberty" as a category of human nature. But my goal is not to demonstrate that Wesley was able to develop full consonance between theology and the science of his day. It is enough to show that he was concerned to *push*

---

101. See Hartley, *Observations*, 1:vi.

102. Wesley, *Thoughts upon Necessity* (London: Hawes, 1774), in *Works* (Jackson) 10:457–74; and "A Thought on Necessity," *Arminian Magazine* 3 (1780) 485–92, in *Works* (Jackson) 10:474–80.

103. Wesley, *Thoughts upon Necessity*, 4.2, *Works* (Jackson) 10:469.

104. See his discussion of "liberty" in ibid., 3.9, *Works* (Jackson) 10:468–69.

105. See ibid., 4.4, *Works* (Jackson) 10:473. Also in "Thought on Necessity," 4.1, *Works* (Jackson) 10:478.

for consonance, in part by encouraging reconsideration of certain models in science.

Wesley's precedent leaves little room for his current progeny to rest content with the supposed peace of a "separate but equal" relationship between theology and science, such as Stephen Gould's proposal of "nonoverlapping magisteria."[106] It would encourage us instead to engage reigning models in the natural sciences in honest dialogue, reflecting on where these models resonate with our deep theological convictions and where they create (or, appear to create) significant dissonance. It would also encourage those among us with the appropriate expertise to engage in the important and difficult work of proposing and building support for alternative accounts, *within the relevant sciences themselves*, in those areas of dissonance.

We could name many examples where this kind of work is underway among Wesley's progeny and in the larger church. To stick to the focus of Wesley's concern relating to David Hartley, I will limit myself to suggesting that Wesley would be gratified by efforts like those of Warren Brown and his associates who are seeking to elaborate a neurobiological account of human experience and volition that takes with full seriousness the determinative elements while also elucidating a modest, but real, element of liberty (or, "agent causation").[107]

COUNTERING THE TENDENCY TO ANTHROPOCENTRIC EXPLOITATION

One of the central dynamics that transformed natural philosophy into modern science over the course of the eighteenth century was the increasing adoption of Francis Bacon's perspective that the value of *any* study of nature was proportionate to the technological benefits it provided for human control and exploitation of the natural world.[108]

---

106. A brief sense of this proposal, and the alternative stress on consonance, can be found in Peters, "Science and Theology."

107. See particularly, Warren S. Brown, "Cognitive Neuroscience and a Wesleyan View of the Person," in *Companions and Apprentices*, edited by Maxine Walker (San Diego: Point Loma Press, 1999) 31–39; and Nancey Murphy & Warren Brown, *Did My Neurons Make Me Do It? Philosophical and Neurobiological Perspectives on Moral Responsibility and Free Will* (New York: Oxford University Press, 2007).

108. For an incisive analysis of this dimension of Bacon, see Carolyn Merchant, *The Death of Nature* (San Francisco: Harper & Row, 1980) 164–90.

Wesley was familiar with champions of this anthropocentric, exploitive emphasis in scientific investigation. He had to look no further than William Derham, who insisted "We can, if need be, ransack the whole globe, . . . penetrate into the bowels of the earth, descend to the bottom of the deep, travel to the farthest regions of this world, to acquire wealth, to increase our knowledge, or even only to please our eye or fancy."[109]

This is another of the passages from Derham that was *not* selected by Wesley for inclusion in his *Survey*. Nor does anything in its vein from other sources appear there. Part of the reason is that Wesley imbibed more deeply than Derham the convictions of the chain of beings model of nature. While this model highlights (as ecologists would today) a range of ways that any particular species might contribute to the well-being of others above or below it in the chain, it also insists that every species has intrinsic value and a right to exist for its own purposes. John Ray, who was deeply shaped by this model, emphasized the relevant implication: "It is a generally received opinion that all this visible world was created for man, that man is the end of creation, as if there were no other end of any creature but some way or other to be serviceable to man. . . . Yet wise men nowadays think otherwise."[110] While Ray went on to insist that, in this interdependent chain, all species are in some sense serviceable to humanity and we would frustrate the purposes of their creation if we did not make appropriate use of them, he offered Wesley a model of *modest* anthropocentrism.[111]

Wesley appropriated this model in a way that moved beyond Ray through his distinctive emphasis regarding our role as "stewards." This emphasis is seen most clearly in his instructions on the use of money, where he criticizes any suggestion that resources put at our disposal are for us to use however we see fit. Wesley insists instead that everything belongs ultimately to God; that it is placed in our care to use as God directs; and that God directs us to use it for the benefit of others once

---

109. Derham, *Physico-Theology*, 112. For perspective on diversity in Derham's context, see William Coleman, "Providence, Capitalism, and Environmental Degradation: English Apologetics in an Era of Economic Revolution." *Journal of the History of Ideas* 37 (1976) 27–44.

110. Ray, *Wisdom of God*, 127–28.

111. See ibid, 176–77 n. 39. Cf. John Hedley Brooke, "'Wise Men Nowadays Think Otherwise': John Ray, Natural Theology, and the Meanings of Anthropomorphism," *Notes Received by the Royal Society of London* 54 (2000) 199–213.

our basic needs are met.[112] Extending this principle to the rest of creation, the focus of Wesley's environmental ethic is better characterized as *theocentric* than anthropocentric. He portrayed the ideal relationship of humanity with creation (modeled by Adam in the Garden of Eden) as one of *modest stewardship*, where we devote our distinctive gifts to upholding God's intentions for the balance and flourishing of all creation.[113]

Most in Wesley's day shared his assumption of the idyllic nature of the original creation, with peace abounding between all creatures and humans possessing the knowledge to promote the thriving of the whole. They also shared the recognition that this was very unlike the world in which we live now, with "nature red in tooth and claw" (Tennyson) and humans largely at the mercy of the forces of nature. Differences emerged around the implications drawn from the present condition for human interaction with the rest of nature. Many resigned themselves to the situation, as long as we are in the present world. Among the ones who believed that change was possible, the most significant distinction emerged between those (like Francis Bacon) who championed the mandate to *reclaim the mastery* over creation that was lost in the fall, and those (like Wesley) who pleaded for *resuming the loving stewardship* of creation that we inverted in the fall.[114] While the first two alternatives could acquiesce to (or even justify) the aggressive domination of other creatures by humans, Wesley is representative of the third alternative in his portrayal of such domination as the epitome of the fallen practices that must be set aside.[115] Deeply aware of how much damage we have done, the stewardship that Wesley called for us to resume is not only modest but *chastened*.[116]

---

112. See Sermon 28, "Sermon on the Mount 8," §§11, 25–26, *Works* 1:618–19, 628–29; Sermon 50, "The Use of Money," *Works* 2:266–80; and Sermon 51, "The Good Steward," §1.1, *Works* 2:283.

113. See Sermon 60, "The General Deliverance," §1.6, *Works* 2:444.

114. This distinction is highlighted in Peter Harrison, "Subduing the Earth: Genesis 1, Early Modern Science, and the Exploitation of Nature," *Journal of Religion* 79 (1999) 86–109; esp. 102–3.

115. See esp. his description of the negative impact of humanity upon creation in Sermon 60, "The General Deliverance," 2, *Works* 2:442–45.

116. For more on Wesley's precedent for environmental stewardship, see Randy L. Maddox, "Anticipating the New Creation: Wesleyan Foundations for Holistic Mission," *Asbury Journal* 62 (2007) 49–66.

This ideal, alongside Wesley naming his compendium of natural philosophy a *Survey of the Wisdom of God in Creation*, suggests a very different rationale for the study of nature (or science) than that of Bacon. We should seek this knowledge not to increase our ability to exploit nature but to increase our awareness of the wondrous range of creation and deepen our sensitivity to our integral connection with it all—so that we might more effectively *imitate the God whose mercy is over all his works.*[117] Progeny like that would surely rejoice Wesley's heart!

---

117. Cf. Sermon 60, "General Deliverance," §3.10, *Works* 2:449.

2

John Wesley's Vision of Science in the Service of Christ[1]

John W. Haas Jr.

The eighteenth century challenged Christians to adapt their ways to new ideas. Many intellectuals in John Wesley's England embraced a widening gap between the natural and the supernatural, natural law and providence, and rational faith and piety, which had roots in the mechanistic interpretations of nature epitomized by Sir Isaac Newton's accomplishments. This study offers an analysis of Wesley's interaction with natural philosophy and the challenges which the new understanding of nature brought to believers.

Wesley's intellectual horizon included a lifelong interest in the progress of science and the ways that science could serve Christian purposes. Although he occasionally dabbled in the field or recommended projects to others, Wesley never had the interest (or time) to devote to serious experimental study and should not be compared with contemporary scientist-clerics such as Joseph Priestley, Stephen Hales, Bishop Samuel Horsley, or William Derham. Mainly, he focused on science to serve his grand purpose of furthering the gospel and helping the sick.

---

1. Originally published in *Perspectives on Science and Christian Faith* 47 (December 1995).

He also wrote inexpensive works on natural science for his constituency. Wesley's sermons and other writings point to an enthusiasm for the natural world as God's World that could be exploited for humanitarian as well as traditional religious purposes.

Wesley's student days at Oxford indicated a more than ordinary attention to science. He was interested in such disparate questions as the nature of "vacuums, the Chain of Being, and the ability of animals to reason."[2] In later travels, he would meet and comment on the work of many individuals working in science. He was particularly concerned with unusual natural phenomena and would often speculate on their causes. An insatiable reader, Wesley read scientific works throughout his life, often from the back of his horse. From his own reading and the advice of others, he developed short lists of scientific works for his correspondents, schools, and lay preachers. These collections included older works by John Ray, Cotton Mather, and Jonathan Edwards as well as current works by Benjamin Franklin, Charles Bonnet, John Hutchinson, and Oliver Goldsmith. Wesley followed the debates that swirled around the various interpretations of Newton's ideas. In the famous Clarke-Leibnitz controversy he would side with Clarke on one question,[3] but at another point in the debate would support Leibnitz.[4]

Wesley's view of the natural world and the position of nature in God's economy was never listed in one place or integrated into a system. In drawing together his ideas from various sources, we recognize that our understanding will be tentative and incomplete . . . an appropriate response to one who dealt with challenges in context rather that from a confession.

---

2. John C. English, "John Wesley and Isaac Newton's 'System of the World,'" *Proceedings of the Wesley Historical Society* XLVIII (1991) 71 and John C. English, "John Wesley's Scientific Education," *Methodist History* 30 (1991) 50.

3. *Journal*, May 22, 1775, *The Works of John Wesley*. Thomas Jackson, editor, 14 vols., 3rd ed. (London: Wesleyan Methodist Book Room, 1872; reprint ed.: Grand Rapids, MI: Zondervan, 1958–1959), IV:45.

4. Sermon: "On the Omnipresence of God," (1788) II.3, *The Bicentennial Edition of the Works of John Wesley*. Editor in Chief, Frank Baker (Nashville: Abingdon, 1984– [Volumes 7, 11, 16, and 25 originally appeared as the *Oxford Edition of the Works of John Wesley*, Oxford: Oxford University Press, 1975–1985]) 4:44.

Wesley's Intellectual Roots

In examining Wesley's interaction with natural philosophy, it is instructive to examine several features in his background which influenced his response to the *Book of Nature*. Wesley never offered a reason for his interest in natural phenomena and scientific activity. John English has suggested that his curiosity may have been stimulated as a child by the "gentlemanly scientific interests of his father and older brother Samuel, members of the Spalding Gentlemen's Society, which also included Alexander Pope and Sir Isaac Newton in its number."[5] Wesley early recognized the impact of the revolution in science on public life and the influence for good and evil that it could offer to Christianity.[6]

Wesley's ideas on the philosophical foundation of scientific and religious knowledge guided his approach to a wide spectrum of questions. He studied and commented on works by John Locke, Rene Descartes, Nicholas Malebranche, John Norris, Isaac Newton, George Cheyne, Peter Browne, David Hartley, David Hume, and Thomas Reid as well as an eclectic range of theological sources.[7]

The Power and Limits of Empiricism and Reason

Wesley assimilated and adapted the ideas of John Locke, Peter Browne, and John Norris in forming an epistemology which valued "spiritual senses as well as those in the physical domain."[8] Orthodox theologians Thomas Bray, William Law, Isaac Watts, Bishop Butler (in part), and William Cowper all affirmed the need for empirical verification expressed in Locke's *An Essay Concerning Human Understanding* (1690). Wesley's practical bent, aversion to metaphysical speculation, and

---

5. English, "John Wesley's Scientific Education," 48–50.

6. Sermon: "The Promise of Understanding," (1730) I.1–II.1 (BE 4:281–285). Richard G. Olson, "Tory-High Church Opposition to Science and Scientism in the Eighteenth Century: The Works of John Arbuthnot, Jonathan Swift, and Samuel Johnson," in James G. Burke, ed., *The Uses of Science in the Age of Newton* (Berkeley: University of California Press, 1983) provides insight into the science/religion context in which the young Wesley grew up.

7. See the Introduction (BE 1:55–69).

8. "An Earnest Appeal to Men of Reason and Religion," (1744) 32–35 (BE 11:56–57), See also the Sermons: "Awake, Thou That Sleepest," (1742) I.11 (BE 1:146), "The Witness of The Spirit," I, (1746) I.12 (BE 1: 276) and "The Great Privilege of Those That Are Born of God," (1748) I.3–10 (BE 1:433–35).

emphasis on facts before theory follows the tradition of Francis Bacon, Locke, and Newton. He singled out Bacon for praise for his emphasis on the inductive method.[9]

Brantley has described the multifaceted nature of Locke's influence. Wesley mastered the *Essay*, followed its principles, spread its message, reconciled it with his faith, and incorporated it into his philosophical theology.[10] "The Lockean language of experience, says Brantley, "enabled him [Wesley] to raise his ineffable experience of grace to graceful and cogent expressions of methodology."[11]

Wesley had an almost obsessive concern with "the littleness of human knowledge in both the natural and supernatural."[12] Two influences on this question were Peter Browne's *The Procedure, Extent, and Limits of Human Understanding* (1728) which Wesley praised[13] and Robert Boyle's *The Skeptical Chemist* (1661) from which he would quote on the lack of knowledge of the properties of the metal antimony in his *Remarks on the Limits of Human Knowledge* (1763).[14] The limits on physical knowledge found parallels in theology for those who felt that some scriptural passages were above reason. Locke had described such propositions as those which cannot be derived from the normal method of discerning truth. Boyle's *Things Above Reason* (1691) followed orthodox Anglican thought in asserting that truths such as God's nature, how God made the world out of nothing, or how he unites an immaterial soul to a human body and maintains that union are "incomprehensible truth."[15]

---

9. "On the Gradual Improvement of Natural Philosophy," (1784) 6 (Jackson XIII:483).

10. Richard E. Brantley, *Locke, Wesley, and the Method of English Romanticism* (Gainesville: University of Florida Press, 1984), 17.

11. Ibid., 22–23.

12. Sermon: "The Imperfection of Human Knowledge," (1784) (BE 2:568–86).

13. John C. English, "John Wesley's Indebtedness to John Norris," *Church History* 60 (1991), 55ff.

14. Stewart Andrews, "John Wesley and the Age of Reason," *History Today* 18 (1969), 27.

15. Robert Boyle, *A Discourse of Things Above Reason*, in Thomas Birch, ed., *The Works of the Honourable Robert Boyle*, 6 vols. (London, 1772) 4:409.

The Organic World

During the early part of Wesley's life England was basking in the triumphs of Newton's physics and the focus was on the physical side of nature. Wesley proved an exception to the rule as his curiosity about nature extended over the spectrum from organic to inorganic . . . from animal psychology to comets . . . from man to polyps. Philip Ott notes that the images that Wesley used to relate body and soul were derived from the Cartesian school and reflect similar seventeenth and eighteenth century physiologies.[16] The link between thinking and acting that was popularly thought to involve some sort of animal spirits was held by such Wesley sources as Descartes, Malebranche, Norris, Locke, and Dr. John Cheyne. Later Cheyne moved toward David Hartley's vibratory theory of motion. Both notions are found in Wesley's writings.[17]

Wesley was impressed by the fact that the natural world . . . from dust to man . . . could be arranged in a gradation of infinitesimally different organisms. This Chain (or scale) of Being concept, held by a long line of thinkers from Aristotle to John Locke, has been viewed as a precursor to the concept of evolution.[18]

High Church Influence

One pervasive influence on Wesley's attitude toward science derived from his High Church Anglican roots. Many High-Churchmen rejected the Newtonian natural philosophy espoused by latitudinarian Low-Church leaders, which they associated with deism and atheism. Richard Olson has argued that High-Church antiscientific attitudes represented a concern that the theories and practices of the new science would either directly or indirectly bring harm to the practitioners and those who read their work. This harm came from "the pridefulness and moral insensitivity that seemed to accompany scientific theorizing, or from attempts to extend scientific approaches to inappropriate domains . . .

---

16. Philip W. Oct, "John Wesley on Mind and Body: Toward and Understanding of Health and Wholeness," *Methodist History* 27 (1989) 62–66.

17. Sermon: "Wandering Thoughts," (1762) II. 3, 5 (BE 2:129–30) and "A Thought on Necessity," (1780) I.3, 1I.I (Jackson X:474, 475).

18. John Hedley Brooke, *Science and Religion: Some Historical Perspectives* (Cambridge: Cambridge University Press, 1991) 175–76.

especially to religious and closely associated moral issues."[19] It was natural that Wesley would be inclined toward the novel system of Francis Hutchinson who offered an aggressive High-Church response to the linking of suspect Low-Church theology and Newtonian science.

Wesley lived during a period where the scriptures were taken at face value. Evidence supplied by miracles, fulfilled prophecy, and ancient records was eagerly adapted to endorse the theory of plenary inspiration of the Bible. High-Church conservatives found no fundamental discrepancy between the Old Testament and modern natural science. Biblical criticism had yet to make an impact on literal interpretation. High-Churchmen based their theology on the tenets of St. Augustine which emphasized those aspects of Christian faith most difficult to defend on rational grounds—original sin, the incarnation, vicarious atonement, and redemption.

A hundred years before, Francis Bacon had offered advice about going to the Old Testament for science. "Some of the moderns have indulged this folly with such consummate inconsiderateness," said Bacon, "that they have endeavored to build a system of natural philosophy on the first chapter of Genesis, the book of Job, and the other parts of Scripture, seeking thus the dead amongst the living."[20] Until the late eighteenth century, there was little reliable scientific evidence to offset the story of early Genesis allowing Wesley to avoid the science-Bible battles of a later day.

The mechanistic triumphs of seventeenth century natural science had offered an impersonal deity who ruled through unchanging natural laws. As Wesley grew up, he faced a new picture of God's ways with man. Now God's care was expressed in ordinary natural processes rather than through one who would intervene in nature to save an individual sinner. Order and a tangible, consistent way of viewing nature and society were preferred to the transcendent mystery of classical Christianity. Wesley's struggles with this new movement and his personal quest in coming to terms with reason and piety reflect the modern dilemma.

---

19. Olson, "Tory-High Church Opposition to Science and Scientism in the Eighteenth Century," 9.

20. Francis Bacon, *Novum Organum*, book i, Aphorism LXI, in Robert M. Hutchens, ed., *Great Books of the Western World*, 2nd ed. (Chicago: Encyclopedia Britanica, 1991), 28:114.

Wesley's Integration of Natural Philosophy and Christianity

John Wesley recognized the accomplishments of the new science and sought to bring its power to serve the church. In typical Wesley fashion he never gathered his thoughts on this subject in one place. Our analysis is further complicated (but made more interesting) by the diverse ways that science both served and influenced his ministry. In seeking to trace and define Wesley's "integrative strategy," I will examine the place of natural phenomena in his sermons, his views on apologetics, and his interest in the application of science for the benefit of humankind.

One tradition has viewed Wesley as holding negative views toward science.[21] In a recent paper, I have shown the opposite to be the case, if one examines the entire corpus of his work and pays attention to the context of his alleged antiscience remarks.[22] His enemies were deism, atheism, materialism, and intellectual pride . . . not natural philosophy! Wesley linked scripture and nature in a non-confrontational way emphasizing the values and limits of each mode of God's revelation. This attitude characterized nineteenth century Methodism which remained friendly toward science even with the publication of Darwin's *Origin of Species* (1859).[23]

Scripture and Nature

Wesley's published sermons reflect an active and appreciative interest in the natural world and scientific progress. He summed things up in *God's Approbation of His Works* (1782): "How small a part of this great work of God is man able to understand! But it is our duty to contemplate what he has wrought, and to understand as much of it as we are able."[24]

This speculative sermon drew on sources ranging from Lucretius, Thomas Burnet, and John Hutchinson to Chambers's *Cyclopaedia*; it

---

21. A. D. White, *History of the Warfare of Science With Theology in Christendom* (New York: Appleton, 1895) 1:128, 148, 220–21, 340, 361, 363.

22. John W. Haas Jr., "John Wesley's Eighteenth Century Views on Science and Christianity: An Examination of the Charge of Antiscience," *Church History* 63 (1994) 378–92.

23. See C. David Grant, "Evolution and Darwinism in the *Methodist Quarterly Review*, 1840–1870," *Methodist History* 29 (1991) 175–83.

24. Sermon: "God's Approbation of His Works," (1782) I.2 (BE 2:387).

detailed a pre-fall world without "violent winter or "sultry summer, "pain, "weeds, and without predators" . . . an interpretation which endures in some religious circles today.

The written sermons were designed primarily for "*nurture and reflection* over against the goals of "*proclamation and invitation* for the oral sermons."[25] His written sermons contain a wealth of scriptural references to natural phenomena and scientific information. Often this material would illustrate and embellish the discussion of a particular passage.[26] Wesley would also use natural phenomena as an analogy for spiritual themes.[27] In other instances, he would speculate on the state of nature before the fall or in the world to come.[28] His favorite scientific topics were astronomy, electricity, earthquakes, physiology, and volcanoes. Some of the sermons went far beyond Wesley's claim that in providing "plain truth for plain people" he abstained from all nice and philosophical speculations; from all perplexed and intricate reasonings; and as far as possible from even the show of learning."[29]

In Wesley's day, there was little geological or biological data to add to the scriptural account of the creation period. Orthodox Christians generally read this portion of the Bible in literal fashion. Wesley felt that scripture did not provide a *scientific* account of nature: "the inspired penman in this history [Genesis] . . . [wrote] for the Jews first and calculating his narratives for the infant state of the church, describes things by their outward sensible appearances, and leaves us, by further discoveries of the divine light, to be led into the understanding of the mysteries couched under them."[30] His comment on Gen. 1:3 notes, "He made the stars also, which were spoken of only in general, for the Scriptures were written not to gratify our curiosity but to lead us to God.[31] Yet he happily noted, "I was strengthened in the belief of the holy word, which

---

25. Cf. Introduction (BE 1:14).

26. Cf. his early sermon "The Image of God," (1730) (BE 4:292–303) and one from late in his life "The Imperfection of Human Knowledge," (1784) (BE 2:568–86).

27. Sermon: "On The Trinity," (1775) I.7–16 (BE 2:380–84).

28. Sermon: "God's Approbation of His Works," ibid. I.1–14 (BE 2:388–97) speaks to the pre-fall world. See the sermon, "The New Creation," (1785) 1–18 (BE 2: 500–510) for his speculations on the world to come.

29. Preface: "Sermons on Several Occasions," 3 (BE 1:104).

30. John Wesley, *Wesley's Notes on the Bible* (Grand Rapids: Asbury, 1987) 25.

31. Ibid., 22.

had so great congruity with these [scientific] truths."[32] It is interesting that the order of creation in his *Survey of the Wisdom of God in Creation* (1763) only roughly follows that of *Genesis*, and there only with respect to the creation of animate nature.

Wesley would occasionally use the "two books to support and interpret one another." He invoked Ecc. 3:11 to argue a static view of nature: "So that all things are still as they were at the beginning."[33] He also used the Chain of Being concept to emphasize the unity of creation and the inability of anything in nature to act independently of God. He provided a gloss to improve Genesis 1:31 by inserting the italicized phrase in the text: "when he saw everything he had made, *all in connection with each other*, behold it was very good."[34]

Wesley articulated a prominent place for God as Creator and Sustainer in his *Sermon on the Mount III* (1748).

> The great lesson that our blessed Lord inculcates here . . . is that God is in all things, and that we are to see the Creator in the glass of every creature; that we should use and look upon nothing as separate from God, which indeed is a kind of practical atheism; but with a true magnificence of thought survey heaven and earth and all that is therein as contained by God in the hollow of his hand, who by his intimate presence holds them all in being, who pervades and activates the whole created frame, and is in a true sense the soul of the universe.[35]

Wesley always described nature as wholly dependent on God . . . a voluntarist God who works above the "laws of nature."[36]

In his *On the Education of Children* Wesley encouraged parents to combat the "natural atheism of their children." He chided them for ascribing the works of creation to nature or "chance" or "good or ill

---

32. John Wesley, *A Survey of the Wisdom of God in the Creation: or, A Compendium of Natural Philosophy*, 3rd ed. (London: Fry, 1777) 2:463.

33. Sermon: "The Wisdom of God's Counsels," (1784) 3 (BE 2:553).

34. Cf. Sermons: "God's Approbation of His Works," I.1 (BE 2:388), 14 (BE 2:396–97) and "On Divine Providence," (1786) 8 (BE 2: 537–38).

35. Sermon: "Upon our Lord's Sermon on the Mount" III, (1748) I:11 (BE 1:516–17).

36. Sermon: "Of Hell," (1782) II.1 (BE 3:36).

fortune." "Nothing comes by chance," said Wesley, "that is a silly word: there is no such thing as chance."[37]

Sermons From Nature

Christian tradition has found a further role for the natural world. Medieval, Renaissance and Puritan natural theology taught that nature was a book which illustrated spiritual themes and offered "moral emblems" and "types of things to come."[38] The eighteenth century offered many examples. Wesley's Lincoln College student, James Hervey's *Meditations and Contemplations* (1748) found that every page of nature is rich with "sacred hints," "lively sermons," and "excellent lessons."[39] John Newton thought that a thorough knowledge of scripture was the best preparation for a firsthand understanding of the book of nature. "The Lord has established a wonderful analogy between the natural and spiritual world," said Newton. "Almost every object they see, when they are in a right frame of mind, either leads their thoughts to Jesus, or tends to illustrate some scriptural truth or promise."[40]

Wesley's sermons exhibit a mind deeply saturated with scriptural texts. These often appear as metaphors of things in nature: "leaf shaking in the wind," "grace seasoned with salt," and "he maketh the clouds his chariots." Much less frequently, he borrowed metaphors from his reading or those of his own inventions. He was not averse to linking faith and nature. "We will learn a lesson of faith and cheerfulness from every bird of the air, and every flower of the field," said Wesley.[41] His *Survey of the Wisdom of God in Creation* was designed to lead the reader to see the power, wisdom, and goodness of God, and increase man's happiness.[42] Yet, Wesley was sparing in the use of typology, metaphor, and emblem. His *Minutes* for 1749 contained the injunction to his preach-

37. Sermon: "On The Education of Children," (1783) 13 (BE 3:352).

38. Richard E. Brantley, *Wordsworth's "Natural Methodism"* (New Haven: Yale University Press, 1975) 143. See also Sermon: "Awake Thou That Sleepest," (1742) I.7 (BE 1:144).

39. Brantley, *Wordsworth's "Natural Methodism,"* 144.

40. Ibid.

41. John Wesley, *Explanatory Notes Upon the New Testament*, new ed. (London: Wesleyan-Methodist Book Room, 1884) Matt 6:31, 18.

42. John Wesley, *A Survey of the Wisdom of God in the Creation*, Preface, 1, 7 (Jackson XIV:300, 302).

ers, "Beware of allegorizing or spiritualizing too much."[43] Wesley opposed interpreting scripture by "any allegorizing method." "No other ideas are to be affixed to the words of scripture than such as occur to one who looks at the thing spoken of."[44] His reticence to engage in such rhetorical devices stemmed from the nature of his typically untutored audience, not from a lack of writing skills.

Wesley and The Apologetic Tradition

John Wesley ministered in an age when scientists and clerics sought to use Sir Isaac Newton's triumphs to serve the cause of religion. Newton's followers were primarily found among Low-Church latitudinarians, the dominant force in early eighteenth century Anglicanism. Newtonian natural theology sometimes took antithetical paths and it is ironic that one who wanted his work to support both general and special revelation would be later exploited by the deists who advocated a creator-mechanic over an active providence. Those who invoked the name of Newton in developing views of science and religion often had little understanding of his science and the central place that theology held in his natural philosophy.[45] Wesley, though a contemporary of Newton, would have learned about his nation's hero more from hearsay and the works of his disciples and opponents than from the writings of one who was inordinately reticent to reveal his thoughts on nature or Christianity.[46] High-Churchman Wesley, put off by the acclaim accorded to Newton's accomplishments, suspicious of the theology of many Newtonians and the direction that Newtonian apologetics were taking, would have a natural affinity for the views of John Hutchinson (1674–1737), a fellow High-Church partisan who led a forceful opposition to Newton's ideas.

Wesley was ambivalent about Isaac Newton, at times harshly critical, but later echoed the adoring rhetoric of the day. The *Concise*

---

43. Albert C. Outler, *John Wesley* (New York: Oxford University Press, 1980) 175–76.

44. *Survey* 1:412.

45. Edward B. Davis, "Newton's Rejection of the 'Newtonian World View': The Role of Divine Will in Newton's Natural Philosophy," *Fides et Historia* 22 (1990) 7.

46. Richard S. Wesphall, "The Rise of Science and the Decline of Orthodox Christianity: A Study of Kepler, Descartes, and Newton," in David C. Lindberg and Ronald L. Numbers, eds. *God & Nature: Historical Essays on the Encounter Between Christianity and Science,* (Berkeley: University of California Press, 1986) 229.

Ecclesiastical History (1781) reflects his mature view. "The immortal man to whose genius and indefatigable industry philosophy owed its greatest improvements, and who carried the lamp of knowledge into paths of knowledge that had been unexplored before, was Sir Isaac Newton," said Wesley, "whose name was revered, and his genius admired, even by his warmest adversaries."[47] Wesley might disagree with the metaphysics that claimed Newton's name but would give him his due in experimental physics, signaling a willingness to separate science from theological considerations and philosophy. Earlier, a July 21, 1758 *Journal* entry reported his reading of Needham's discovery of the spontaneous generation of life. Wesley said the "tract confounded all my philosophy" but thought it "highly probable that this particular class of animals existed."[48] In this case, Wesley may not have considered the theological implications of *natural creation* of life; still, this incident offers a further example of his willingness to allow science to speak without religious strictures.

Wesley and other High-Churchmen were attracted to the apologetic line of Bishop Joseph Butler's *The Analogy of Religion, Natural and Revealed, to the Constitution and Course of Nature* (1736).[49] Butler's work was a popular tool in combating deism and became a fixture at the English universities until the age of Darwin. Wesley affirmed Butler's concerns with the limitations of natural knowledge and emphasis on the importance of scriptural knowledge.[50] While Wesley found few deists in mines or fishing villages, he recognized their force in the intellectual life of his nation. He confronted them in his sermons, in his *Arminian Magazine,* and other works directed to a more literate readership.[51]

Wesley entered the apologetic fray at several key points. One question involved the deist view that man could arrive at the essential truths of religion by reason alone. Low-Churchman Richard Bentley's *Boyle*

---

47. John Wesley, *A Concise Ecclesiastical History, From the Birth of Christ to the Beginning of the Present Century* (London: Paramore, 1781) 3:332.

48. *Journal*, August 17, 1758 (Jackson II: 454).

49. *Journal*, February 21, 1746 (Jackson II:7) and *Journal*, May 20, 1768 (ibid. III:323–24).

50. M. Elton Hendricks, "John Wesley and Natural Theology," *Wesleyan Theological Journal* 18:2 (1983) 12–13.

51. See his "An Earnest Appeal to Men of Reason," (BE 11:45–94) and "A Further Appeal to Men of Reason and Religion," (1745) (BE 11:105–331).

Lecture (1692) argued for man's self-sufficiency: "God hath endowed Mankind with powers and abilities, which we call Natural light, and Reason, and Common Sense: by the use of which we cannot miss the discovery of His Being; and this is sufficient."[52] Wesley joined Butler in valuing a limited role for natural theology by emphasizing the inherent uncertainty and limited power of human knowledge.[53] His sermon *The Case of Reason Impartially Considered* (1781) represents an attempt to find a middle ground between the extremes of undervaluing and overvaluing reason.[54] Wesley shared a commitment to the traditional evidences for theism but felt that Holy Scripture has a priority over the witness of nature.[55] The wisdom of God in creation was available to all men but insufficient to gain saving faith. Newton's triumphs derived "independently of revelation and Church tradition undermined this view."[56]

John Hutchinson felt that Newtonian philosophy gave comfort to deists and dissenters by what he saw as excessive stress on God's *immanence* over His *transcendence*.[57] Curiously, Hutchinson's alternative system postulated a self-contained world without need for a divine agency that effectively supported the same pantheistic-materialistic accounts of nature which Boyle and Newton had sought to offset.[58] By the 1740s British natural philosophers were less concerned to demonstrate God's providence and direct role in nature's laws and the violation of these laws and turned instead to explanations based on active powers *immanent* in matter.[59] God's volition was no longer necessary. In an attempt to stem this anti-theistic flow Wesley turned to Hutchinson's full-blown anti-Newtonian system of scriptural science.

---

52. As quoted in C. B. Wilde, "Hutchinsonianism, Natural Philosophy, and Religious Controversy in Eighteenth Century Britain," *History of Science*, xviii (1980) 8–9.

53. Sermon: "The General Deliverence," (1781) III. 7–8 (BE 2:448–49).

54. Sermon: "The Case of Reason Impartially Considered," (1781) 5 (BE 2:588–89).

55. Letter: John Wesley to Dr. Middleton, January 24, 1748–49 (Jackson X:76).

56. Wilde, "Hutchinsonianism," 8.

57. Ibid., 5.

58. Steven Shapin, "Social Uses of Science, from G. S. Rousseau and Ray Porter," *The Ferment of Knowledge* (Cambridge: Cambridge University Press, 1980) 110.

59. P. M. Heinman, "Voluntarism and Immanence: Conception of Nature in 18th Century British Thought," *Journal of the History of Ideas* 39 (1978) 277.

Hutchinson's approach was based on two concepts; (1) that all the operations of nature can be explained in terms of a *triune fluid* which appears as fire, light, and air, and (2) the notion that scripture (the Hebrew Language) "contained the indispensable key to all knowledge, both natural and spiritual."[60] Hutchinson's physico-theology was attractive to Wesley because his natural philosophy and theology were based on scripture. Difficult doctrines such as the Trinity were shown to be both scripturally based and empirically verified in nature . . . accomplishments which restored "the credibility of Church doctrine and the philosophical integrity of the Bible."[61]

Wesley often referred to Hutchinson's work, primarily in critical terms. In 1758 after conferring with a leading Hebrew scholar on Hutchinson's Hebrew treatment, he concluded "his hypothesis is unsupported by scripture; very ingenious, but quite precarious."[62] A 1770 *Journal* entry notes "his whole hypothesis, philosophical, and theological is unsupported by any solid proof."[63] Brooke has suggested that Wesley's skepticism of Hutchinson's system may have come from his aversion to *any system* of natural philosophy.[64] Yet Wesley inevitably referred to Hutchinson in his critical discussions on astronomy and adopted his unique translation of the early verses of Genesis.[65] It is not obvious why Wesley kept coming back to one whose system he rejected. Hutchinson's High-Church orthodoxy and good intentions appear to have won the day over what he knew was poor exegesis and highly idiosyncratic natural philosophy.

A further eighteenth century problem involved the perennial tension between providential and natural law explanations of phenomena . . . the way that God dealt with nature, society, and individuals. At the time of Newton's death a delicate balance was maintained between a general providence which created the world *ex nihlo* and established and maintained the laws by which it operated, and a special providence which produced miracles and intervened to fine-tune the workings of

---

60. Wilde, "Hutchinsonianism," 3.

61. Ibid.

62. *Journal*, December 12 and 22, 1756 (Jackson II:389).

63. *Journal*, February 13, 1770 (Jackson III:387).

64. Brooke, *Science and Religion*, 190.

65. Sermon: "God's Approbation of His Works," I.1 (BE 2:388) and "On the Fall of Man," (1782) 6 (BE 2:409).

nature. This balance would swing in the direction of a watchmaker God who worked through the laws of nature rather than an interventionist deity.[66] Joseph Priestley's materialist world view was an extreme example of the use of Newton's ideas to argue for the *self-sufficiency* of matter and the laws of motion.[67]

John Wesley joined a growing High-Church and evangelical effort to counter this trend with an apologetic which gave greater emphasis on an *immediate* and *observable* providence. This natural theology would emphasize natural history and the biological sciences over astronomy and the mathematical sciences reaching a climax in Paley's *Natural Theology* (1802). In a 1753 letter to Dr. John Robertson, Wesley had commented on Andrew Ramsay's *Philosophical Principles of Natural and Revealed Religion, unfolded in a Geometrical Order* (1748–49), "The treatise itself gave me a stronger conviction than ever I had before both of the fallaciousness and unsatisfactoriness of the mathematical method of reasoning on religious subjects."[68] His assertion, "we can have no idea of God, nor any sufficient proof of his very being, but from the creatures; and that the meanest plant is a far stronger proof than all Dr. Clarke's or the Chevalier's [astronomical] demonstrations," is telling.[69] Robert Boyle writing before the time of Newton had said essentially the same thing: "that the situations of the celestial bodies do not afford, by far, so clear and cogent arguments of the wisdom and design of the author of the world, as do the bodies of animals and plants."[70]

Wesley's view on providence took a radically different turn, first, by rejecting any distinction between particular (special) and general providence and then by focusing attention on the human dimension of providence over the physical. "For as a general providence (vulgarly so called) counterdistinguished from a particular, it is only a decent well-sounding word, which means just nothing."[71] He was even more explicit in his sermon *On Divine Providence*. "I hope to show it [General Providence] is such stark, staring nonsense as any man of sense ought

66. John C. Gascoigne, "From Bentley to the Victorians: The Rise and Fall of Newtonian Natural Theology," *Science in Context* 2.2 (1988) 230.

67. See Brooke, *Science and Religion*, 177–80.

68. Letter: John Wesley to Dr. John Robertson, September 24, 1753 (BE 26:515).

69. Ibid., 516.

70. As quoted in Gascoigne, "From Bentley to the Victorians," 232.

71. Sermon: "Wandering Thoughts," III.1 (BE 2:132).

to be utterly ashamed of."[72] Wesley agreed "that in the common course of nature God does act by general laws, but he has never precluded himself from making exceptions to them whensoever he pleases; either by suspending the law in favor of those who love him, or by employing his mighty angels; by either of which he can deliver out of danger them that trust in him."[73] Wesley saw no distinction between usual and unusual events. Wesley's particular focus was on the "superintending providence which regards the children of men" rather than "that overruling hand which governs the inanimate creation."[74] He reserved the term *works of providence* to refer to the nations and individuals and *works of creation* to address the natural order.[75]

The preface to Wesley's *Survey of the Wisdom of God* notes his desire to "recite both uncommon appearances of nature, and uncommon instances of art . . . for surely in these appearances also, the wisdom of God is displayed."[76] His *Journal* (1755) devotes several pages to speculation on the cause of a spectacular fall of rocks which he had seen in his travels. He considers various scientific causes before concluding that the cause could only be God, "who arose to shake terribly the earth; who purposely chose such a place, where there is so great a concourse of nobility every year; and wrought in such a manner, that they might see it and fear," an approach which would later be called *God of the Gaps*.[77] He (as did Newton) first considered scientific explanations before adopting a theological explanation. In his work on electricity he describes a lightening conductor but argues that use of such a device did not deny God's providence.[78]

The London earthquakes of 1750 and the destructive 1755 earthquake in Lisbon offered the clergy a golden opportunity to denounce the infidelity and immortality of the day. Wesley's pamphlet *Serious Thoughts on the Earthquake at Lisbon* (1755) forcefully spoke of a Divine visitation over against the notion that the event was "purely natural and

---

72. Sermon: "On Divine Providence," 23 (BE 2:546).
73. Ibid., 22 (BE 2:546).
74. Ibid., 16 (BE 2:542).
75. Sermon: "The Imperfection of Human Knowledge," II.1 (BE 2:577).
76. The Preface, 4 (Jackson XIV:301).
77. *Journal*, June 2, 1755 (Jackson II:330–33).
78. Andrews, "John Wesley and the Age of Reason," 28.

accidental; the result of natural causes."[79] For Wesley "nature is the Art of God, or God's method of acting in the material world;" earthquakes emerge from the "hand of the Almighty, arising to such an effect."[80]

All of God's providences, said Wesley, "be they mild or severe, are all designed either to wean us from what is not, or to unite us to what is worthy of our affection. Every pain cries aloud, 'Love not the world, neither the things of the world.' And every pleasure says, with a still small voice, 'Thou shalt love the Lord thy God with all thy heart.'"[81]

His orthodox attitude toward angels, demons, witches and other supernatural beings went against the grain of enlightenment naturalism.[82] He saw the Devil as active in causing damaging natural events such as storms, wind, and fires as well as disease and mental instability. For Wesley "With my latest breath will I bear my testimony against giving up to infidels one great proof of the invisible world: I mean that of Witchcraft and apparitions, confirmed by the testimony of all ages."[83]

Wesley's sermon *Spiritual Worship* contains the core of his views on God's role in the natural world.[84] While affirming the orthodox view of God as creator and sustainer of all that is, he speculated that causal agency could be transferred to supernatural beings such as angels as well as humankind. Wesley, searching for some breathing room for human will suggested that God "imparts a spark of his self-moving nature to created spirits [human souls]."[85] He argued that man has "an innate principle of self-motion because he was created in the image of God."[86] For Wesley, "God is a Spirit: So therefore was man." [87] In the end, knowl-

79. "Serious Thoughts Occasioned by the Late Earthquake at Lisbon," 1755 (Jackson), 11:6.

80. Ibid., 6–7.

81. Sermon: "The One Thing Needful," (1734) II.4 (BE 4:356–57).

82. Sermon: "Of Good Angels," (1783) 1–10 (BE 3:4–15). See also Sermon: "Of Evil Angels," (1783) II.10–13 (BE 2:25–27).

83. "Preface to a true Relation of the Chief Things which an Evil Spirit did and said at Mascon, in Burgundy," (Jackson XIV:290).

84. Sermon: "Spiritual Worship," (1780) 1.2–10 (BE 3:91–95).

85. "A Thought on Necessity," V.1 (Jackson X:476–77).

86. Sermon: "The Great Deliverance," (1782) I.4 (BE 2:440–41) and "Some Thoughts on an Expression of St. Paul, in the First Epistle to the Thessalonians," Chapter V, Verse 23, (1786) 1 (Jackson XI:447).

87. Sermon: "The Great Deliverance," I.1 (BE: 2:438–39). Sermon: "The Great Deliverence," I.1 (BE: 2:438–39).

edge of the vital link between material and nonmaterial (body and soul) falls beyond the limits of understanding.[88]

Wesley's notion of secondary causes has a deist tone:

> Will you suppose that it derogates from the glory of the Divine presence, to represent the great engine of this visible world, as moving onward in its appointed course, without the continual interposture of his hand? It is granted, indeed, that his hand is ever active in preserving all the parts of matter, in all of their motions, according to these uniform laws: but I think it is rather derogatory to His infinite wisdom, to imagine that He would not make the vegetable and the animal as well as the inanimate worlds, of such workmanship, as might regularly move onward in this manner five or six thousand years; without putting a new hand to it ten thousand times every hour: I say *ten thousand times every hour*; for there is not an hour or a moment passes, wherein there are not millions of plants or animals forming in southern or northern climates.[89]

John English suggests that Wesley devised the notion of spiritual senses to appeal to the enlightenment demand for facts obtained through the physical senses. Spiritual senses would be complementary to physical senses by describing the knowledge that comes by faith thus offering a link to modern science.[90] Sara Miles argues that Wesley's notion of spiritual senses capable of *immediate* response to God's mediate revelation to man supported not only the contentions of those who believed in a continuing revelation to the people of God, but prepared the way for "a view of nature in flux which became the paradigm for Nineteenth Century natural history."[91] Wesley allowed reason a valid but very restricted role in describing human experience, assigning to faith the principle part in integrating the scattered forces of man's personal life. Wesley's appeal for a living faith over abstract theory offered an evangelical counter to the dominant rationalism of his age.

---

88. Sermon: "On the Trinity," 10–12 (BE 2:381–83). Also, Sermon: "The Heavenly Treasure in Earthern Vessels," (1790) II.1–2 (BE 4:164–66).

89. *Survey* 1:372.

90. John C. English, "John Wesley's Indebtedness to John Norris," *Church History* 60 (1991) 60ff. See also the sermon: "On the Discoveries of Faith," (1788) 12 (BE 4:34–35).

91. English, 64. See also Sara J. Miles, "From Being to Becoming: Science and Theology in the 18th Century," *Perspectives on Science and Christian Faith*, 43 (1991) 222.

Wesley's Confronts Scientism

Wesley did not back off from a confrontation with the interpreters of science . . . especially where there was a presumption of materialistic determinism in human affairs or natural systems. His *Thoughts Upon Necessity* (1774) analyzed Dr. David Hartley's "sensationalist view of brain function" which Wesley admitted "is now adopted by almost all who doubt of the Christian system."[92] He agreed that Hartley's physiological scheme contains a great deal of truth but balked at his notion that "men have no more liberty than stones."[93] For Wesley, the case turned on the point that necessity cannot exist "if there be a God in the world."[94] God has control over matter and spirits, over our souls and bodies. "Cannot He cut off, or suspend, in any degree, the connexion between vibrations and sensations, between sensations and reflections, between reflections and judgements, and between judgements and passions or actions?"[95] God's free choice stands between man and materialistic necessity . . . between human freedom and man as a "wheel fixed in a universe consisting of one immense machine."[96] God "is not only the true *primum mobile,* containing the whole frame of creation, but likewise the inward, sustaining, acting principle, indeed the only proper agent in the universe; unless so far as he imparts a spark of his active, self-moving nature to created spirits."[97]

Science in the Service of Humanity

Francis Bacon's concern that science serve humankind bore significant fruit in eighteenth century England. Problems such as the determination of longitude at sea, improvements in agriculture, bleaching, and the production of chemicals were practical outcomes. John Wesley was particularly interested in medical applications of the new science. At one point he encouraged the use of blood transfusions in normal medical practice.[98] His *Desideratum or Electricity Made Plain and Useful*

---

92. "Thoughts Upon Necessity," 2–5 (Jackson X:469–74).
93. Ibid., 476.
94. Ibid., 473.
95. Ibid.
96. Ibid., 476.
97. Ibid., 476–77.
98. *Survey* (1777), 1:16–17.

(1859) described the properties of electricity and the therapeutic effects of electrical shocks. He bought four of these electrostatic machines for use in his medical clinics. When asked by the Dec. 12, 1760 *London Magazine*, "Why do you meddle with electricity?" He replied, "To do as much good as I can."[99]

Wesley's most enduring scientific interests were in the medical field. His *A Plain Account of the People Called Methodists* claimed "For six or seven and twenty years, I had made anatomy and physick the diversion of my leisure hours."[100] He experimented on his patients and himself often describing the results in his *Journal*. His *Primitive Physick or An Easy and Natural Way of Curing Most Diseases* first published in 1747 went through twenty-three editions in his lifetime. This work challenged contemporary medical practice for its obsession with theory and lack of interest in developing practical medical treatment. Wesley's listing of remedies encouraged experimentation and the use of alternative approaches.

Conclusion

Wesley engaged many of the issues of the Enlightenment which touched on Christianity. He maintained an active interest in the development of the new science valuing it for the benefits it brought to human happiness and the way that it could support religion, yet was unwilling to subscribe to the antiscientific sentiments expressed by leading Tory intellectuals of his day. He encouraged his preachers and broader constituency to gain an understanding of the new science from a world view which saw God as creator and sustainer and nature as both dependent on and (in concert with scripture) exhibiting some of the attributes of God. Wesley was alert to the problems that natural theology could pose for the Christian and sought to counter them in his voluminous publications. He pursued a middle road that considered both faith and reason. In assuming this position he offers a pattern for those, two centuries later,

---

99. *The Letters of the Rev. John Wesley, A. M.* John Telford (London: Epworth, 1931). Volume 4, 123. Samuel J. Rogel, "Electricity: John Wesley's 'Curious and Important Subject,'" *Eighteenth-Century Life* 13 (Nov. 1989) 79–90, summarizes Wesley's views on electricity. See also H. Newton Malony, "John Wesley and The Eighteenth Century Therapeutic Uses of Electricity, *Perspectives on Science and Christian Faith*, 47 (1995) 244–255.

100. "A Plain Account of a People Called Methodists," 2 (Jackson VIII: 264).

who seek to remain responsive to Christianity in a culture infinitely more attuned to science. Wesley's sometimes erratic views on theories of natural philosophy reflect the limitations of one who read widely but was hampered by a lack of time and associates with whom he could carefully hammer out his ideas. Margaret Jacob's description of the typical High-Churchman as offering "ignorant and obscurantist opposition to everything new and modern" could not be applied to Wesley.[101]

Wesley maintained a high view on the value of history in an age that deprecated historical knowledge, recognized the limitations of reason and scientific method in an age which deified reason, and offered a critique of the use of science when used to attack religion. Wesley did not invoke moralistic attacks on natural philosophy but disparaged those theories or activities that would directly or indirectly bring harm to humankind or keep one's eyes from God. He adroitly mixed rationalistic orthodoxy and pietistic theology with natural philosophy in ways that allowed his followers to appreciate and participate in the study of God's creation. He offered a response to modernity that constructively, but selectively engaged science from a perspective of theological conservatism.[102]

---

101. Olson, "Tory High-Church Opposition," 27.

102. John W. Haas Jr., "Eighteenth Century Evangelical Responses to Science: John Wesley's Enduring Legacy," *Science & Christian Belief* 6 (1994) 83–102, describes ways that his ideas were adopted and transformed by later generations of Methodists.

3

Degrees of Certainty in John Wesley's Natural Philosophy

Laura Bartels Felleman

Natural Philosophy, as defined by the historian of science Andrew Cunningham, is an archaic argument best characterized by a particular assumption and a specific aim. Natural philosophy assumes that God's attributes are evident in the works of creation, and it aims this argument at atheists who reject physical evidence of the existence God.[1] Cunningham distinguishes natural philosophy from modern science (a view of the world that does not implicitly see the natural order as the creation of God and definitely does not understand its purpose to be the refutation of atheism). As the study of the natural world became more secularized and less and less about a divine creation between 1760 and 1848, according to Cunningham, science began to replace natural philosophy.[2]

---

1. Andrew Cunningham, "How the *Principia* Got Its Name; or, Taking Natural Philosophy Seriously," *History of Science* 29 (1991) 381, 383, 388; Andrew Cunningham, "The Identity of Natural Philosophy: A Response to Edward Grant," *Early Science and Medicine* 5 (2000) 264; and Andrew Cunningham, "A Reply to Peter Dear's 'Religion, Science and Natural Philosophy: Thoughts on Cunningham's Thesis,'" *Studies in History and Philosophy of Science* 32 (2001) 390.

2. Andrew Cunningham and Perry Williams, "De-Centring the 'Big Picture': *The*

The first edition of John Wesley's book, *A Survey of the Wisdom of God in Creation* (1763), was published within the timeframe Cunningham marks as a transition period between natural philosophy and science. However, Wesley's natural philosophy is neither a secular argument nor is it an attack on atheism. The *Survey* provides example after example of the ways in which God's wisdom, goodness, and power are evident in the creation, but Wesley did not then go on to suggest that atheists should be converted to faith by such natural evidence. Instead, when the *Survey* is compared to the sources Wesley relied upon to compile his natural philosophy, an obvious and intentional removal of condemnatory language directed at atheists can be noted.

In my earlier work, I argued that Wesley's editorial decision was consistent with his religious epistemology. In this essay, I add to that earlier argument by setting his theory of sacred knowing within a broader historical framework.

There are theological reasons why the *Survey* does not fit Cunningham's paradigm. In order to account for the difference between conventional natural philosophy arguments and the one in the *Survey*, this essay focuses on the Appendix to the *Survey* and compares it to Wesley's 1788 sermons on faith. Those sermons clarify his perspective on a controversy over kinds of knowledge, types of evidence, and degrees of certainty in the area of religious epistemology that had embroiled Christian writers for over a century. Although Wesley did not explain his decision to redact atheism from his natural philosophy sources, by investigating the intellectual history behind the *Survey* a highly probable—if not infallibly certain—explanation can be posited.

Certain Matters of Fact

The terms "highly probable" and "infallibly certain" are an intentional allusion to the scholarship of intellectual historian Barbara Shapiro. Shapiro's work revises an earlier thesis of Richard Popkin and Henry Van Leeuwen, which argued that British theories on the nature, limitation, and validity of human knowledge were influenced by developments in science and religion. In *Probability and Certainty in Seventeenth Century England* (1983), Shapiro builds upon this thesis and gives

Origins of Modern Science and the Modern Origins of Science," *British Journal for the History of Science* 26 (1993) 418, 424.

examples from legal theory, history, and literature that reflect similar epistemological models. She shows that in the seventeenth century, a broad cross-section of writers shared "a common set of assumptions about the nature of truth, the methods for attaining it, and the degree of probability or certainty that might be attributed to the findings produced by those methods."[3]

The highest degree of certainty was divine knowledge, which was absolute and infallible and only attainable by God. Mathematical knowledge and, to some extent, metaphysics occupied the next level of certainty. These were the only types of infallible, unquestionably certain knowledge that humans had the means to attain. Knowledge based on firsthand, direct sensory experience was less definitive than theorems and axioms but more reliable than knowledge dependent on another's testimony. Testimonial-based knowledge, which was placed in a middle epistemological space between highest human certainty and probable opinion, was labeled "moral certainty." A conclusion reached in science, religion, history, or jurisprudence was considered morally certain and beyond a reasonable doubt as long as the credibility of its evidence could be verified.[4]

The reasonableness of accepting and acting upon truth-claims established to a degree of moral certainty was defended with examples from everyday life. A willingness to believe there is a place called America without ever visiting it in person, the certainty that an unfamiliar road does indeed lead to the desired destination, the confidence that satisfactory reasons exist to trust that Queen Elizabeth was a real person—such beliefs posited that first-hand and demonstrative evidence was not necessary in the conduct of everyday life. If these matters of fact could be trusted, reasoned the defenders of moral certainty, so too should scientific, religious, historical, and legal claims.[5]

Shapiro revised this thesis in a later work, *A Culture of Fact* (2000), and instead asserted that legal theory, not science and religion, was

---

3. Barbara J. Shapiro, *Probability and Certainty in Seventeenth-Century England* (Princeton: Princeton University Press, 1983) 1.

4. Shapiro, *Probability and Certainty*, 28–35.

5. Shapiro, *Probability and Certainty*, 103–4; Barbara J. Shapiro, *John Wilkins, 1614–1672: An Intellectual Biography* (Berkeley: University of California Press, 1969) 230–31; and Henry Van Leeuwen, *The Problem of Certainty in English Thought 1630–1690* (The Hague: Martinus Nijhoff, 1963) 23–24.

the original source for this British emphasis on the category of moral certainty. After describing the methods of sixteenth-century trial juries, specifically the methods of evaluating the credibility of written evidence and eyewitness accounts, determining the facts in a case, and confidently rendering an impartial verdict with a clear conscience, Shapiro documents the broader application of these methods in history, literature, science, and religion.[6]

Three avenues for the cultural diffusion of legal epistemology are suggested. First, jury duty required more and more men to put into practice the methods of evaluating evidence, determining fact, and rendering verdicts. Another, the popular reading of late seventeenth century published trials, included the judge's instructions to the jury on the methodology to follow in deliberation. And the third avenue was the number of individuals engaged in cross-disciplinary interests and investigations (the bishop who conducted experiments, the judge who wrote religious tracts, or the natural philosopher who researched history).[7]

Practitioners of these disciplines were all confronted with the difficulty of knowing the truth about events they had not personally observed. Historians, scientists, and theologians were much like jurists in the sense that they often did not have first-hand experience of the facts in questions on which they could base their ideas, nor could their reasoning be grounded in a mathematical formula. Nevertheless, these practitioners asserted, this did not mean the judgments and conclusions of these fields were irrational or mere opinions. They could not offer infallible evidence in support of their ideas, theories, and doctrines, but they could cite evidence that an impartial audience should find intellectually persuasive.[8]

The book *The Religion of Protestants, a Safe Way to Salvation* (1638) marks the beginning of the cross-over of legal epistemology into Anglican theology. Written to defend Anglicanism against Catholic criticism, its author, William Chillingworth (1602–1643), was a protégé of Wil-

---

6. Barbara J. Shapiro, *A Culture of Fact: England 1550–1720* (Ithaca, NY: Cornell University Press, 2000) 1–9, 26.

7. Barbara J. Shapiro, *Beyond Reasonable Doubt and Probable Cause* (Berkeley: University of California Press, 1991) 1–13; Shapiro, *Probability and Certainty*, 69; and Shapiro, *A Culture of Fact*, 9–13, 30–33, 37, 169, 177.

8. Shapiro, *A Culture of Fact*, 27–35; 45, 47, 111.

liam Laud and a convert to Catholicism who later rejoined the Church of England.

The book quotes one section of *The Truth of the Christian Religion* (1624) by the Dutch jurist Hugo Grotius. Section 19 of Book II, entitled "Answer to Them that Require More Forcible Reasons," alludes to the Aristotelian principle that recognizes the different standards of proof required for different subjects (e.g. mathematics, physics, ethics, matters of fact like history) and uses this to defend the credibility of Christianity. Because Christianity bases its arguments upon credible testimonies, it can meet the verification level set for matters of fact.[9]

Catholic controversialists responded to this correlation of doctrine to matters of fact with their own interpretation of Aristotle. They argued that Catholic teachings were infallibly certain, because they were based on an unbroken line of authoritative interpreters who accurately identified the first principles of Christianity and who demonstrated by syllogistic argumentation how their system of belief was logically derived from these truths. The Catholics, acknowledging no middle epistemological ground between infallible certainty and opinion, relegated Protestant teachings to the latter.[10]

Anglican theologians of the seventeenth century continued to employ the themes of legal epistemology in their polemical writings against Catholics as well as against atheists and enthusiasts. A common vocabulary is noted between Anglicans such as Edward Stillingfleet, John Wilkins, Seth Ward, and John Tillotson. Their writings identify degrees of certainty, equate religious principles with matters of fact that are verifiable to a level of moral certainty, defend Scripture as a sufficient guide to salvation and a credible record of events based on eyewitness testimony, and define faith as uncompelled intellectual assent to religious teachings that have been confirmed beyond a reasonable doubt.[11]

---

9. Van Leeuwen, *Problem of Certainty*, 21, 22 n. 18; and Shapiro, *A Culture of Fact*, 169.

10. Van Leeuwen, *Problem of Certainty*, 25, 26; and Dorothea Krook, *John Sergeant and His Circle: A Study of Three Seventeenth-Century English Aristotelians* (Leiden: Brill, 1993).

11. Van Leeuwen, *Problem of Certainty*, 33–43; Shaprio, *Probability and Certainty*, 85–103; and Shapiro, *Culture of Fact*, 169–72. Wesley's agreement with this Anglican definition of faith as an intellectual assent can be found in a letter he wrote to his mother, November 22, 1725.

An Appendix on Human Understanding

Some of these terms retain their meaning and are used for similar apologetic ends in the eighteenth century. One example of this is *The Procedure, Extent, and Limits of Human Understanding* (1728) by Peter Browne, Anglican Bishop of Cork and Ross. Browne equated religious knowledge with moral certainty and distinguished it from the demonstrative certainty of science and mathematics.[12]

The vocabulary of legal epistemology can also be found in the Wesley's *Survey*, particularly in its Appendix. This treatise on human understanding can be divided into three parts: Wesley's paraphrased and greatly truncated version of Browne's *Procedure*, a second section drawn from the essay "The Account of the Good Steward" written by a seventeenth-century British judge, and a final section original to Wesley. The theme of certainty appears in all three sections of the Appendix, but its meaning is not identical.

Browne's Scale of Knowledge

The first section of the Appendix, which drew from Browne, goes into the most detail concerning the degrees of certainty associated with each kind of evidence-based knowledge. In addition to moral certainty, Browne identified the categories of sensitive, self-conscious, demonstrative, opinion-based, and testimonial knowledge.[13]

The highest degree of certainty is associated with the first three kinds of knowledge, because these kinds of knowledge are grounded in self-evident substantiations—either in external evidence perceived by the five physical senses or in the internal evidence of consciousness. The simple ideas of sensation (colors, temperatures, textures, etc.), self-awareness of one's mind, will, passions, and affections, and axioms deduced by logic or mathematics are obvious and compel the assent of the observer's intellect. As long as its access to sensory data is unhampered and the brain is properly functioning, the mind will form accurate ideas,

---

12. Peter Browne, *The Procedure, Extent, and Limits of Human Understanding* (London: Printed for W. Innys and R. Manby, 1737) 231–45.

13. Browne, *Procedure, Extent, and Limits*, 214–75. Compare to Wesley, *Survey*, 5: 192–205.

judgments, and abstractions about the outside world and will maintain an honest self-assessment.[14]

Knowledge rooted in opinions is at the opposite end of the certainty scale. If the evidence is inconclusive, the intellect can only reach conclusions that range from plausible to doubtful. Testimonial knowledge is of a higher degree of certainty than that of opinion if the eyewitness account on which it is based is reliable. Authenticated testimony of matters in religion or ethics crosses over into the category of moral certainty. Christianity, natural religion, and moral teachings are examples of this kind of knowledge, because one can cite evidence so persuasive and believable that the mind voluntarily assents and the will consents to its propositions.[15]

This active rather than passive concurrence of the will is part of what distinguishes moral certainty from mathematical certainty for Browne. Disagreements can arise between reasonable people when the evidence offered in support of a position persuades the will of one person but not that of another. Such a conflict of wills could not happen at the demonstrative level, because the propositions associated with this category are so obviously consistent with observed reality that the will is powerless to overturn the compelled intellect.[16]

The lack of self-evident truth at the level of moral certainty would be another discrepancy between the two kinds of knowledge. Religious faith cannot be presented as a syllogism or mathematical formula. Instead, its truth was established either by analogical reasoning (inferring from the visible world the qualities of the spiritual) or by truths deduced from scriptural revelation. The *Procedure* points to these differences as the reasons why neither revealed nor natural religion should be conflated with demonstrative knowledge.[17]

After differentiating kinds of knowledge and their associated types of evidence and degrees of certainty, the role of revelation in human

---

14. Browne, *Procedure, Extent, and Limits*, 55, 147, 155–57, 175–204, 216, 224. Compare to Wesley, *Survey*, 5:172, 187–93.

15. Browne, *Procedure, Extent, and Limits*, 246, 247, 264–68, 274, 275. Compare to Wesley, *Survey*, 5:199, 200, 202, 205.

16. Browne, *Procedure, Extent, and Limits*, 265–67. Compare to Wesley, *Survey*, 5:203, 204.

17. Browne, *Procedure, Extent, and Limits*, 114, 132–46, 217–19, 231–41. Compare to Wesley, *Survey*, 5:184, 194, 196–99.

understanding is explained in more detail. Moral certainty in the existence of a Creator who provides for the creation can be obtained through observation, judgment, and reasoning, Browne argued, but the tenets of revealed religion (e.g., the one God who creates and sustains through the Word, humanity created in the image of God, the final judgment) are matters of faith that can only be known through divine disclosure. Through analogies, the faculties of the mind can comprehend the "general and imperfect" degree of knowledge available in natural religion or "the light of nature," as Browne referred to it. In contrast, knowing particular details like the nature and will of God requires the testimony of Scripture.[18]

Wesley placed an asterisk next to the phrase "light of nature" in his redaction of this section of the *Procedure*. At the bottom of the page, Wesley inserted this footnote: "I believe all 'the light of nature,' so called, to flow from preventing Grace."[19] The comment is not explained, preventing Grace is not defined, its relationship to revealed or natural religion is not clarified, and its category (kind of knowledge, type of evidence, degree of certainty?) is not identified. This interruption in the flow of the *Procedure* marks the first unresolved epistemological tension in the Appendix. The second section of Wesley's Appendix to the *Survey* contains another.

Hale's Demonstrative Certainty

The next part of Wesley's Appendix to his *A Survey of the Wisdom of God in Creation* is taken from the writings of Matthew Hale (1609–1676). Hale was the most respected judge of the mid-seventeenth century, advancing in his profession to the position of Lord Chief Justice of King's Bench. Hale counted among his friends and associates the Anglican theologians already cited for their use of legal epistemology: John Wilkins, Seth Ward, John Tillotson, and Edward Stillingfleet.[20] He wrote authoritative interpretations of English criminal law and the his-

---

18. Browne, *Procedure, Extent, and Limits*, 290–93. Compare to Wesley, *Survey*, 5:210–12.

19. Wesley, *Survey*, 5:211.

20. Gilbert Burnet, *The Life and Death of Sir Matthew Hale* (London: printed for William Shrowsbery, 1681) 74; Shapiro, *Intellectual Biography*, 175, 176; and Alan Cromartie, *Sir Matthew Hale (1609–1676): Law, Religion, and Natural Philosophy* (Cambridge: Cambridge University Press, 1995) 140.

tory of the common law, in addition to works on science, religion, and witchcraft.

The most infamous episode of his career is the trial of the alleged witches Amy Duny and Rose Cullender. Unsurprisingly, the vocabulary of legal epistemology is present in his instructions to the jury for this case, as well as an assertion of the reality of witchcraft. Belief in witchcraft was unusual for a judge of this time, but it reflects a commonly-held religious conviction that to do otherwise was an indirect support to materialism and atheism. The refutation of atheism and the synthesis of religious doctrine and legal theory can also be found in his defense of the Mosaic Creation story.[21]

Wesley read Hale's *Contemplations Moral and Divine* in 1731 and Gilbert Burnet's biography of Hale in 1726.[22] The essay Wesley included in the Appendix is taken from the *Contemplations* and is based on the parable of the talents, Mt 25:14–30. God requires an account from the steward detailing how he has employed the talents entrusted to him. In Hale's retelling, the talents include the gift of wealth, together with those of the understanding, the body, speech, life, reputation, education, the Scriptures, ministers, and the animate and inanimate parts of creation. For the Appendix, Wesley brought together the steward's description of his use of creation and education.

The steward reports that he "studiously and diligently" observed the works of creation. He used his intellect to understand creation's physical aspects and natural causes, an investigation into causation that in the end brought him to a "demonstrative conviction" in the First Cause.[23] The steward's search for demonstrations and Aristotelian causes should not be interpreted as a sign that Hale harbored secret Catholic tendencies. On the contrary, there was another interpreter of Aristotle that Anglicans could look to for guidance when attempting to reconcile their theology with legal epistemology. William Harvey (1578–1657), the first person to accurately describe the circulation of the blood, was a

21. Cromartie, *Sir Matthew Hale*, 1–11, 237–39; Shapiro, *Probability and Certainty*, 98, 206–7; and Shapiro, *Culture of Fact*, 177, 181, 182. A paraphrase of Hale's instructions to the jury can be found in *A Tryal of Witches at the Assizes Held at Bury St. Edmonds* (London: Printed for William Shrewsbery, 1682) 56.

22. Richard P. Heitzenrater, *John Wesley and the Oxford Methodists, 1725–1735* (PhD diss., Duke University, 1972) 499, 506. Excerpts from both books are included in *The Christian Library*.

23. Wesley, *Survey*, 5:225, 226.

strong advocate for the Aristotelian research method, a method that he set out in the introduction to his book *De Generatione* (1653).

Harvey reminded his readers that Aristotle had taught that "all certain knowledge is gained by syllogism and demonstration," and that certainty depended upon accurate principles, which in turn had to be formed out of sense data, because "nothing is in the understanding, which was not before in the sense" (another Aristotelian maxim). Knowledge, according to this theory, proceeds from sense perceptions of a Singular (the color yellow) to an internal sense that judges the Singular and forms from it an abstract idea, a Universal (Yellow), by means of the imagination or memory. Abstracted sensory impressions give rise to experience and then to reason, definitions, and principles.[24] The rational soul is the efficient cause behind mental processes, and the brain—the physical organ where ideas are conceived—is the soul's material instrument of operation.[25]

This viewpoint sees science as ultimately dependent upon the five physical senses, and Harvey proposed a new "surer path to the attainment of knowledge" based on this perspective. If knowledge proceeded from the senses, so would his experiments. He described how his investigations began by witnessing animal dissections, a step he encouraged his readers to repeat in order to verify his findings with their own eyes. Once this physical evidence was gathered, he sought to discover the material, formal, efficient, and final causes that gave rise to the generation of animals.[26]

He admired those experimenters "who, following Natures conduct with their own eyes, have at length through a perplexed, but yet a most faithful tract, attained to the highest pitch of Truth." With his own eyes, he observed fetal development in the egg and, by tracing out its causes, came to the final cause: God. For it is God who is the proper end towards which all nature works, and thus his research method, is directed.[27]

---

24. William Harvey, *Anatomical Exercitations Concerning the Generation of Living Creatures* (London: Printed by James Young, 1653) Preface, n.p. Compare to the reasoning process in Browne, *Procedure, Extent, and Limits*, 155–57, 175–204 where simple apprehensions developed into ideas, judgments, and abstraction.

25. Harvey, *Anatomical Exercitations*, 543–47.

26. Harvey, *Anatomical Exercitations*, Preface, 264–71, 551–54. Hale used different terms, referring to the natural causes of frame, motion, order and Divine economy, Wesley, *Survey*, 5:225.

27. Harvey, *Anatomical Exercitations*, Preface, 52, 203, 207, 248.

Judge Hale read *De Generatione* and most likely would have noticed the use of legal terminology in the text: "a right verdict of the senses controlled by frequent observation and valid experiences," "unless sense give a right verdict," "making a trial," "the faithful testimony of thy own eyes."[28] The Good Steward follows the Harveyan method, conducts his own trial, makes physical observations, and follows nature's appearance down a causal trail that ultimately leads to its Creator.

Because this demonstrative knowledge is based on sensory information, it is certain and compelling knowledge. Even so, it is not the highest form of human knowledge the mind can attain. The knowledge of natural and divine causes is not the ultimate purpose for which our intellectual powers were prepared, Hale concluded in the voice of the Steward. It was given instead "for a certain, useful and becoming object," the knowledge of God and of Christ Crucified.[29]

Hale did not elaborate on the nature of this category of knowledge in "The Good Steward," but such an explanation can be found in his essay "Of the Knowledge of Christ Crucified." In this work, useful knowledge is differentiated from that which is not. For instance, familiarity with the exact time when a particular event took place is not in and of itself useful, studying "the progression of generation in an Egg" and discovering from that "the wisdom of the great Creator," (an obvious reference to *De Generatione*) is more useful. But there is only one thing that is *necessary* to know, "Jesus Christ, and Him Crucified."

This kind of knowledge is more certain than the others including sensory-based (which is dependent on a limited range of sense perceptions), experience-based (which can never eliminate the possibility of drawing false conclusions from sense data), history (which depends upon credible eyewitnesses), and even doctrine (which is based upon human opinions). Knowledge of Christ, unlike the other kinds, is confirmed by an abundance of reliable sources. Examples of this evidence include prophecy, biblical witnesses, miracles, the Transfiguration, and the witness of the Spirit. Hale called the latter a type of evidence that is "beyond all the Moral persuasions in the world, beyond the conviction of demonstration."[30]

28. Harvey, *Anatomical Exercitations*, Preface; Cromartie, *Sir Matthew Hale*, 221; and Shapiro, *Culture of Fact*, 111.

29. Wesley, *Survey*, 230, 235.

30. Matthew Hale, *Contemplations Moral and Divine* (London: Printed by William Godbid, 1676) 159–64.

There is no "the witness of the Spirit" category in the types of evidence and kinds of knowledge identified by Browne and the other Anglican writers who tried to work out the relationship between religious principles and moral and demonstrative certainty. This reference to the witness of the Spirit may reflect Hale's Puritan upbringing or the influence of his friendship with Richard Baxter.[31]

The *Procedure* is highly critical of theories similar to those of Hale that posit the existence of extra-sensory mental abilities. Browne rejected the theory that there is a faculty in the mind capable of receiving accurate impressions of spiritual objects, because it could not be supported by common experience. "But every one may be conscious," said Browne, "that immaterial objects were never so present to any faculty of his mind, as to imprint and leave upon it any just and real similitude or resemblance of themselves." The theory that the mind has an inherent power capable of forming spiritual ideas independent of object impressions is also contrary to experience.[32]

Another theory, that God has the power to give the mind ideas of the immaterial, is beyond the scope of the *Procedure*, which is limited to a discussion of ordinary mental processes. Browne pointed out that if God did "imprint upon our minds any *Direct* Idea of himself," proofs for the existence of God would not be necessary. Direct evidence would compel assent. Disagreements about the existence of God prove that this type of evidence is not available.[33] This observation is absent from Wesley's Appendix.

Sensitive knowledge and self-awareness provide sufficient proofs to discredit those claiming extra-sensory perception of the immaterial, in Browne's opinion. He equated such assertions with religious enthusiasm:

> Men's endeavoring to abstract the Intellect from all Objects of Sense, so as to take a *Direct View* of spiritual things; and work-

---

31. Cromartie, *Sir Matthew Hale*, 2, 156–91; and Shapiro, *An Intellectual Biography*, 176. The 1570s saw the beginning of a renewed interest in the doctrine of the Holy Spirit among Puritan writers, Baxter included. Owen C. Watkins, *The Puritan Experience: Studies in Spiritual Autobiography* (New York: Schocken, 1972) 11, 12, 83–88; Norman Pettit, *The Heart Prepared: Grace and Conversion in Puritan Spiritual Life* (Middletown, CT: Wesleyan University Press, 1989); Geoffrey F. Nuttal, *The Holy Spirit in Puritan Faith and Experience* (Chicago: University of Chicago Press, 1992).

32. Wesley, *Survey*, 180. Compare to Browne, *Procedure, Extent, and Limits*, 92–95.

33. Browne, *Procedure, Extent, and Limits*, 94.

ing up their Minds to an opinion and belief that they have some degree of *Intuitive Direct* knowledge of them tho' *Imperfect* and obscure, hath proved a fatal Delusion, and never served an real and substantial *End* of Religion. I believe I may safely appeal to the Experience of the best of Men, whether they ever found any the least *Glimmerings* of such celestial Light in their most exalted Contemplations? Many who never aspired to this *Immediate* and familiar Intercourse with heavenly Objects, have arrived to great degrees of habitual Virtue and Holiness; whereas the contrary Opinion doth but puff Men up with spiritual Pride; and too often ends in rank *Enthusiasm*.[34]

The Appendix does not include this paragraph, which is so contradictory to the claims of Hale. Deleting the paragraph does not resolve this tension between the Browne and Hale sections, however. A reconciliation of their conflicting definitions of demonstrative certainty is not offered. Instead the treatise makes an abrupt transition into the final section of the Appendix and its definition of certainty.

Wesley's Wise Limits

Wesley ended his survey of the wisdom of God displayed in creation with a final example of God's wisdom. After compiling his ideal natural philosophy according to the standards set forth in the Preface—a concise treatment of whatever "is know with any degree of certainty" and nothing that is "false or uncertain," written in simple prose, directed to its right end, reporting the latest findings, and thoroughly covering every work of creation—the last section of the Appendix concludes with a list of all the things in the natural world that are still left unexplained.[35]

The inability of human understanding to account for every natural cause, whether material, efficient, formal, or final, is interpreted as a sign of God's wisdom: "What cause have we then to adore the wisdom of God, who has so exactly proportioned our knowledge to our state? We may know whatever is needful for life or godliness, whatever is necessary either for our present or eternal happiness. But how little beside can the most penetrating genius know with any certainty?"[36]

---

34. Browne, *Procedure, Extent, and Limits*, 95, 96.
35. Wesley, *Survey*, 1:i–v.
36. Wesley, *Survey*, 5:255.

The "littleness of knowledge" is briefly commented on in the Preface in connection with a discussion on methodology that reflects the language of legal epistemology. Only the facts as they appear to the senses would be reported in the *Survey* and not a convoluted search for causes: "The *facts* lie within the reach of our senses and understanding; the *causes* are more remote. *That things are so*, we know with certainty: but *why they are so*, we know not."[37] Unlike Hale, Wesley defined natural philosophy as a matter of fact with a degree of certainty based on reliable sensory evidence and not as a demonstration capable of infallible abstractions.

These limits on human knowledge are part of God's design: "Such pains, so to speak, hath God taken to *hide pride from man!* And to bound his thought within that channel of knowledge, wherein he already finds eternal life."[38] With these words, Wesley concluded his survey of the wisdom of God displayed in the works of creation.

The *Procedure*'s section on the littleness of human understanding concludes that even though exact knowledge of natural causes is impossible, we can know and practice morality with certainty.[39] Wesley did not include this section in his paraphrase, and he appears to be referring to something more than moral behavior in his 1777 introduction to the Appendix. That Appendix declares that, though we may understand very little about the nature of natural objects, we may love much and know "with the greatest certainty" our whole duty to God.[40]

The bracketing of Wesley's essay on human understanding between two statements detailing its littleness but sufficiency in matters of faith leaves us with unresolved tensions and unanswered questions. What kind of knowledge and what type of evidence are needed to discover life, godliness, present happiness, whole duty, and eternal life? Is this certain knowledge of salvation based on the assent of the intellect, the consent of the will, both, or something else entirely? Catholics, Anglicans, and Puritans had been debating for decades which doctrines were essential, sufficient, and necessary for saving faith. The *Survey* has nothing to say on this matter.

37. Wesley, *Survey*, 1:vi.

38. Wesley, *Survey*, 5:255. Wesley's 1784 sermon "The Imperfection of Human Knowledge" states that we know just enough to maintain our health and comfort and avoid evil, but that there are many things we know very little of besides the fact of their existence.

39. Browne, *Procedure, Extent, and Limits*, 205–13.

40. Wesley, *Survey*, 5:169, 170.

The *Survey* does not contribute to these debates, because those debates are beyond the scope of Wesley's natural philosophy. Wesley limited the *Survey* to matters of fact, moral certainty, and faith as assent. As he stated in the language of the *Procedure*: "we are now speaking what our perceptions are, in the ordinary way of nature."[41] A discussion of extra-ordinary ways of knowing the Divine—one that ties up the loose ends of the Appendix and explains the relationship between preventing grace, religious epistemology, and the essentials of saving faith—will be offered in 1788. To expect it in the *Survey* is to violate the Aristotelian principle of different types of evidence for different kinds of knowledge. Natural philosophy is one kind of knowledge. Christian faith, from Wesley's perspective, is another.

The 1788 Sermons

The eight sermons Wesley wrote four years after the release of the 1784 *Survey* develop the category of faith as an avenue for knowledge and cover epistemological concerns similar to those found in the Appendix. The sermons contrast the limitations of knowledge based in sensitive and matters-of-fact evidence with what can be known by faith about God and the things of God. The language of legal epistemology is present in such phrases as "reasonably doubt" and "highly probable," as well as in the distinction made between the possible, the probable and the certain. References to the sensory basis of knowledge—"nothing is in the understanding which was not first perceived by some of the senses"—and perceptions coming together to form judgments and reasoning are also asserted. The sermons do not, however, equate Christian faith with moral certainty as had the Anglican theologians named above.[42]

Wesley first explained his definition of faith as a kind of knowledge and a type of evidence in *An Earnest Appeal to Men of Reason and Religion* (1743). That treatise defines accurate reasoning as a process that moves from clear sensory apprehension to definite ideas to true judgments and finally to reasonable argumentation. John Locke argued that without some prior apprehension of an object or subject, it would

---

41. Wesley, *Survey*, 5:180.

42. Wesley, *Works*, Sermon 115 "Dives and Lazarus," Sermon 116 "What is Man?", Sermon 117 "On the Discoveries of Faith," and Sermon 119 "Walking By Sight and Walking By Faith," 4: 6, 17, 21, 29, and 51. The inferences drawn from the 1788 sermons are influenced by and indebted to the scholarship of Barbara Shapiro.

be impossible to judge or reason on it. Browne challenged this definition of reason when applied to matters of religion by countering that reasoning on immaterial things is not limited to sensitive knowledge because religious reasoning can be carried out by means of analogies.[43]

Browne agreed that religious ideas grounded in sensory apprehensions were not attainable. All that human reasoning on spiritual ideas could do, in his opinion, was infer a similarity between the faculties of the mind (e.g., thinking, feeling, desiring), the complex notions formed by the mind (justice, gladness, mercy), and the nature of God. The Holy Spirit assisted the mind with this ordinary mental operation, which encompassed knowledge of such things as God's wisdom, goodness, and power, the mystery of the Trinity, and the rewards of heaven and the punishments of hell.[44]

Wesley's *Earnest Appeal* acknowledges the dilemma posed by Locke but it does not follow Browne's solution. "What then will your reason do here?" asked Wesley. "How will it pass from things natural to spiritual; from the things that are seen to those that are not seen; from the visible to the invisible world? What a gulf is here! By what art will reason get over the immense chasm? This cannot be till the Almighty come in to your succour, and give you that faith you have hitherto despised."[45] For Wesley, it is faith, not analogy that supplies the reliable evidence the mind needs to reason with certainty about religious truths.

The 1788 sermons repeat the definition of faith found in the *Earnest Appeal* and include additional discussions of preventing grace, natural religion, and the essentials of saving faith in relationship to religious knowledge of the highest degree of certainty. These discussions help to resolve the tensions between the sections of the Appendix and suggest a plausible explanation for the elimination of references to atheism in Wesley's natural philosophy.

Preventing Grace

Wesley divided faith-based knowledge into seven different degrees or "species" in his sermons. At the lowest level is the Materialist, who has

---

43. Wesley, *Works*, 11:56; John Locke, *An Essay Concerning Human Understanding* (London: Printed by Eliz. Holt, 1690) 341, 344. Browne, *Procedure, Extent, and Limits*, 421, 422, 439–47.

44. Browne, *Procedure, Extent, and Limits*, 133–39, 201, 202, 470–75.

45. Wesley, *Works*, 11:57.

no sense of God or the things of God and limits knowledge to physical matters of fact. The Deist intellectually assents to the idea of a Creator. The Heathen can deduce from observation of the natural world that there must be a Creator who is wise, good, and powerful. Jewish judgments about God are more accurate, because they are based on divine revelation. The faith of a Roman Catholic adds extracanonical human opinions to revelation, unlike the Protestant who only accepts teachings that are found in Scripture.[46]

The first degrees of faith are six versions of faith as an intellectual assent. The facts about divine matters may get clearer and more accurate from one degree of faith to the next, but they are simply ideas produced by ratiocination. God's grace can give those at the lower end of the faith scale an idea of morality, but this is still only the level of moral certainty. This grace (which Wesley identified as preventing grace), besides acting as the voice of conscience, can also allow those with a lower degree of faith to infer the general knowledge of the divine from the creation. Unlike Hale, Wesley did not equate this knowledge with demonstrative certainty.[47]

THE CATEGORY OF CHRISTIAN FAITH

The faith of a Christian exceeds belief in the tenets of natural religion and encompasses the particulars of revealed religion. Faith according to Hebrews 11:1 is "the evidence of things hoped for, the conviction of things not seen." Wesley interpreted this to mean that faith gives Christians spiritual senses that provide personal, first-hand evidence of the Divine. This evidence has the same intellectually self-evident quality as the evidence of sensory knowledge and rises to a similar level of highest certainty. Those with lower degrees of faith have spiritual senses, but they are closed and not functional. Only after repentance and justification are the spiritual senses of Christian faith opened by grace, after which the believer is able to discern the invisible, eternal, and spiritual worlds.[48]

---

46. Wesley, *Works*, Sermon 106 "On Faith," and Sermon 119, 3:493–96, 498–55, 4:51, 52.

47. Wesley, *Works*, Sermon 105 "On Conscience," and Sermon 119, 3:482, 4:57.

48. Wesley, *Works*, Sermon 105, Sermon 106, Sermon 117, and Sermon 119, 3:484, 492 4:34, 35, 49, 52–54.

The reality of invisible things like the human soul and the presence of God, Christ, the Spirit, angels, and demons are all known by faith. The spiritual senses perceive the truths associated with the eternal world: the wonders of paradise, the torment of the unholy, and the awe of the Second Coming. Discernment of the spiritual world, "the kingdom of God in the soul," is also possible once the spiritual senses become operational.[49]

The differences between Wesley's understanding of Christian Faith and the kinds of knowledge discussed in the Appendix can be illustrated diagrammatically (Fig. 1).[50]

FIGURE 1

Kind of Knowledge	Type of Evidence	Degree of Certainty	Response of Intellect	Response of Will
Christian Faith	spiritual sense perceptions (Wesley) witness of the Spirit (Hale)	highest	voluntary submission	voluntary submission
Sensitive	physical sense impressions	highest	irresistible	Passive
Self-knowledge	Consciousness	highest	irresistible	Passive
Demonstration	Syllogisms, Mathematical formulas, Natural philosophy (Hale)	highest	compelled	Overwhelmed
Matters of Fact	written record, Nature testimony, Scriptures, conscience (Wesley)	moral	voluntary	voluntary
Opinion	Inconclusive	probable to doubtful	voluntary	voluntary

49. Wesley, *Works*, Sermon 108 "On Riches," Sermon 117, and Sermon 118 "On the Omnipresence of God," 3:521, 4:30–35, 45, 47.

50. Compare to Shapiro, *Probability and Certainty*, 29, Fig. 1.

The Essentials of Saving Faith

The reaction of the intellect and will to the evidence of the spiritual senses is different than their reactions in the categories of sensitive knowledge and matters of fact in Wesley's scale of knowledge. Mental responses to physical sensation are so instantaneous and immediate that there is little to no involvement of the intellect or will. In matters of fact, the faculty of liberty ensures free, voluntary responses to evidence, including that which is offered by preventing grace. The will has the capacity to resist the witness of the conscience and refuse to repent and conform to the religious principles taught in Scripture.[51]

The voluntary submission of both the intellect and the will distinguishes Christian Faith from other kinds of knowledge and different species of faith. The Muslim, Jew, Catholic, and Protestant are morally persuaded by religious teachings. But in Wesley's opinion, a system of beliefs and ethics does not rise to the level of saving faith. This act of intellectual assent must be coupled with the submission of the will in order to advance to the higher degrees of faith.[52]

Rational conviction of the truth of Scripture is the foundation of saving faith, but it is not equivalent to saving faith. The individual must repent of sin and believe in Christ. "Divine confidence in a pardoning God" is Wesley's definition of faith in the "proper Christian sense." And the spiritual senses are the only avenue available by which this knowledge of reconciliation can be communicated to the mind.[53]

A developmental model of salvation is described in the 1788 sermons, and each stage of development is marked by a different degree of certainty or assurance of pardon. *Fathers in Christ* experience no spiritual doubt or fear, can resist sinful influences by God's grace, continue to increase in the knowledge and love of God, and have "full assurance of hope" that they will attain heaven after death. *Young men* in faith are also free from doubt and fear, are certain their sins are forgiven, and have "full assurance of faith," or a continuous consciousness of reconciliation. Babes in Christ are weak in faith, doubt their salvation, and fear God's judgment even after their repentance and justification.[54]

---

51. Wesley, *Works*, Sermon 115 and Sermon 117, 4:5, 11, 14, 15, 16, 29.
52. Wesley, *Works*, Sermon 106 and Sermon 119, 3:494–97, 4:57.
53. Wesley, *Works*, Sermon 108 and Sermon 115, 3:521, 4:18 n. 76.
54. Wesley, *Works*, Sermon 106 and Sermon 117, 3:497–98, 500, 4:36, 37.

The latter stage represents a change in Methodist teachings on the level of certainty an individual needed to experience to be assured of salvation. Early in his career, Wesley equated the sense of the spiritual world with the Spirit's direct, inward witness that one was forgiven and reconciled to God through Christ. Later, he accepted a fear of God that inspires the living of a righteous life as experimental proof that the spiritual senses had been opened up following repentance and that the individual had a degree of faith that facilitated the perception of the spiritual world or the "Kingdom of God within." Based on this evidence, Wesley concluded that even those with the faith of a servant were accepted by God.[55]

The Deletion of Atheism

The definition of faith as a spiritual sense of the invisible, eternal, and spiritual worlds of God evident in the 1788 sermons is similar to the means of sacred knowledge postulated in the natural philosophy of Dr. George Cheyne (1671–1743). Cheyne, a well-known physician and medical writer, was critical of the limitations Locke placed on the certainty of religious knowledge. Cheyne argued that Locke only considered human understanding in the unregenerated, and that he failed to take into account the spiritual and divine senses that allow a justified person to have accurate ideas about the divine. Cheyne did not relate these senses to faith, and this marks an important difference between the two religious epistemologies.[56]

For Wesley, only God, through faith, can give an individual certain knowledge of spiritual matters. An unbeliever could be frightened with stories of eternal punishment or intrigued by speculative reasonings, but such evidence only produces an intellectual assent that is incapable of regenerating the spiritual senses and does not rise to the level of a faith conviction. A system of morality based on natural religion could also not produce a personal, inward faith experience of the things of God on which to ground accurate ideas of the divine.[57]

---

55. Wesley, *Works*, Sermon 106 and Sermon 117, 3:497, 4:34, 35.

56. George Cheyne, *Philosophical Principles of Religion: Natural and Revealed* (Printed for George Strahan, 1715) 108–16.

57. Wesley, *Works*, Sermon 106 and Sermon 115, 3:499, 4:16.

Wesley's conception of faith as a spiritual sense provides a theological explanation for the difference between his natural philosophy and that of Cheyne (and those analyzed by Cunningham, as well). The preface to Cheyne's *Philosophical Principles* includes an anti-atheist reproach typical of this genre: "Atheism may be eternally confounded, by the most distant approaches to the true causes of Natural Appearances. And that if the Modern Philosophy demonstrates nothing else, yet it infallibly proves Atheism to be the most gross ignorance."[58]

Such condemnatory language against atheism is not found in Wesley's *Survey*, and it would be inconsistent with Wesley's religious epistemology. In the 1788 sermons, Wesley defined an atheist as someone who had no sense of divine things, who had forgotten God, and who was unmindful of the invisible, eternal, and spiritual worlds.[59] The atheist was ignorant of immaterial reality, and the modern philosophy of experiential knowledge would not provide enlightenment, because it could not transform the soul, open up the spiritual senses, and impart belief. In spite of all its evidence of the wisdom, goodness, and power displayed in the Creation, the *Survey* could not help the atheist attain Christian faith. Natural philosophy was a type of evidence appropriate for matters of moral certainty, but it could not offer adequate proof to substantiate faith-based knowledge.

This is not to say that Wesley's theological writings restrict scientific theories to the realm of matters of fact. They also contributed to his analysis of religious experiences.[60] In particular, the influence of medical science on Wesley's understanding of assurance can be seen in his 1768 letter to the Reverend Dr. Thomas Rutherforth, Archdeacon of Essex. In the letter, Wesley stated that a few people have an assurance of "everlasting salvation," and more have an assurance that they are currently reconciled to God. The common Christian experience, however, is one that fluctuates between consciousness of God's favor and fear of God. Those who never feel assurance because of bodily disorders that depress the soul constitute an exception to this general rule, which led

---

58. Cheyne, Preface, n.p.

59. Wesley, *Works*, Sermon 108 and Sermon 119, 3:523, 4:58.

60. Wesley, *Works*, "Heaviness through manifold temptations," 2:226, 227, pars. 3.1, 2; See *Works* (Jackson) 4:63; 12:379; 13:27, 47, and 76 where the spiritual heaviness of Jane Binknell, Jane Hilton Barton, Mary Bishop, Damaris Perronet, and Hester Ann Roe is attributed to bodily disorders.

Wesley to conclude, "Therefore I have not for many years thought a consciousness of acceptance to be essential to justifying faith."[61]

Wesley's understanding of the relationship between the brain, the nerves, and the soul contributed to his decision to revise his teachings on the essentials of saving faith. A steadfast, unwavering conviction of salvation may not be possible for some bodies, he realized, due to an impairment of the brain or nervous system that degraded the function of the soul's spiritual senses and its ability to discern the spiritual world. Such a disorder would explain why some experienced temporary or permanent loss of the witness of the Spirit.[62]

The atheist, whose spiritual senses are also nonfunctioning, is in a different predicament. A physical ailment is not the cause of the problem but a failure of the will. Unless the individual works together with God, even the influence of preventing grace will diminish, the conscience will harden, and the spiritual senses will remain closed. Reading books of natural philosophy will not change this condition. The atheist does not lack information about God; the atheist lacks the will to yield to God.[63]

A section of the Appendix, taken from the *Procedure*, is the closest Wesley comes to criticizing atheists. He sounds like a prosecuting attorney delivering a summation to the jury: "Here we are to fix our foot, and join issue with all ranks of unbelievers; the ground of whose condemnation will be, that they willfully with-held their assent from the truths of revelation, when they had the same evidence which would have fully convinced them in matters merely human."[64]

The legalese is even more apparent in the original Browne version of the *Procedure* from which Wesley was drawing (complete with capitol letters and italics to ensure the point does not go unnoticed!):

> This shows the strange inconsistency of those men who reject the faith of Christian Mysteries, under color of wanting *Strict*

61. Wesley, *Works* (Jackson) 14:348. This is consistent with the degrees of saving faith (Fathers in Christ, Young Men in faith, and Babes in Christ) discussed in the 1788 sermons.

62. For more on Wesley's familiarity with medical theories about the brain see my "A Necessary Relationship: John Wesley on the Body-Soul Connection," in *Inward and Outward Health: John Wesley's Holistic Concept of Medical Science, the Environment and Holy Living* (London: Epworth, 2008) 140–68.

63. Wesley, *Works*, Sermons 105 and Sermon 108, 3:487, 523.

64. Wesley, *Survey*, 5:200.

> *Reason* and *Evidence*; for as it is their present guilt, so the ground of this condemnation hereafter will be their *Want of Knowledge*, when they had all the proper *Means* of attaining it; and that they did not yield the *Assent* of the *Understanding* upon the same or greater Moral Certainty and Evidence, than would be a full conviction to them in Matters merely Human of the same sort. That they withheld that Assent either through *Passion* or *Prejudice*; or for want of *Application* to weigh and consider the Force of that Evidence; and that they insisted upon a *Sort* of Proof and Evidence, which is proper only to a quite different *Kind* of Knowledge, and such as would render all *Religious Faith* impracticable.[65]

Browne argued that the method practiced in jury deliberations (and in other areas of life) of weighing and considering whether or not "Sufficient, Undoubted Evidence or a Moral Certainty" has been provided in support of a claim is the same type of procedure that should be followed in questions of religion.[66] For their insistence on a higher level of certainty than the one they accept in other instances of moral certainty, the ranks of unbelievers stand accused of unreasonable prejudice against religion.

Browne included within these ranks such heretics as Arians, Socinians, Deists, Freethinkers, and Atheists. The *Procedure* is introduced in its first chapter as a successful argument against the irrational demands of these adversaries of Christianity.[67] Wesley did not retain this chapter in his *Survey* Appendix, and he did not include the steward's comment that natural philosophy saved him from atheism.[68] Wesley did not leave behind a record detailing his reasons for deleting these and other references to atheism from his *Survey*. Whether he had his category of faith-based knowledge in mind as he crafted his natural philosophy is a matter of opinion. All that can be determined with certainty from the surviving documents is that this action is in keeping with his definition of faith as a spiritual sense.

---

65. Browne, *Procedure, Extent, and Limits*, 250, 251.
66. Ibid., 249.
67. Ibid., 27–32, 35–41.
68. Hale, *Contemplations*, 283.

4

Mystery and Humility in John Wesley's Narrative Ecology

Marc Otto and Michael Lodahl

*In this our infant state we cannot know much:
but we may love much.
Let us secure this point and we shall soon be swallowed up
in an ocean of both Knowledge and Love!*

—John Wesley

This study is an attempt to unearth John Wesley's contributions to one of the most persistent questions in Western thought from the eighteenth century to the present: What is the nature of God's relation to the world in which we live?

We undertake this "unearthing"—which, happily, will turn out to be a kind of "earthing" of Wesley—by exploring a somewhat unexpected and generally overlooked source, *Survey of the Wisdom of God in Creation*, which Wesley cobbled together from the works of several contemporary natural philosophers. We will focus our attention on Wesley's interpolations and emendations of his sources, ferreting out those textual junctures in which Wesley's own voice is discernible. In particular, we hope to show how the stories of natural oddities and "believe-it-or-not" occurrences that were Wesley's own distinct contributions were intended to function in his readers' experience of the book, and of the mysterious world they, and we, inhabit.

By the eighteenth century, natural philosophy had reconceived God as a mechanical clockmaker rather than the freely interactive God of the Bible. The critical blow that tipped the new European consciousness was Newton's discovery that planetary motion could be described by a mathematical formula. This discovery struck at the heart of a widely embraced conviction that God's finger was the direct cause for any movement within the heavens. Amidst the onslaught of this and other discoveries, Christianity was quickly becoming viewed as inadequate to provide the best picture of reality. Thus, Wesley's work reflects a passionate, scholarly attempt to defend the God of the Bible during a rapidly crumbling Christian understanding of God's relationship to the natural world.

The publication of *Survey* in 1763 "was so favorably received, far beyond his expectation," that the whole work went through seven editions in England, three editions in America until 1823 and then a final edition in London in 1835.[1] Wesley required the work to be read by his ministers, listed it among other recommended reading of natural philosophy, read it to his preacher classes and printed extracts from it in the *Arminian Magazine* until his death.[2]

Despite *Survey*'s popularity during Wesley's lifetime, it attracts little scholarly interest today. *Survey* cannot (at least yet) be found within *The Complete Works of Wesley*, and it is difficult to obtain. In the initial stages of research, we found no book, or any article of great length, devoted to understanding the work of *Survey*. Soon after and only by the gracious direction of Randy Maddox did we learn of Laura Bartels Felleman's recent doctoral dissertation at Drew University that engages *Survey* extensively.

There are understandable reasons for this reticence regarding research of *Survey*. Wesley's natural philosophy fades into the shadows of his other more distinctive ideas about prevenient grace, the witness of the Spirit and Christian perfection. Additionally, some scholars may be reluctant to attribute any great significance to Wesley due to his prolific

---

1. Robert E. Schofield, "John Wesley and Science in 18th Century England," *Isis* 44 (1953) 3:336.

2. Ibid.

reliance on the writings of others in this work. Nonetheless, our working assumption is that Wesley worked carefully and intentionally in his editing of the works he effectively plagiarized; thus, it requires no great leap to credit to Wesley the theological reflections within *Survey*. If an idea from one of his sources escaped the editing pen, we assume it is because Wesley wanted to leave the idea intact. Indeed, Wesley himself wrote that he had "found occasion to retrench, enlarge, or alter every chapter and almost every section."[3]

Further, we believe that Wesley's insistence upon the limits of human knowledge has not been sufficiently appreciated as one of the primary theological aims of *Survey*, representing a crucial component of his orientation toward this mysterious world. This frank insistence upon human limitation and humility bespeaks a greater significance for this work in relation to Wesley's intellectual milieu. Our argument is that *Survey*, to a great extent, appears to be Wesley's evangelical response to the mechanistic philosophy and deism of his day. Notably, this may help to explain Felleman's observation that Wesley's intentionally deleted the word "atheism" from some his original sources.[4] We suspect that Wesley's deletion of "atheism" demonstrates that he would not have wanted to restrict his concern to atheism, very likely because mechanical philosophy and deism were as great a concern as atheism, if not greater. Wesley's reading of Scripture, his Aristotelian commitment to the nature of matter, and his sympathy with British empiricism encouraged him to emphasize the limits of human knowledge. These equipped him to respond to the growing trend in his day that "all things might be accounted for."[5] In *Survey*, Wesley describes a picture of the universe that is full of the uncommon—a place much bigger than math and human understanding. The universe is not merely a machine or math or mechanism of a Watch Maker, for God's Spirit, the utterly mysterious "Soul of the universe," fills and enshrouds all of creation.

While many of the scientific assumptions within the work are outdated and inadequate and our knowledge of the universe has moved

---

3. John Wesley, *A Survey of the Wisdom of God in Creation: A Compendium of Natural Philosophy*, 4th ed. (London: J. Paramore Upper-Moorfields, 1784) 1:v–vi.

4. Felleman observed that Wesley intentionally deleted the word "atheism" from some of his original sources in her dissertation, "The Evidence of Things Not Seen: John Wesley's Use of Natural Philosophy" (PhD diss., Drew University, 2004).

5. Wesley, *Survey*, 1:21.

far beyond what Wesley thought possible, there are some fascinating insights from *Survey* that are similar to some of our contemporary concepts in science today. Further, this paper explores the significance of Wesley's natural philosophy in light of his emphasis on the limits of human knowledge. In short, *Survey* remains a significant work of faith resonating with Scripture and the science of the eighteenth century. Yet, it contains some significant thinking that can reshape some of our theological views today. Wesley stands out in history as one the greatest evangelists the world and yet he also had an uncommon curiosity in nature's ability to reveal the mysterious presence of God within nature. Surely we have much more to learn about the ways that Wesley's love for God and nature fueled and shaped each other.

Wesley alone writes the preface to his *Survey*. Following the preface, much of the basic structure of the work regarding human beings is taken directly from the prominent Genevan biologist Johann Franz Buddeus, although Wesley vastly shortens the length and offers his own reflections.[6] In particular, Wesley's appears to rely upon Buddeus's outline in *Elementa Philosophiae*. Wesley translated the work from Latin. Overarching the entire work, Wesley follows a structure more similar to the work of William Derham in *Physico-theology* and to a lesser degree, Noel Pluche in *Nature Delineated*.[7] Wesley also weaves in the contributions of the biological discoveries of William Harvey (1658–1657) and, toward the end of his work, theological reflections from Lord Justice Matthew Hale (1609–1676). Wesley's goal was to "display the invisible things of God, his Power, Wisdom and Goodness," from the visible parts of nature.[8]

Why Wesley Undertook *Survey*: The Challenge of Newtonian Physics in Natural Philosophy

Preparation for *Survey* began in 1758 when John Wesley spent a full week away from his vigorous preaching schedule to compile materials for the work.[9] From Wesley's journal, no other statement regarding

6. Schofield, "John Wesley and Science," 336–37.
7. Ibid.
8. Wesley, *Survey*, 1:iii.
9. *The Works of John Wesley, Journal* (11 Dec. 1758), 3rd ed. (Grand Rapids: Baker, 1991) 2:464.

Survey would appear until 1764, one year after publication, when he writes, "At ten (and so every morning) I met the preachers that were in town and read over with them the 'Survey of the Wisdom of God in the Creation.'"[10]

Thus, our exploration of context begins with a question. Why would one of the greatest evangelists of the eighteenth century take on the immense task of summarizing all the major discoveries in nature?

Before any suggestion, it may be helpful to examine Wesley's context and then to explore some of his own interactions with nature. Yet, the growing belief that God was not essential to explain nature's operations, as well as Wesley's discontent with the current works of natural philosophy, led him to publish his thoughts on the interactions between nature and God. Here we examine some important contextual details for the work, including Wesley's personal interest in nature.

In the seventeenth century, natural philosophy was optimistic that nature might confirm the truth of Scripture. A number of Anglican clergy and Puritan philosophers offered a set of values that encouraged scientific inquiry—more properly understood as natural philosophy. Yet in Wesley's day, this very pursuit grew to question whether God was necessary to explain the behaviors observed in nature.[11] By the eighteenth century, Galileo's theories of the solar system, Kepler's work regarding the motion of planets, Boyle's work in chemistry and Newton's study of physics all marked a key departure from traditional thinking about God and nature.[12] Understandably, for some, these new theories replaced God's finger as the direct source of power in the universe. By this time, many of the new discoveries by Newton and others had challenged traditional assumptions about God's relationship to the universe; thus, some philosophers saw evidence for atheism, others deism and still a few others, like Wesley, further evidence of God's presence in nature.

Within Europe, the city of London offered a particular focal point for the growth of information relating to the development of science. One reason for this is the early seventeenth century work of Francis

---

10. See *Journal* (8 November 1964), Wesley, *Works*, 3:201.

11. David Lindberg and Ronald L. Numbers, editors, *God and Nature: Historical Essays on the Encounter Between Christianity and Science* (Berkeley: University of California Press, 1986) 4. See also essays by Webster and Westfall.

12. Ian Barbour, *Religion and Science: Historical and Contemporary Issues* (New York: Harper-Collins, 1997) 19–20.

Bacon (1561–1626). Born in this great city, it was here that Bacon developed and popularized a new method for observing nature and collecting knowledge. This method was a precursor to the scientific method that developed shortly after Wesley's passing in the late eighteenth century. Notably, Wesley credits Bacon with the development of natural philosophy within Europe as he "incited lovers of philosophy to diligent research into natural history. And he himself led the way, by many experiments and observations."[13]

Another reason for the shift from God's power to the power of nature was the development in 1660 of The Royal Society of London for the Improvement of Natural Knowledge. This band of religious inquirers grew to become one of the most well respected sources for publishing new information relating to observations in nature and medicine. Composed primarily of Anglican and Puritan ministers, the society directed its study of nature "to the glory of God and the benefit of the human race" by establishing a set of standards by which one could publish works of new observation and critique theories.[14] Wesley himself read the publications and several of the Society's notices and articles appear within *Survey* nearly unchanged in their wording.[15]

Not surprisingly, the Royal Society would come increasingly to imbibe the naturalistic spirit of the Enlightenment. Natural philosophy had begun in earnest to turn God into a mechanical clock maker rather than the freely interactive God of biblical faith. Again, to a growing group of philosophers, Newton's physics had replaced God's finger as the direct cause for planetary motion. Some philosophers like as Pierre-Simon Marquis de Laplace (1749–1827) claimed that the God hypothesis was no longer any use to astronomers.[16] Interestingly, in 1758, the same year Wesley began preparing for *Survey*, the Catholic Church reversed its condemnation of Galileo's sun-centered universe. While the effect of this on Wesley is only speculative, natural philosophy was in need of a new direction in order to reaffirm the God of the Bible amidst a wave

---

13. Wesley, *Survey*, 1:15.

14. Ibid.

15. There are several instances in *Survey* where the *Philosophical Transactions of the Royal Society* Wesley is mentioned; furthermore, Wesley mentions the Royal Society by name in Wesley, *Survey*, 3:280.

16. Lindberg, *God and Nature*, 12.

of new discoveries from the telescope, microscope and mathematical descriptions for planetary movement within the universe.

In Wesley's time, though, the Royal Society appears to have been more interested in collecting knowledge than in developing new theologies in response to the new discoveries. Wesley, however, displayed greater sensitivity to the broader currents of this philosophical drift toward deism and mechanical conceptions of nature in his natural philosophy.

The Experiential Wesley and the Purpose of *Survey*

Several fascinating accounts about John Wesley's life indicate that he had an intense, even uncommon interest in nature. In one account, Wesley attended the Tower Zoo with a flutist to watch the animals respond to the music.[17] Similarly, within *Survey*, Wesley describes watching the great old lion in Edinburgh roar with fierceness to the sound of music.[18] Another time, Wesley writes, "I have seen all the horses and cows in a field, where there were above a hundred, gather round a person that was blowing a French horn and seeming to testify to an awkward kind of satisfaction."[19] Further illustrations of his observations in nature include Wesley going to see "a monster" and a pelican near Bath and a cactus that bloomed at night. In December of 1759, Wesley spent a morning translating Greek from the New Testament, followed by an afternoon visit to a British Museum where he saw Sir Hans Sloane's collection of "shells, butterflies, beetles, grasshoppers etc.," and other curious, "uncommon items."[20]

Wesley worked diligently to observe the work of God in nature. While it was customary for an Anglican gentleman in the eighteenth century to give some thought to these phenomena, Wesley's level of interest in the study of nature appears unusual when one considers his work within *Survey*, his significant contribution to educate people about nature and his own careful observations of the natural world.

In short, the work of *Survey* arises from the context of his dissatisfaction with other natural philosophies, his own curiosity and a

17. Schofield, "John Wesley and Science," 338.
18. Wesley, *Survey*, 2:68.
19. Ibid.
20. *Journal* (12 Dec. 1759), *Works* 2:520.

concern to preserve God's place within a growing system of knowledge that had little apparent room for the idea of God. We now examine the theology in *Survey* from this context.

The Three Primary Theological Themes Within *Survey* [21]

The first crucial theological theme in Wesley's *Survey* can be summarized as the *economy, design and providence* of God's creation—the way God has created the world to sustain and provide for itself. The second examines *the limits of human knowledge*—the way God has created the world (human beings) so that we may be in responsible relationship with God, without fully understanding God's ways. And the last theme reveals *God's call, through creation, to wonder and worship*—or, the way God has created the world to inspire worship from human beings. While we shall give attention to all three themes, we will give greater attention to the second, on the limits of human knowledge, as a call upon humans to exercise humility and a sense of wonder in the face of the far-more-than-human world.

Theme One: Design/Economy/Providence

Wesley refers to God's design, economy and providence frequently throughout *Survey*.[22] These three specific themes are often woven together, making them hard to distinguish from each other at times. However, generally speaking, *design* reveals God's purposeful intention to create and sustain life. *Economy* reveals the interconnectedness of all the parts in design to sustain the whole. And *providence* reveals God's wise, powerful and good intentions to supply all that is needed for life in nature. Collectively, the sub-themes represent the idea that God was intentional in formation of life.

In opposition to some forms of deism, Wesley emphasizes God's continual touch in the created plant world, where "there is not an hour nor moment passes, wherein there are not many millions of plants and animals forming" in just one part of the world. Wesley, then, purports

---

21. By "primary" we mean the terms and ideas most frequently employed by Wesley as they develop his larger theological arguments discussed in this chapter.

22. We have identified some 140 explicit instances of this theme in *Survey*.

that it would be derogatory to believe that God's hand touches the vegetable world any less than "ten thousand times every hour."[23]

Through the lens of Scripture upon nature, Wesley observes the Psalmist's statement that God grows the grass for the cattle as revealing a "singular wisdom of the divine economy" and "the care of a wise and condescending Providence, even over these lowest formations [in the chain] of nature."[24] For Wesley and for other thinkers of the time, all things in creation were connected to each other in an ascending order of complexity. They were links in a great chain ultimately leading to our connection to God. Furthermore, God filled every particle of Creation with a fire-fluid-spirit and life-giving presence, called the principle of life. Electricity, Wesley surmised, is God's presence within the fabric of creation.

The links of the great chain are infused with electricity, which Wesley again suggests is the "soul of the universe" that pervades and surrounds every part of earth, every particle and ultimately connects all things.[25] That Wesley understood this electric-fire to be God's glory or presence is clear by his belief that God was the immediate cause of all motion.[26]

In a philosophy of nature, Wesley could not conceive of anything as separate from God. From the words of Bonnet, the great chain reveals this interrelatedness of all things:

> The Divine Mind has so closely connected every part of his work, that there is not one which has not a relation to the whole system. A mushroom, a mite, are as essential parts of it as the cedar or elephant. So that those minute productions of nature which unthinking men judge to be useless, are not mere particles of dust on the wheels of the machine of the world; they are small wheels intermixed with the greater. There is nothing by itself.[27]

---

23. Ibid., 2:258–59.
24. Ibid., 3:270.
25. Ibid., 3:215–16.
26. Ibid., 4:6.
27. Ibid., 4:68.

Theme Two: The Limits of Knowledge and Humility

While theme one reflects upon intentional design, theme two suggests that God limited the knowledge of human beings to humble us. For this reason, nature in all her design, economy and providence was beyond comprehension. "God is the center of all knowledge," Wesley wrote, so humans, not being God, cannot have this full knowledge.[28] If nature was the realm for God's presence then it follows that nature, too, could only be understood in part.

Wesley aims for greater humility among the "children of pride"—the beginning place for a relationship with God.[29] However, a historical consideration reveals another purpose for insisting upon limits in the knowledge of human beings. If theme one confronts the atheist with the evidence of design, then theme two might be said to be the wrench of mystery thrown into the gears of the philosophy of deism. If developing philosophies in Wesley's day described away God's power, then the evangelist would confront the foundation of this supposed progress. Thus, Wesley's target audience for theme two is likely the deistic philosophy of pure mechanistic thinking. While it may not be a strong apologetic, he clearly responds to his context. Wesley's theological aim in stressing the limits of human understanding may have been a move *against* mechanical philosophy.

Wesley perceived the human body as a site of inescapable mystery, writing, "How little do we know even of our own frame!"[30] He then offers several accounts of uncommon appearances in the human body, sounding at times like he's writing for *Ripley's Believe It or Not*. A man without any arms was observed to ride a horse for 40 miles a day, holding a brush between his chin and shoulder to care for his horse.[31] Another man, 28 years of age, lost his speech due to a sore throat and never regained his speech until four years later when he fell from his horse and dreamed that he was falling into boiling wort—an infusion of malt in the formation of beer. From his sleep, he cried out loud for help.[32] This wild story is told in the context of Wesley's bewilderment about the

---

28. Ibid., 1:10.
29. Ibid., 1:vi–vii, and 5:229–32.
30. Ibid., 1:47.
31. Ibid., 1:96.
32. Ibid., 1:72.

phenomenon of sleep. "I apprehend that nothing can be known with any certainty upon the head.... who can give a satisfactory account of sleep ... we are ignorant of the whole affair."[33] He calls dreams a mystery and wonders how curious it is that when one awakes all the faculties of human reasoning have been perfectly restored. He states, "Surely this is the Lord's doing. And it is marvelous in our eyes!"[34]

Animals, too, reveal the limits of our knowledge, giving evidence of something like a soul, something "not commonly known."[35] Elephants, for example, "appear delighted with music and readily learn to beat time, to move in measure and even join their voice with the drum and trumpet."[36] They have a discerning sense of smell:

> This animal's sense of smelling is not only exquisite, but it is pleased with the same odors that delight mankind. The elephant gathers flowers with great pleasure; it picks them up one by one, unties them in a nosegay and seems charmed with the perfume ... it seeks in the meadows the most odoriferous plants to feed upon; and in the woods it prefers the coco, the banana, the palm and the sage tree to all others.[37]

They have the ability for touch: "By means of this [trunk], the elephant can untie the knots of a rope, unlock a door and even write with a pen."[38] But even more confounding to the human mind is the great care they develop for their trainers, seeking their caress, obeying them and anticipating their desires. Yet even more remarkable is the following:

> ... he [the elephant] frequently takes such an affection for his keeper that he will obey no other; and it has been known to die for grief when in some sudden fit of madness, it has killed its conductor.[39]

Another account describes how an elephant in Delhi, passing by a shop, stuck his trunk in a place of business. A person within the shop pricked the elephant's nose with a needle. Wesley notes that without any

33. Ibid., 1:147.
34. Ibid., 1:151.
35. Ibid., 1:203.
36. Ibid., 1:204.
37. Ibid., 1:205.
38. Ibid., 1:206.
39. Ibid., 1:208.

sign of resentment, the elephant calmly removed his nose, walked to a puddle of dirty water, filled its trunk and returned to spray the interior of the shop.[40] Animals are a more-than-mechanical mystery surpassing human understanding, the elephant being just one example.

Similarly, for Wesley no natural philosophy adequately accounted for underwater animal behavior. One man observed the social behavior of fish when he kept two fish together during Christmas and separated them in April, noticing that upon separation, one fish became melancholy and would not eat for three weeks. Yet it fully recovered when it was put back with the other fish. Wesley told another story about a fish that loved to look at its master "with pleasure" when the latter entered the room.[41] Birds, like fish, reveal the limits of human understanding: "What master has taught the birds, that they have any need for nests?"[42] Wesley's curiosity recounts how a man bonded with a frog for 36 years, meeting each evening for a feeding.[43] Wesley's view of nature, by his stories of the uncommon, reveals a strange, wonderful and more-than-mechanical world.

By his own account, our evangelist witnessed the uncommon mystery of animals and music:

> We have many other odd accounts of the power of music: and it must not be denied, but that on some particular occasions, musical sounds may have a very powerful effect. I have seen all the horses and cows in a field, where there were above a hundred, gather round a person that was blowing a French horn and seeming to testify an awkward kind of satisfaction. Dogs are well known to be very sensible of different tones in music; and I have sometimes heard them sustain a very ridiculous part in a concert.[44]

In this section of *Survey*, Wesley also recounts a story referred to earlier about the great old lion in Edinburgh who roared with fierceness to the sound of music as further evidence that animals are more than machines. For Wesley, they appeared to have some sense of reason:

40. Ibid., 1:208.
41. Ibid., 1:330.
42. Ibid., 1:312.
43. Ibid., 2:54.
44. Ibid., 2:68.

> Several eminent men have been of opinion, that all brutes are mere machines. This may be agreeable enough to the pride of man; but it is not agreeable to daily observation. Do we not continually observe in the brutes which are round us, a degree of reason? Many of their actions cannot be accounted for without it: as that commonly noted of dogs, that running before their masters, they will stop at the parting of the road, till they see which way their masters take.[45]

Wesley appears to have delighted in these stories in order to demonstrate that humans grasp in vain at nature's knowledge and may discover that the very purpose for this mystery is God. Accordingly, he offers a significant and broad theological reflection regarding the philosophy of nature:

> And this is the substance of true philosophy. We cannot know much. In vain our shallow reason attempts to fathom the mysteries of nature and to pry into the secrets of the Almighty. *His ways are past finding out.*[46]

For Wesley, this abiding sense of mystery is not restricted to living things. The primary elements, the building block of all things in creation, display curious phenomena and confound reason. The presence of the primary elements within the larger order of creation also displays the limits in human understanding. While mountains are said not to move, a mountain of sand, Wesley reports, traveled four miles over 30 years and buried a town near Lakenheath.[47] In the same way, no theory of mountains can explain the formation of Iron Mountain, near Taberg in Sweden, for there is no other iron in any other mountain surrounding. Yet stranger, a bed of sand surrounds it although the mount is far from the sea.[48] Thus, in affirmation of Scripture, Wesley infers that God not only can move mountains, but that God already has.

Like comparing a grain of sand to the number of grains on a beach, Wesley wonders at the depth of the sea, perhaps more than 3,000 fathoms, and marvels that water on the tip of a needle contains no less than 13,000 globules. We grasp this knowledge in vain, said Wesley, "and if

---

45. Ibid., 2:139. Of course Wesley would make a similar point in his sermon "The General Deliverance."

46. Ibid., 2:252.

47. Ibid., 3:9.

48. Ibid., 3:15–19.

so many thousands exist in so small a speck, how many in the unmeasured extent of the ocean? Who can count them? We may as well grasp the wind in our fist, or measure out the universe with our span.[49]"

Notably, several lengthy and emotion-filled accounts of the uncommon occur in the second chapter concerning "fire." They provide a link between theme two and theme three by revealing the uncommon enshrouded by a sentiment of wonder and worship within the story itself! One story is about a man who survived an earthquake. Barely able to move upon the violent land, he escaped to a boat in which he confessed his sins and watched the justice of God shatter the town. Ten years later, a fire destroyed the town and after this, a hurricane. All the public officials were removed from office and no market was to be held in the future of that town.[50]

Irregular tides, the curious patterns of water freezing and evaporating, the curious properties of mercury, strange appearances in water and subterranean trees all reveal the smallness of human knowledge. The uncommon reveals more than human limitations, for these accounts gave Wesley reasons to admire and wonder in God's presence with nature. He offers them to others in *Survey*, writing, "Job considered this [the elements of nature] with holy admiration. 'Dost thou know the balancing of the clouds? How such ponderous bodies are made to hang in even poise and hover like the lightest down?'"[51]

Survey contains significant sections of unanswered questions reminiscent of those found in the book of Job. In fact, Wesley makes specific references to Job within *Survey*. Questions serve an important theological aim within the work to reveal the limits of human understanding and to proclaim the wisdom of God.

Wesley framed the current debate on motion by saying, "The motion of [all things in the universe] . . . must be guided at every moment by either mechanism or by a spiritual power."[52] He then explains that Newton himself believed the power behind the mechanical theories was a "subtle, ethereal medium, diffused through the whole universe,"

---

49. Ibid., 3:68 (wording slightly changed but meaning preserved.)
50. Ibid., 3:143
51. Ibid., 3:264.
52. Ibid., 3:340.

a spiritual power.⁵³ As we have mentioned already, this was Wesley's view.⁵⁴ Notably, Wesley attacks a Newtonian mechanical philosophy on the grounds that Newton himself believed that any mathematical descriptions of the universe rest upon a spiritual foundation. For this reason, Wesley's reverses the idea of progress. Newtonian physics, for Wesley, was little more than "a step further in the dark."⁵⁵ He states, "the knot does not lie in gravitation or attraction, or any particular kind of motion, but in finding powers to produce and maintain motion in general."⁵⁶ And later, "It can be no mechanical power. It must be the finger of God . . . the direct, immediate power of God operating through the whole universe."⁵⁷

In short, Wesley believed that Newton's physics, contrary to popular opinion, did not fundamentally advance human knowledge, because the latter's principles rested upon an unexplained spiritual principle. Newton's work describes but does not explain, Wesley argued. In this view, Newton does not so much remove God's finger from nature, but instead does show that nature points further into the mysteries of human understanding. In so arguing, Wesley offers an important response to the direction of natural philosophy in eighteenth century England.

Survey, then, reveals that nature *had to* be unpredictable for God's mystery has been infused throughout the fabric and flow of creation. Because humans cannot fully understand God, it followed that we could never fully understand nature. God had not abandoned nature to mathematical formulas but filled it with God's own glory, a divine mystery.

Wesley's inclusion of accounts of the uncommon, inserted intentionally by Wesley into his mix of natural philosophers, is significant precisely because he collected these narratives and intentionally added to his natural philosophy. Thus, accounts of the uncommon offer today's Wesleyan scholar a direct link to the evangelist's own aim and voice, even if only in his function as editor of *Survey*. Wesley states that he intentionally added the stories as a "proper digression," for they too

---

53. Ibid.
54. See n. 25 above.
55. Ibid., 3:340–41.
56. Ibid.
57. Ibid., 4:37.

illustrate the wisdom of God. The uncommon, Wesley states, reveals the mystery where the Creator "'hath so done his works,' that we may admire and adore, but 'we cannot search them out to perfection.'"[58] In the preface, he writes: "For when we have finished our *Survey*, what do we know? How inconceivably little! . . . It may be a means, on one hand of humbling the pride of man, by showing that he is surrounded on every side, with things which he cannot account for . . .[59]"

Furthermore, by calling these accounts a "digression" Wesley implies they were atypical from the common arguments and functions of natural philosophy in his time. Again, this points to the significance of theme two and further distinguishes his natural theology from the works of others.

Remarkably, it appears that theme two has not been given adequate attention as a perspective from which the work should be understood. For example, Felleman's work, in agreement with Andrew Cunningham, differentiates Wesley's natural philosophy by comparing it to the normative function of natural philosophy in Wesley's day to combat the enemy of atheism.[60] However, Felleman does not comment on a relationship between *Survey* and the growth of mechanical philosophy and even implies that Wesley was comfortable employing mechanical descriptions as evidence of God's wisdom.[61] Unfortunately, scholarly descriptions of *Survey* have often overlooked the significance of theme two. For this reason, *Survey* has not been accurately understood as Wesley's corrective response to growing trends in deistic thinking and mechanical philosophy.[62]

Thus we propose that *Survey* had for Wesley the fundamental purpose of evoking in his readers a profound sense of the limitations of human understanding. It should be clear, additionally, that Wesley was *not* comfortable with mere mechanical descriptions of God and nature.

---

58. Ibid.

59. Ibid., 1:vii–viii.

60. Felleman, "The Evidence of Things Not Seen," 96.

61. Laura Bartels Felleman, "John Wesley's *Survey of the Wisdom of God in Creation*: A Methodological Inquiry," *Perspectives on Science and Christian Faith* 58 (2006) 72.

62. Barbour, *Religion and Science*, 42. While Barbour does not offer the limits of human understanding as a primary way of reading *Survey*, he does suggest that Wesley's concerns with Newtonianism may have been due to its association with deism and claims of knowledge beyond human possibility.

A proper understanding of theme two demonstrates that, for Wesley, mechanical descriptions were only a starting place in the knowledge of God and nature. While Wesley, at times, employs mechanical descriptions they become the ground from which he moves beyond them or offers criticisms of them. God and nature, for Wesley, were always more than purely mechanical. And lastly, from a contextual analysis, Wesley's emphasis on theme two appears to be in direct response to the growth of mechanical philosophy and deism.[63]

These themes in conjunction suggest that God's intentional design confronts the atheist while the limits of human understanding confound the deist. Wesley's common sense approach to the philosophy of religion, his commitments to Aristotelian empiricism and his inclusion of Brown's epistemology within the work adequately equipped him to describe nature in ways contrary to atheism and mechanical philosophy.[64]

Theme two, in this view of Wesley's theological aims, was not accidental as though having only an unintended consequence to respond to deism. As demonstrated early in this thesis, Wesley's aim that humility be instilled within humankind would confront the growing assumption that a human philosophy or principle might account for *all* the secrets of nature.[65]

In sum, this is the significance of theme two within *Survey*: mystery confronts the machine. Wesley builds a natural philosophy sufficient to confront atheism with the evidence of design (theme one) and challenges deism with the evidence of a more-than mechanical universe (theme two). He appears concerned that the God of the Bible should be preserved in the light of the revolution of information initiated by Copernicus, Galileo and Newton.

While the discoveries of the seventeenth and eighteenth fueled the growth of mechanical conceptions of nature, in Wesley's view, God's freely interactive presence filled the very fabric of creation. Matter was not merely matter, for it contained this mysterious presence of God. In *Survey*, Wesley describes this most frequently as the principle of life—a

63. Ibid. Barbour's comments support the connection between theme two and Wesley's concern with deism.

64. Peter Brown's work allowed Wesley to conclude that Scripture represented an improvement upon the knowledge of human beings.

65. Wesley, *Survey*, 1:21.

spirit-fire-fluid—in a God infused universe. And, more radically, by emphasizing theme two, the confidence in progress itself seemed to be brought into question.[66] For Wesley, progress lay not so much in answering questions as in raising new greater questions. This was a function of his argument that there is a profoundly unknowable element within nature.

Understandably, in Wesley's view, God was not a Clock Maker who had stepped away from the daily sustenance of his wild, curious and wonderfully strange order. If God is beyond comprehension and nature is infused with God's active presence, then it followed that nature too would hide a full knowledge of her ways. Thus, any mechanical philosophy was going to fall short of explaining nature. It might describe but could not account for everything.

Theme two also points to the significant role of Scripture within Wesley's natural philosophy. Clearly, Scripture was a source of Wesley's thinking about this theme, in addition to the works of philosophers.[67] If Scripture contained appearances of the uncommon—like a continually burning bush or an unusual star above Bethlehem, for example—then Wesley's observations of nature should and would also display the uncommon. If the Bible was true, then the study of nature would *have to* display a more-than-mechanical world—a world full of the mysterious Divine. The Bible described this, so Wesley's world would reflect the same.

Wesley created philosophical room for the idea of a God in an intellectual context that challenged this traditional assumption. In *Survey*, the God of Nature could surprise us, call us to wonder and worship and even confound our senses for the benefit of our humility. Notably, Wesley believed that one day God would increase our human understanding. In the closing remarks of one of the abridgements, our evangelist exclaims, "In this our infant state we cannot know much: but we may love much. Let us secure this point and we shall soon be swallowed up in an ocean of both Knowledge and Love!"[68]

---

66. See Wesley's abridgement of Dutens's *Discoveries of the Ancients* within *Survey*.
67. Examples abound on virtually every page of Wesley's *Survey*.
68. Ibid., 5:170.

Theme Three: The Call to Wonder and to Worship

While theme two suggested that the limits upon our knowledge were designed to reveal God, theme three calls human beings to respond in wonder and worship, celebrating both the knowledge and mystery of God. Thus, theme three builds upon the previous themes, for Wesley believed that the knowledge of God's character was sufficient to call human beings into the wonder and worship of God despite our limited understanding of how God works within creation.

A natural philosophy only addressing atheism had little need to describe God's character. Deism, on the other hand, demanded a bit more theological sophistication with a natural philosophy. God's presence in nature was mystery but God's character of goodness, wisdom and power were on display—calling us past the limits of our understanding to worship the Creator.

Therefore, in Wesley's view, God's character was sufficient to overcome all our doubts and call us to wonder and worship:

> I trust therefore the following sheets may, in some degree, answer both these important purposes. It may be a means, on one hand, of humbling the pride of man, by showing that he is surrounded on every side, with things which he can no more account for, than for immensity or eternity: and it may serve on the other, to display the amazing Power, Wisdom and Goodness of the great Creator; to warm our hearts and fill our mouths with wonder, love and praise![69]

God created human beings to enjoy God's presence in nature. As noted earlier, nature could instill human beings with a sense of wonder at the uncommon. For example, Wesley tells a story about a person without eyesight who could see when his nose was pinched, and another about a maid of 23 years of age who was colorblind yet could read in the dark for nearly 30 minutes.[70] Yet more, Richard Clutterback of Redborough was also blind but could hear a single grain of sand fall within an hourglass and could put together a watch.[71] At times, these accounts might encourage an emotional or experiential reaction in the reader, like a preacher using stories to illustrate his or her point.

---

69. Ibid., 1:vii–viii.
70. Ibid., 1:62.
71. Ibid.

One such story is of a man whose nursing wife tragically died, yet he was able to care for the child by breastfeeding from his own chest.[72] In a similar wonder of God's providence, an older woman of 68 cared for a child in the same way.[73]

The call for wonder and worship can also be seen in Wesley's reflections on the human body. "With what holy fear," said Wesley, "we should we pass the time of our sojourning here below. Trusting for our continual preservation, not merely to our own care, but to the Almighty Hand, which formed the admirable machine, directs its agency and supports its being!"[74]

At times, Wesley used accounts of the uncommon, as above, to move the reader past pure reason to feel and sense the universe, perhaps even God. The death of the young boy might invoke sadness, or perhaps even hope as the men searched for their lost loved ones in the snow. In short, Wesley, in some accounts, unexplained and uncommon, may have sought for the reader to experience the wonder and worship of God in a more-than-mechanical universe.

Wesley believed that nature was sufficient to call human beings beyond the limits of their understanding into a trusting relationship with God. Humility was the ground from which human reasoning could turn to wonder in the handiwork of God and God's character. This revelation through nature, by God's design, was not simply a function of nature but the result of God's own active presence within nature. Nature is God's own voice that calls human beings into a saving relationship with God's own self. As we shall see, this light of nature that guides the pathway to God, Wesley also called prevenient grace.

Theme three reaches a summit in *Survey's* Appendix. Upon an examination of different types of knowledge, Wesley argues that Scripture is an improvement upon the limited knowledge of humankind.[75] As such, this knowledge comes from a revelation from heaven. Wesley explains that human reasoning upon the work of nature, "the light of nature," offers a limited "general knowledge" of God—that God is the

---

72. Ibid., 1:87.

73. Ibid.

74. Ibid., 1:132.

75. Ibid., 5:192–221. (Wesley borrows in part from Peter Browne's *The Procedure, Extent and Limits of Human Understanding* which appears in an edited form within the Appendix.)

Creator of all things. However, by a greater light, the light of Scripture, the improved "Gospel-Revelation" reveals that nature is calling humankind into a responsible relationship with the one true God of the Bible—the Father, Son and Holy Spirit. As such, the substance of true religion is where the light of nature and Scripture uncovers the relations we bear to God and each other.

In a fascinating footnote, Wesley states, "I believe all 'the light of nature,' so called, to flow from preventing Grace."[76] For Wesley, preventing grace was God's work in human beings, freeing them from utter determination under the weight of sin's curse, and calling them to respond in worship. It may be that the light within nature is possibly the same as the spirit-fire-fluid that gives motion and life within the universe. If this is true, then every part of nature has been infused with God's prevenient grace moving before human beings and setting them free to know the Creator's grace and love.

Wesley concluded that the human ability to reason, enlightened by prevenient grace, has a design: "Upon all these considerations I concluded, that my intellectual power and the exercise of it in this life, was given for a certain useful and becoming object, even to know thee, the only true God and Jesus whom thou hast sent."[77]

Thus, it might be said that Survey's last theological purpose was not simply to confront the atheist or to correct the deist, but by the means of God's character to call human beings into a greater knowledge of the God of the Bible. By the lens of Scripture upon the links of the great chain in every part of each link, creation calls human beings into a responsible relationship with the Creator and all of creation.

Conclusion: Love God, Love God's Creation

As we have seen, Wesley's most frequent theological reflections may be categorized into three major themes: theme one, the design/economy/providence supporting life; theme two, the limits of human knowledge; and theme three, wonder and worship. Together they reveal a larger theological argument that moves from evidence to mystery to worship. The goal of this paper was to offer the reader a clear understanding of the primary theological themes within *Survey*.

76. Ibid. (Preventing grace is also termed prevenient grace in Wesley's writings.)
77. Ibid., 5:235.

Beyond a summary of the three primary themes and Wesley's typical employment of them, we trust that the reader will understand the significance of the second theme. Stated simply, Wesley's emphasis upon "the limits of human understanding" is vital to understanding the theological aims in *Survey*. In fact, any scholarly summary of *Survey* that ignores the significance of theme two has not properly understood the work.[78] Unfortunately, it appears that previous scholarship has often overlooked this theme. Thus, many working with *Survey* have not drawn the line and connected the dots between Wesley's emphasis upon the limits of our understanding and his opposition to the rise of mechanical philosophy.

Furthermore, attention to Wesley's use of the stories of the weird and uncommon is well past due. Overlooking these odd and wonderful accounts would be tragic. They offer a critical means by which one may understand Wesley's theological aims within *Survey*. These narratives offer theological and perhaps even an experiential type of support for Wesley's reflections. They are further evidence of Wesley's own voice within the work.

Thus, Wesley wrote *Survey*, in part, to respond to the rise of mechanistic philosophy and deism in the eighteenth century. His passion to share the gospel is clear from his frequent use of Scripture. His goal was to reveal that the God of nature was the God of the Bible. And his theological reflections move from intentional design to mystery and finally to wonder and worship.[79] As noted earlier, God's attributes in nature were calling upon humans to trust in the character of God despite the limits of understanding. The Bible was clearly Wesley's lens upon nature. It revealed God's desire to be in a redemptive relationship with human beings and indeed with all of creation—clearly an evangelistic motif. Notably, Wesley is clear within *Survey* that nature offers only a general knowledge of God. Thus, within *Survey*, Scripture expands the study of nature and God and reveals that nature's God is really the God of the Bible.

78. The evidence for the primacy of this theme can be observed by the great frequency with which Wesley employs it (roughly 100 times), his use of supporting Scriptures, the editorial inclusion of the uncommon in nature (and art) and by the abridgements of Dutens' *Enquiry Into the Origin of the Discoveries Attributed to the Moderns* and Browne's *The Procedure, Extent and Limits of Human Understanding*.

79. Again, this is not the only direction of his theological movement but the most common.

Yet, Wesley's curiosity in nature was more than evangelical; it was personal. To illustrate this, the great evangelist offered several first-person stories in *Survey*, including his personal observations of animals and music, published several significant works on nature and medicine, required the reading of natural philosophy by his clergy, met with several significant natural philosophers in person and credited himself with the discovery of a small animal, the "marine glow worms."[80] He loved learning about the uncommon in nature and read accounts from the Royal Society's *Philosophical Transactions*. Consequently, *Survey* describes a more-than-mechanical universe full of God's glorious and mysterious presence. This was like the God of nature Wesley read about in Scripture. Nature could not be fully comprehended for Wesley because it was full of God. Thus, the evidence of God's reality was apparent in the design of nature but also in the strange and uncommon operations of nature.

In a culture where math appeared to replace mystery and reason the sense of wonder, *Survey* was Wesley's response. It was—and perhaps we can say *is*—a call for all of humankind to see the wisdom, power and goodness of God on display within nature. By observing how all the interconnected parts of nature are so mysteriously knit together for life, the reasonable person discovers the evidence for God and God's character. In Wesley's view, a person's only true response, by the grace-saturated light of nature and the further illumination of Scripture, was to fall on his or her knees in wonder and worship—returning God's original breath in praise.

Wesley's goal, then, was always to look and love beyond the surface of nature. This, in fact, was his very goal in *Survey*—to begin with the visible creation and move toward a greater knowledge and love for that which is invisible. Importantly, Wesley never describes nature as empty: "Yet all these are the works of God's hands and are full of his presence!"[81] He believed that a proper study of God and nature would teach us to be humble and would "warm our hearts and fill our mouths with wonder, love and praise."[82] Therefore, a proper love for nature must move past the surface of nature and recognize the presence of God that

---

80. Ibid., 3:213.
81. Wesley, *Survey*, 3:319.
82. Ibid., viii.

is within all things. While many Christians worry that loving nature is wrong, it seems that loving God without loving creation may equally miss the mark. As noted previously, the direction of love must make a difference on the way to God. Our ability to enjoy God's presence in the world is our best hope to save the world.

All too often, however, we overlook the beauty of plants, ignore the trees, miss the sound of leaves in the wind and drive too fast—eyes safely on the cars surrounding us. We forget the trees, these gentle giants that still provide us shelter; they have been cut down into little pieces and hidden behind our chalk white walls. We listen to TV more than we listen to the songs of birds and sounds of crickets. We no longer consider the lilies and our language is descriptive of our life indoors. We ask, "Do you want to go out somewhere?" This usually means moving from one building to another—"out" rarely means outside. Birds nest in buildings and we nest upon two by fours. The sun and stars no longer give us a sense of direction—we are lost. Our map, however, is not simply the words of Scripture but the words from God who spoke into being the night and day, the waters of heaven, the land, the birds of the field and the animals the cover the earth. The language of *Survey* is not the language of a science book, although it is similar at times; it is a wedding of observations and reflections and of facts and faith. *Survey* reminds the reader that the world is far more than what he or she sees. We touch nothing separate from God and God's care. This is clearly an ecological ethic. It is our map.

So how do we move forward? Surprisingly enough, Wesley's example in *Survey* suggests the importance of stories in helping us more accurately to know and understand the world around us. While much of Western culture and the church are guilty, on different counts, for the general apathy towards care for the environment, the church has a key historical tradition of telling stories about God's healing presence in the world. The language of the church is free to dance and sing with poetry. Perhaps we can tell stories similar to Nathaniel Hawthorne's narrative about a great stone face where the movement of the sun and shadows upon the knotty hills reveals the wise and great face that watches over the town. By reconnecting language and landscape, our own words can reorient us to experience the world in a new way. Scripture works in this same way and offers stories, wisdom and poetry that can guide our interactions with nature.

Thankfully, Wesley never sought to treat Scripture like a science book. The distinction offered in *Survey* between moral certainty and mathematical certainty would imply that treating Scripture like a book of science (math) would reduce Scripture to a lesser form of certainty. Instead, Scripture must guide our sense of how to live before the Creator. And the consequences are real if we don't begin to care for our environment.

For this purpose, Scripture must be our lens upon the world. It has the power to open our hearts to God's presence and mystery in a more-than-machine world. This is vital because many in Western culture appear to have lost their sense of wonder toward creation. Perhaps the most obvious reason is because our communal and economic structures often place us in closer relationship to houses, cars and office buildings rather than to the forests, a muddy trial or the mountains. Yet Scripture can help us find our way back to a view of the universe as full of God's active presence. It provides us with divinely inspired stories, wisdom literature and poetry that can shape our daily interactions and care for creation. For this purpose, Wesley's *Survey* provides a fascinating lens for reading Scripture's testimony to the wisdom of God in creation.

5

Sighs, Signs, and Significance

Natural Science and a Hermeneutics of Nature

Jürgen Moltmann[1]

Do We Understand What We Know?

Jakob von Uexküll was one of the first biologists to investigate the habitats of living things. He followed up his *Streifzügen durch die Umwelten von Tieren und Menschen* ("Brief Surveys of the Environments of Animals and Human Beings") with *The Theory of Meaning*.[2] He didn't just want to observe what *is*; he also wanted to understand what it means. In a dispute with a famous contemporary chemist, he gave the following example.

---

1. This paper was delivered as a keynote address at the joint annual meetings of the Wesleyan Theological Society and the Society of Pentecostal Studies, convened at the Divinity School of Duke University, March, 2008. Initial editing of this essay was done by Barry Callen.

2. Jakob von Uexküll, *The Theory of Meaning*, trans. B. Stone and H. Weiner (Amsterdam, 1982).

Let us assume that a chemist stands in front of Raphael's Sistine Madonna in Dresden and analyses it with a chemist's eye. What does he perceive? He perceives the colors, but he doesn't see the picture. He is "blind to its meaning." And this is the way he confronts "the face of nature" too. He sees a great deal, but understands very little. Yet—so von Uexküll concludes—life can only be understood if we understand its meaning. All the acts of living things are determined by "perceiving and acting accordingly." They are "determined by their significance, not mechanically."[3]

Today, if we are to believe the journalist prophets in the German news magazine *Der Spiegel*, we are at a turning point. We are "from the society of knowing to the society of understanding."[4] True, today our scientific knowledge doubles every five years; but do we understand what we know? Excellent research certainly provides data, numbers, and diagrams, but it does not provide meanings. A computer can store all the data, but it doesn't understand them, because it is unable to interpret them. Mere collections of data are not yet knowledge. At bottom, a person only knows what he or she has appropriated and understood. It is only when I have understood the significance of something that I know it.

Consequently, we can venture to say that sciences only emerge from a hermeneutics of nature. The concern of the sciences is, therefore, to perceive the meaning of natural phenomena for each other, in their interrelations, and, not least, for human culture. Every perception presses towards understanding, and it is only what we have understood that we can say we know.

What Is Our Knowledge—Our Leading Interests?

Primal scientific curiosity desires to know nature for nature's sake. We want to know more than we need to know in order to survive. Primal perception is based on *wonder*, as Plato stressed so unforgettably. In wonder we perceive natural phenomena for their own sake, and forget ourselves. Pragmatic concerns only follow later. In view of today's economization of the sciences, a hermeneutics of nature which wants to do justice to nature will restore to their origin the interests of the mod-

---

3. German edition (1940) 161.
4. *Der Spiegel* 30 (2007) 125–26.

ern sciences which are dominated by the need to know. There is indeed a modern anthropocentric and utilitarian hermeneutics of nature. But we call the original hermeneutics of nature *the natural hermeneutics of nature*. Whereas in the one case the aim is *to know so as to dominate nature*, in the natural hermeneutics of nature the aim is *to know so as to understand*.[5]

The modern method for dominating nature has often been compared with the Roman recipe for government: *divida et impera*—divide and rule. This method led to the splitting of the atom and to the search for the ultimate, indivisible components of matter, the "elementary particles." Scientific reductionism is then inescapable. Every attempt to understand natural processes leads in the opposite direction. We then understand something when we perceive its function for its relative whole, and see its relative whole in its environment, and thus see the living thing in its habitat, the space in which it lives, and the spaces in which the living things live in their interactions with our human spaces for living. In this way we pass from the nucleus to the atom, from the atom to the molecule, from the molecule to the cell, and so forth, until we arrive at the whole organism of the earth, and to the horizons of value and belief of human culture.

Do the natural sciences do violence to nature? Where it is a matter of the nature over which human beings can acquire power, violence has not merely been employed but also justified. For Francis Bacon, the sciences bring Mother Nature and her children to humans as their slaves. The image is drawn from the colonialism and slave trade of Bacon's time. According to Immanuel Kant, nature is passive material, where "reason has insight only into that which it produces according to its own concepts . . . constraining nature to answer reason's own questions." This constraining of nature was also compared with torture, through which secrets are extorted. These images of the imposition of force on nature are in line with the technology with which nature is exploited. If, on the other hand, we assume that nature has in its own way its own subjectivity, the consequence is a dialogue and exchange between human beings and nature, and a technology allied with natural forces, such as Ernst Bloch envisaged.

---

5. Jürgen Moltmann, *Science and Wisdom*, trans. Margaret Kohl (Minneapolis: Fortress, 2003) 141–57.

If we want to understand, our aim should not be to dominate and exploit nature; after all, our goal is community with nature. We investigate complex interactions, and see ourselves as part of nature. The object of our understanding is *complexity*. We do not set ourselves up as absolutes over against the nature we can perceive, as Descartes recommended; we understand our perception as a participatory link. *We want to know in order to participate.* We understand the knowability of nature as an act of its participation in us or, as people used to say, as "the language of nature" addressed to human beings.

The hermeneutics of the relationship between nature and human beings corresponds to the relationship in the human being between body and soul.[6] In the early modern world, we find that a parallel was made between the subjugation of the body and the subjugation of nature, as well as between the body as a machine and the cosmos as a clockwork mechanism. But now we are becoming aware of the psychosomatic totality of the human gestalt (or total configuration) and the inner orientation of the body; this awareness gives us a better understanding of natural environments and habitats. Says Uexküll, "Every environment is filled only with symbols of meaning.... Every symbol of meaning of a determining subject is also a symbol of meaning for the bodily gestalt of that subject."[7]

The Idea of the "Two Books"

What can theology contribute to the present-day development of a scientifically acceptable and fruitful hermeneutics of nature? The idea of "the two books" refers to the Holy Scriptures and the "book of nature." It derives from Christian tradition, and was widespread in the era before the scientific revolution.[8] Does it offer us an acceptable point of departure for a theological hermeneutics of nature?

Generally speaking, this idea points to a comparison between the Jewish-Christian revelatory Scriptures and the scientific knowledge

---

6. Jürgen Moltmann, *God in Creation: An Ecological Doctrine of Creation* (The Gifford Lectures 1984-85), trans. Margaret Kohl (San Francisco: SCM, 1985) 244-75.

7. Uexküll, *Theory of Meaning*, 158.

8. Peter G. Hetzel, "Interpreting the Book of Nature in the Protestant Tradition," *The Journal of Faith and Science Exchange* (2000) 223-39; Giuseppe Tanzella-Nitti, "The Two Books Prior to the Scientific Revolution," *Annales Theologici* 18 (2004) 51-83; H. M. Nobis, "Buch der Natur" in *Hist W. Ph.* (Basel and Stuttgart, 1971) 958-59.

of nature, and allows us to see as God's creation the nature which the scientists investigate. More precisely, this metaphor lets us understand nature as a "book" whose characters we can learn to read. Nature is intelligible just as the human mind is rational. The metaphor assumes that nature has a language, and it calls the signatures of nature a "script" which human beings can read. The interactions in nature are viewed on the analog of linguistic information. Kepler and Galileo, however, thought that "the book of nature" was written in numbers, not letters: the language of the great book which we always have before our eyes is mathematics. John Polkinghorne thought the same, calling mathematics "the language" in which the cosmos speaks to human intelligence. But is mathematics really a science? Does it not rather belong to the humanities or to art?

Nature speaks to human beings through a language of signs which can be deciphered in the way that an unknown language can be deciphered. To put it theologically, all created things are creations of the divine Word: "God said: Let there be light! And there was light." What we get to see in nature are therefore creations of God's Word. In the beginning was the Word "and all things were made by him that were made" (Jn 1:1, 3). Their perceptible reality is an expression of the eternal Logos, in which the human mind and spirit also shares.

The Syrian Fathers of the church and the Cappodicians used the idea of the two books. A certain third-century Abbot Anthony said: "My book is the created nature, one always at my disposal whenever I want to read God's words." Basil the Great believed that our reason was so perfectly created by God that "through the beauties of created things we can read God's wisdom and providence as if these beauties were letters and words." For Augustine, although only the person who has learned to read can read Holy Scripture, even the illiterate can understand the book of the universe. For Maximus the Confessor, nature and Scripture are the two robes of Christ which shone bright in his transfiguration, his humanity and his divinity. In Christ the "two books" have the same content.

The Celtic theologian Scotus Eriugina thought that the two books were two theophanies, the one through the medium of letters *(apices)*, the other through forms *(species)*. This tradition talks about the book of nature, or the book of the world or the universe, less often about a book of creation. So ever since Raimundus Sebundus the reading of the book of nature has been called *theologia naturalis* (natural theology). The idea of the two books and their inner harmony was also supposed to express the harmony between faith and reason, and was directed against the separation of the two made by the Islamic philosopher Averroes.

Theologically, the book of nature was always read in the light of Holy Scripture. Through revelation, the wisdom hidden in nature becomes legible as the wisdom of God--which means, conversely, that only what corresponds to God's revelation according to Holy Scripture can be read and understood as divine wisdom in nature. The distinction and the correspondence are important: through the natural knowledge of God we become wise, but not saved; through the knowledge of revelation we will be saved, but unfortunately do not yet become wise. All knowledge confers community, but the direct knowledge communicated through revelation confers a fellowship with God different from the indirect knowledge of God given through nature.

Must we also be able to reverse this order of things? Must be able to read the Bible in the light of the book of nature? Many ideas about nature found in the Bible prove to belong to the superseded world pictures of the past eras in which the biblical writings originated. Can only that which is compatible with scientific reason and opens up for science new horizons of interpretation count as divine revelation?

I should like to draw attention to another point of comparison between the "two books": *memory*. The Jewish-Christian writings are undoubtedly an essential component in our common religious and cultural memory. We remember and make present to ourselves the divine revelations given to those before us. We remember their faith, the perils and the liberations they experienced, and the successful and unsuccessful forms of life which they created. In order to awaken faith and experience life for ourselves, we interpret these things for the present and the future. Without cultural memory, the peoples fall sick with Alzheimer disease. To destroy their memory is to rob them of their identity. The art of interpreting religious and cultural memory in the light of its importance for the present and the future is what we call *hermeneutics*. Every culture is a universe of signs, and is therefore dependent on hermeneutics for its survival.

The sciences are concerned in a comparable way with "the memory of nature."[9] When we gaze into the universe at night, we are looking into

---

9. Rupert Sheldrake, *The Presence of the Past* (New York: Times Books, 1988) to

its past. Stars whose light arrives with us now can already have been extinguished light years earlier. Out of the background radiation, the time shortly after the Big Bang comes to meet us. We perceive subsequently, not simultaneously, because the speed of light is finite. What we perceive is not the universe that *is*, but the universe that *was*. What we see is "the presence of the past." In the build-up of matter and living things, nature has acquired a memory that must be called wise, because it has expelled conjunctions hostile to life and has promoted others which are compatible with it. In the cosmos since the Big Bang, and in life on earth since the beginning of evolution, nature has been involved in an irreversible "history of nature."[10]

Cultural and natural memories are not as far apart as are science and the humanities in our universities today. They have always influenced each other mutually, for ultimately speaking the cultural code of human beings is also part of the natural code, if indeed human beings and their brains are part of nature. But because of the subjugation and domination of nature by the scientific and technological culture of human beings, the consonance between the cultural and the natural memory is not sufficiently regarded. Yet, ultimately, modern science belongs to the culture of humanity. It is to a high degree conditioned by culture, and is to an enduring degree even conditioned by the Jewish-Christian religion, as we can easily see if we compare it with Indian and Chinese sciences and the attitude to nature that underlies them.

The General Doctrine of Signs: *Signatura Rerum* or the Signature of All Things

"The book of nature" can only be read if we regard nature not as a world of facts but as a world of meanings.[11] It is only when everything is full of signs that everything is also full of significance. Consequently,

---

which I am indebted. I should also like to point to Ilya Prigogine and Isabella Stengers, *Order Out of Chaos: Man's New Dialogue with Nature* (London: Heinemann, 1984); based on the authors' *La nouvelle alliance*. For insights into the various connections between science and religion I am indebted to John Polkinghorne, *Exploring Reality: The Intertwining of Science and Religion* (New Haven: Yale University Press, 2005).

10. Carl Friedrich von Weizsäcker, *Die Geschichte der Natur* (Goettingen: Vandenhoeck & Ruprecht, 1964).

11. Gernot Böhme, *Für eine ökologische Naturästhetik* (Frankfurt: Suhrkamp, 1989) esp. 121–40: Sprechende Natur. Die Signaturenlehre bei Paracelsus und Jakob Böhme.

the hermeneutics of nature is the art of interpreting the natural world of signs. In Germany this doctrine of signs in nature goes back to Paracelsus, and especially to Jakob Böhme's 1622 book *De signatura rerum oder von der Geburt und Bezeichnung aller Wesen* ("On *de sgnatura rerum* or the birth and description of all things"):

> And there is nothing in nature created or born which does not reveal its inner form (Gestalt) externally as well, for the innermost part always thrusts towards its revelation. . . . Hence there is in the signature the greatest reason, in which a man may not only know himself but may also learn to know the nature of all things. . . . Every thing has its lips open for revelation; that is the language of nature.[12]

What Are Signs or Signatures?

In the doctrine of signature or signs, nature is understood as *expression*. According to ancient Platonic teaching, every individual thing is an expression of its innermost essence, its idea. That is the inward dimension of things as a sign of something in them or above them, either the eternal ideas or the creative words of God. Consequently, natural configurations are read in a physiognomical sense: just as a face expresses the particular character of the soul, so general physiognomy is the art of interpreting configurations in the face of nature.

It is the character of every natural sign to be a *pointer* showing the links between things and their relationships. The signs also point to the relative whole, of which the things are only parts. The cross-references in the network of interrelationship, and the "bottom-up" or "top-down" pointers in the relative wholes, are interlaced.

Not least, nature's world of signs is related to the human beings who observe and who act. The signs then become *signals* and say what the natural environment means for human beings. In its signs, nature is a transmitter of its own signals, and not merely a receiver of the signals of human beings. That presupposes recognition of a graduated subjectivity in nature, in its living things and its various habitats.

Because "the great whole" of a rounded-off and completed cosmos is not yet existent, all individual signs must also be interpreted as *prefigurations* of a future that is possible but not yet present, a future towards

---

12. G. Wehr, *Jakob Böhme* (Hamburg: Rowohlt, 1971) 93–96.

which everything that is already existent points. All the totalities we know are fragments of what is to come, and are therefore *anticipations* open to the future. Paul knew this: "For we know in part and we prophesy in part. But when that which is perfect is come, then that which is in part shall be done away" (1 Cor 13:9–10). It is worth noting that the part-perfect relationship corresponds subjectively to the knowledge-prophecy relationship. We know what exists, and we prophesy what will come. It is also important that the perfect does not *develop* out of what is in part, but comes to meet it.

If we set aside magic, arts of divination, and astrology, which were bound up with the ancient doctrine of signatures or signs, what remains for our modern understanding is the fact that nature is a *world of forms*, and that the connections in nature consist in the exchanges of *energy* and *information*. The ancient doctrine of signs can easily be translated into the modern informatics of nature. The art of receiving information, interpreting it, and assimilating it is hermeneutics. The primal matter of the universe is information, which is simply to say that information and reality are the same.[13]

Taking up this approach, we might say that at the beginning of nature stands the form, and form both as *forma informata* and as *forma informans*: the form is both shaped and shaping. We live in a world of reciprocal informational effects and participations. We also discover a world of *performative anticipations*: reality is formed from potentialities. That is the creative part of reality as efficacy. As Goethe wrote, life is "shaped form which develops as it lives."

We can grasp the sign language of the forms of life and their meaning if we consider our own bodies. We perceive internal illnesses from their outward *symptoms*. A symptom is the sign and expression of an illness. But these signs must not only be noted; they must also be interpreted. The interpretation takes place when the symptoms are *diagnosed*. They must not only be precisely observed; they must also be correctly interpreted, and the illness which they signify and express must be identified. Once we have understood the symptoms correctly, the *therapy* can begin. This closes the hermeneutical circle of perceiving and acting. I believe that this diagnostic-therapeutic circle can also be applied to the sciences and the hermeneutics of nature.

13. Thomas and Brigitte Görritz, *Der kreative Kosmos. Geist und Materie aus der Quanteninformation* (Elsevier, Spektrum Akademischer 2007).

The Theological Doctrine of Signs

With the beginning of the modern world, the theological doctrine of signs was transferred from the cosmos to history, for in Europe, after the French Revolution, "history" came to be the concept for reality as a whole. But if the stars no longer provide any orientation, what should we hold on to in history? We must interpret "the signs of the times" in order to know what hour has struck.[14] The "signature of history" is interpreted in the light of "the signs of the time." According to the Second Vatican Council in *Gaudium et Spes*, "the Church carries the responsibility of reading the signs of the time and of interpreting them in the light of the Gospel." Whereas earlier, grace presupposed nature, now it has to presuppose history. So the historical interpretation of the signs of the times takes over the function of the old *theologia naturalis*. But what Kant called the "historical signs" which have to be interpreted are extremely ambivalent.

On the one hand, there are *signs of hope*, like the "signs and wonders" in the Old Testament—in modern terms, signs of "human nature's capacity for betterment" (which was the way Kant interpreted the French revolution), that is to say, historical signs can be seen as *signs of progress*. On the other hand, there is the apocalyptic orientation towards *signs of the end*: "When will this be, and what will be the sign when these things are all to be accomplished?" is the question in the Little Synoptic Apocalypse (Mark 13:4). And this is the way earthquakes, tsunamis, wars, the climate catastrophe, and homosexuality are interpreted in apocalyptic communities; they are read as advance signs of the imminent end of the world.

For Christian theology, the coming of Christ and his gospel is the one true sign of the times: "But what are the signs of the time?" asked Rudolf Bultmann, replying in his *Theology of the New Testament*: "He himself! His appearance and ministry, his proclamation."[15]

For Christian theology, the centre of its doctrine of signs is the realized presence of Christ in the Eucharist. According to Thomas Aquinas and the general Christian view, the Eucharist or Lord's Supper is: 1) a sig-

---

14. Jürgen Moltmann, *The Church in the Power of the Spirit*, trans. Margaret Kohl (London: SCM, 1977) The church under the spell of "the signs of the times," 37–50.

15. Rudolf Bultmann, *Theologie des Neuen Testament* (Tübingen: Scribner, 1953). Translated by K. Grobel as *Theology of the New Testament* (New York: Scribner, 1951–55).

num rememorativum of the passion of Christ; 2) a signum demonstrativum of present grace; and 3) a signum prognisticon of coming glory—a commemorative sign, a demonstrative sign, and a forward-looking sign (Aquinas, S.Th. III, q 60, a 3). In the unison of remembrance and hope, Christ becomes present. The presence of the Christ who has come is at the same time the presence of the coming Christ.[16]

The Christian doctrine of the signs in history and nature will always take its bearings from this unique sacrament of Christ. Then nature appears in the light of a sacramental interpretation. By virtue of the presence of the creative, life-giving Spirit, the presence of God will be perceived *in all things*, just as the body and blood of Christ is present in bread and wine, and the whole Christ is present in the whole celebration of the Supper. These are the traces of God, *vestigial Dei*, in the history of nature and civilization. These are the correspondences between created beings and their Creator, and the anticipations of their future true form or gestalt.

The World as Nature and as Creation: Theological Interpretative Patterns

Let us look briefly at what changes in the concept of nature. In Latin philosophy, *natura* means the essential nature of something. Today when we talk about the nature of something, we mean its essential character, not its appearance. In contrast, the concept of nature in the modern sciences is aligned exclusively to the side of the thing which can be apprehended by the senses. The empirical concept of nature has no longer anything to do with the metaphysical concept of being or essence. In order to understand something, one must observe it exactly, weigh it, measure it, and so forth, but one does not think about its nature. How did this radical transformation in the concept of nature come about? It is a historically established fact that the change arose under the influence of the theological concept of creation.

The ancient Greece concept of *physis* does not make any distinction between what is divine and what is worldly. *Physis* is the power of producing, of generation, and it is hence divine. Understood as *physis*, the cosmos is of divine perfection. The world is a "sphere," a self-contained system. Its time is circular, for the circle is the image of

16. Jürgen Moltmann, *Church in the Power of the Spirit*, 242–60.

eternity. The Yin/Yang dynamic in Asia is also visually represented by the closed circle.

If the world is understood as *creation*, it cannot be divine like its Creator, but has to be understood in a worldly sense. Consequently, it cannot possess any divine attributes. Creation does not have the form of a sphere; its time is not circular; it is not a self-contained system. It is finite, temporal and contingent. Its foundation is not in itself but in another. As the creation of a transcendent God, it issues from God's free will and is not a necessary expression of his being, although it corresponds to the goodness of that being. So it is contingent (*contingentia mundi*). It can be known only through observation and investigation, not deduced from a being or an idea. That was the theological reason for the transformation of the metaphysical concept of *natura* into the modern empirical concept of nature. This by no means contradicts the theological concept of creation, as the creationists assume; it corresponds to the theological concept and results from it.

According to the first creation account (Gen 1), the whole creation is aligned towards a goal and is in no way a primal condition complete in itself. In the beginning *of what* did God create heaven and earth? Every beginning raises the question about its goal, every *bereshith* (genesis) has its corresponding *acharith*, or end. Even the sabbath of creation, with which the Genesis account closes, points beyond itself, for it has no evening.

"Thou hast created us for thyself, and our hearts are restless until they find rest in thee," declared Augustine, thus basing the restlessness of the human heart not on the Fall but on creation. This proposition became the principle of Western anthropology right down to the present day. And not only that: it is also a principle of the Western worldview. To the restless, self-transcending human mind there corresponds in a graduated way a restless, self-transcending world of nature (*mundus inquietus*) that is open to future possibilities. A self-transcending nature, open to the future, is the correspondence to the human soul's openness to the world. Self-transcendence is, in its always specific way, characteristic of all created things, because it is already given to them "in the beginning." All those God has created are *beginners* of their own future in God.

If, as Augustine maintained, time was created together with creation, and not just after the Fall and the banishment from an unchanging and quiescent paradise, then creation is from the beginning a changeable world (*mundus mutabilis*), a world in movement, in which every living being can distinguish between past and future, reality and potentiality. If the world were suddenly to stand still, we should no longer be able to perceive time.

If we call the present state of the world "God's creation," then theologically we have to be precise: the present state of the world no longer corresponds to conditions as they were "in the beginning," nor is the world as yet the kingdom of God, as it will be at the end. Whatever is between the beginning and the end is on the way and caught up in the transition.

If, then, we talk theologically about the present state of the world as "nature," we mean a creation spoiled and disrupted by chaos (Rom 8:19). It is full of beauties and full of catastrophes. And yet we believe that this world of earthquakes and tsunamis, of Aids and other plagues, and of death, is nevertheless God's good creation, because we trust in the faithfulness of its Creator, and know that he will bring it to its appointed goal.

Why is this creation of God threatened by chaos and why has it fallen victim to annihilation? Because the Creator is by no means "the all-determining realty" of what he has created—in that case creation would be itself divine—but because he has conferred on it its own scope for freedom and generation.[17] According to tradition, these are the so-called secondary causes (*causae secundae*) of creation. Gen 1:11: "Let the earth bring forth vegetation, plants yielding seed, and fruit trees"; Gen 1:24: "Let the earth bring forth living creatures . . ."; Gen 1:26: "Let us make man. . . . And let them have dominion over the fish of the sea, and over the birds of the air, and over the cattle, and over all the earth. . . ." It is an interwoven fabric of relatively independent creative activity on the part of the earth and human beings. But in these free spaces, the earth and human beings are creations that stand on the edge of chaos and are threatened by the forces of annihilation (Gen 6). So in the completed and perfected creation there will be, symbolically speaking, no "sea" and no "night"—or, to put it realistically, no more death and no more sin.

---

17. Michael Welker, *Schöpfung und Wirklichkeit* (Neukirchen: Neukirchen-Vluyn, 1995). Translated by J. F. Hoffmeyer as *Creation and Reality* (Minneapolis: Fortress, 1999) 64ff.

In view of the present state of the world, which lies between order and chaos, between being and non-being, creation is theologically ascribed to continuous creation (*creation continua*). In continuous creation God preserves those he has created in spite of everything that threatens them and in spite of their sins. In it he anticipates their future in his kingdom. By virtue of the patience with which he endures and sustains his fallen creatures, he does not give up their future, but continually gives them new time and new future. "Our God is a God who sustains."[18] It is true that we are used to thinking of a God who rules from above just as he likes, and whose will is for us human beings as inscrutable as fate. But a closer glance at the biblical testimonies shows us that the God of Israel and Jesus Christ is a sustaining, patient, enduring and suffering God. His rule is not a rule that commands; it is a rule of love. His almighty power shows itself in his all-enduring patience.

If we look at Israel's Exodus history, which is what stands behind the first commandment, we perceive on the one hand his liberating power, which destroys the army of the Pharaoh, and on the other hand his sustaining power, which saves the people: "You have seen what I did to the Egyptians, and how I bore you on eagles' wings" (Exod 19.4) For this sustaining power of God, Scripture uses a feminine image—"Carry them in your bosom, as a nurse carries the sucking child" (Num 11:12)—and a male one too: "You have seen how the Lord your God bore you, as a man bears his son" (Deut 1:31). The true revelation of the sustaining God is the suffering Christ on the cross. "He has borne our sicknesses" (Isa 53:4) and has taken on himself the sins of the world, in order to heal and to redeem. "He upholds the universe through his word of power" (Heb 1:3). The God who upholds the world in this way is like the Greek *hypokeimenon*, the sustaining foundation of all things.

We read the signs of what God has created as reminders of God's good foundational conditions, as an expression of his sustaining energies, and as advance signs of his saving future.

The Threefold Sighs of the Divine Spirit

The "sighs of the time" are in fact the cries out of the creaturely depth reaching the ear of God. At the beginning of every experienced divine

---

18. Cf. Dietrich Bonhoeffer, *Nachfolge* (Geneva: 1945). Dietrich Bonhoeffer Works 4, ed. J. D. Godsey and G. B. Kelly (Minneapolis: Fortress, 2000) 45.

salvation there is this cry from the depth (*de profundis*). There was the cry of the tortured people of Israel in the slavery of Egypt. There is the death cry of the crucified Jesus on the cross. And here is the groaning creation around us. And God hears the cry from the depth. God brings his people into the freedom of the promised land. God brings his son Jesus Christ into the glorious life of resurrection. And this God will bring his groaning creatures into the new and everlasting world. Sadness and expectancy both lay heavy on the whole unredeemed earth. But, in winter's expectation of spring, the spring of life already heralds its own coming.

I am assuming familiarity with the wonderful eighth chapter of the Epistle to the Romans and would recall: 1) The sighings and yearnings of creation for liberty in its sufferings from transience; 2) The yearning of human beings for the redemption of the body in the torments of death; and 3) The sighs of the divine Spirit, who intercedes for us.[19] On all three levels it is a matter of the torment and the hope of God's Spirit. The Spirit itself is the force of this universal hope. It both torments and encourages, for where freedom is near, the chains begin to chafe. What ferments and torments in believers is the Spirit of freedom, which fills body and soul. What makes all creation sigh and yearn is the indwelling Spirit of life. The divine Spirit itself, which fills the whole world, is seized by a driving force and torment, for it is beset by the birth pangs of the new creation.

Paul interpreted the deathly torments of this transitory world as the birth pangs of the future world. The sufferings of this present time which interpenetrate the world are the sufferings of an all-embracing divine dynamic.

We must translate this worldview of the apostle Paul's into our own language. We might say that the immanence of the transcendent divine Spirit is the foundation and driving power for *the self-transcendence* of all open systems of matter and life, and of all human forms of life in process. If the infinite is to indwell the finite, the finite is drawn into the movement where it oversteps its own bounds. In this movement, the finite anticipates a future condition in which the infinite can come to rest in the finite and enduringly indwells it. "God *in* creation" makes creation a world open to the future possibilities. That is the *universal*

---

19. Ernst Käsemann, "The Cry for Liberty in the Worship of the Church," in *Perspectives on Paul*, trans. Margaret Kohl (Philadelphia: Fortress, 1971) 122–37.

Exodus of all created beings out of chaos and the destiny of death. The goal is the final and enduring *cosmic Shekinah*: and God will be "all in all" (1 Cor 15:28).

The immanence of the transcendent Spirit is also the foundation and driving power of the *history of life* into ever richer and more complex forms and syntheses. The so-called "self-organization of the universe" is nothing other than the resonance of the universe as it responds to the immanence of the divine Spirit that drives it. Why else should life organize itself? Why else its torment of chaos and death, if there is not something present in all things which desires to endure and not pass away, which wills to live and not die? Why the struggle for survival if life does not promise more than it can give?

The immanence of the transcendent Spirit makes the sign language of nature and of our own bodies legible. In all things we see the many-faceted *expression* of the divine Creator. In everything that is, the eternal Being manifests itself. Everything living is a resonance responding to the living God. Through his creative Spirit, God is already present in all things. His presence is the presence of his coming. Consequently, every *expression* of the divine is at the same time a *prefiguration* and *advance radiance* of the glory of God which will be manifested to everything.

God's Spirit in all things makes the world in which we live a *spiritual world*. Our human spirituality must adapt itself to it. It will become the resonance of a *cosmic spirituality*. It will become a pentecostal spirituality of the wakened senses and the attentive heart. It will be a spirituality not only of the soul but of the body too. Not least, in an *ecological spirituality* we shall rediscover the worship of the earth. That is the sabbath which, according to biblical tradition, the earth is supposed to celebrate in the years of release, during which its fertility will be restored in a realistic way. The *sabbath of the earth* will be an anticipation and a foretaste of "the new earth" on which "righteousness dwells."

6

The Consonance of Wesleyan Theology and Modern Science

Timothy Crutcher

In the twentieth and twenty-first centuries, the clash of religion and science has been a major feature of the culture and religion conflict that began in the Enlightenment. For much of that time, the conflict was accepted by many on both sides as a fundamental clash of method. To many scientists, the scientific approach represented the dispassionate and objective approach to figuring out reality on its own terms. Religion, thought some scientists, only credulously repeated mythic explanations of reality from the past. To many believers, however, science represented the height of human *hubris*. Science seemed to exclude God from any meaningful participation in the world. And because God was useless as an explanation, there was no need for theistic belief any longer.

Not everyone feels this tension so starkly, but its cultural by-products still affect a large number of churches and their institutions, particularly Christian colleges. Much ink has been spilt over, and no few careers threatened by, the way students think about, administrators react to, and constituencies hear about the ideas coming from departments of theology and of science.

But what if the assumptions that drive these tensions are erroneous? What if science and theology are not as far apart methodologically as people tend to think? What if those two disciplines actually share a common methodological core? This essay contends that science and theology share a common methodology. With a Wesleyan approach to theology and a properly reflective approach to science, the gulf between these disciplines narrows. Each even finds some positively beneficial reinforcement precisely because of their methodological similarities.

Without minimizing the real differences that exist between religious and scientific approaches to reality, we want to explore the idea that both enterprises can be seen as differing expressions of a similar methodological or epistemological dynamic. Late twentieth century philosophers of science like Imre Lakatos, Michael Polyani, and even Thomas Kuhn have pointed out that belief systems embedded in science require something very similar to what believers call "faith." John Wesley, two hundred years before these thinkers, modeled an approach to theology in which empirical factors played an enormous role in how he understood the central ideas of his religion. Seen together, both of these movements converge on a common understanding of how human beings pursue and acquire knowledge—of either divine or earthly origin. Appreciation of this commonality could ease tensions and even expand the scope of future interactions between science and religion.

We begin our investigation with a brief exploration of how some form of belief grounds all knowledge structures—even scientific ones. We will lay out a general model of epistemology that can be seen as resonating both with the concerns of contemporary thinkers like Polyani and Lakatos and also with the concerns of ancient philosophers like Aristotle. On the basis of this formulation, we will engage John Wesley's approach to theology, showing that his method is really a specialization of this broader approach to the particular domain of revealed religion. Finally, we will conclude with a few thoughts on how the recognition of this common model of epistemology can be used to defuse some of the more contentious battles between religion and science today.

Belief and the Scientific Method

In the early days of modern science and its concomitant thinking about scientific knowledge, it was common to assume some form of "pure empiricism." Championed by folks like Francis Bacon, John Locke, and the British Empirical tradition, this kind of empiricism stated that the human mind was a *tabula rasa*, a blank slate that automatically and passively accepted data from its senses. All operations of the mind followed upon the acquisition of this data, and there was no role for any *a priori* belief or construction.

By the late nineteenth and early twentieth century, this experiential line of thinking had developed, largely under the influence of Auguste Comte, into scientific positivism. Positivism set up the scientific method as the only reliable means of finding truth, restricting knowledge to that which can be empirically demonstrated in some sense. Although Comte himself recognized the interdependence of scientific theory with scientific observation, positivism would not articulate any role for "faith" in the knowing process. The restriction of knowledge to scientific knowledge also excludes *a priori* any supernatural religion from the domain of knowledge, and this approach has set the stage for much of the science-religion conflict as we now know it.

Positivism, however, begins to break down in the mid-twentieth century as more and more people notice that scientists are, in fact, human beings and not observation-processing automatons. Michael Polanyi discusses how knowledge can only be acquired within a set of tacit assumptions, intellectual passions, and commitments to other people that he calls a "fiduciary framework."[1] Imre Lakatos has a similar understanding, involving what he calls "research programs." These are essentially faith commitments that one must accept as true in order to craft testable hypotheses about the nature of reality. One does not test these faith assumptions; they form an unquestioned core around which a belt of testable predictions are made and through which the results of those experiments are processed.[2] Even Paul Feyerabend's critique of scientific method is based on the tacit recognition that much of that method is grounded in unjustified acts of trust (as in preferring an old theory to a new one).[3]

---

1. Michael Polanyi, *Personal Knowledge: Toward a Post-Critical Philosophy* (Chicago: University of Chicago Press, 1974).

2. Imre Lakatos, *The Methodology of Scientific Research Programs: Philosophical Papers Volume 1* (Cambridge: Cambridge University Press, 1978).

3. Paul Feyerabend, *Against Method* (New York: New Left, 1975).

All these thinkers recognize certain *a priori* conditions that are (or must be) in place before one's experience of reality can be properly processed into knowledge of reality. Recognizing the importance of these *a priori* conditions is not an innovation, however. It is a return to a pre-Enlightenment orientation to science as represented by the ancient scientific philosopher Aristotle.

For Aristotle, the basic *a priori* that one needs prior to experience —and the thing for which Enlightenment thinkers like Bacon and Locke hated him—was logic. In his *Organon*, Aristotle sets out both his *Categories*, which provides a pre-experiential structure to what we can experience, and his *Prior Analytics*, which provides an *a priori* method for moving through the inductive data of sense experience. Although there was a good deal of experiential induction involved in Aristotle's formation of his classifications and his method, the deductive element is nevertheless strong. Bacon reacts against deductive element in his own *Novum Organon*.

This combined inductive-deductive approach to empirical epistemology, whether it employs Aristotelian logic, Polanyian Personal Knowledge, or Lakatosian Research Programs, is best understood as a hermeneutic circle that moves back and forth between the data and interpretations that are accepted as true from an external source (i.e., trusted or accepted "on faith") and the data and interpretations made on the basis of personal experience. On the one hand, we cannot experience anything at all unless we have a framework for organizing those experiences. Language typically serves as that framework. However, that framework only comes to us in the midst of our experience, and it is not so rigid that it cannot be challenged when other personal experiences do not integrate well within it. New or incongruous experiences force us to find or develop new frameworks of interpretation, which we then put back to work in our own experience and—if successful—eventually hand on as *a priori* frameworks someone else might trust.[4]

As an example of this in science, one can look at the developments in astronomy from the complex spheres-within-spheres of the Ptolomaic system to the contemporary understanding of the relativity of all frames of reference. The Ptolomaic system had the weight of

---

4. For a further explanation of this development, particularly in its linguistic frame of reference, cf. Timothy Crutcher, "The Relational Linguistic Spiral: A Model of Language for Theology," in *Heythrop Journal* 43 (2002) 463–79.

ancient authority and seemed to match three common inductions: the earth did not feel like it was moving; it did not leave the birds or clouds behind as one might expect if it moved; and there was in the stars no detectable parallax to indicate any movement. When Copernicus first published his work *On the Revolutions of Celestial Orbs* in 1543, there was no immediate wholesale conversion to his theories, because it could not predict the movement of the planets any better than the accepted Ptolomaic system. Additionally, it seemed to challenge other accepted authorities, like Scripture. Eventually, however, observational ability (mainly the invention of the telescope) allowed Galileo in 1610 to detect real phases in the brightness of Venus that simply could not be explained on a purely geo-centric model. Several new models competed for attention (research programs, Lakatos would have called them), including both Copernicus's helio-centric model and the hybrid model of Tycho Brahe. Eventually, Copernicus's model just worked better. It was therefore adopted and improved by the work of people like Isaac Newton and thereafter accepted as an authority on the basis of their genius until still new observations (this time the temporal variations in the orbit of Mercury) forced a new re-evaluation of the matter, which resulted in the acceptance of Einstein's theory of relativity.

What is so fascinating about this inductive-deductive cyclical approach to the empirical world is that it also works equally well for the construction of theology. The implicit recognition of this is one of the things that makes Wesley's theological method one of his most significant contributions to theology today. We now turn to an exploration of that method to see how this inductive-deductive cycle aids the development of theology.

Theological Method and John Wesley

With Wesley coming as he did several centuries too early to take advantage of the challenges to Enlightenment thinking offered by Polanyi and others, it has always been easy to paint him as an Enlightenment figure in the mold of John Locke, whose empiricism Wesley obviously shares. However, a closer investigation of Wesley's own epistemology shows that he has more in common with the pre-modern approach of Aristotle's thought (and its medieval expression in the Church) than with his more immediate British forbearer. The difference is precisely this interaction between the deductive and inductive elements of Wesley's thought. For Wesley, the mind was no *tabula rasa*, merely passively receiving sensory data from experience. Wesley was also not a rationalist who believed, with Descartes, that the mind had *a priori* knowledge of indubitable first principles from which the rest of knowledge could be deduced. Instead, both experience and reason formed part of a larger unified dynamic that, along with Scripture and tradition, led progressively toward true knowledge and better understanding.

Since Albert Outler first made the observation back in the 1960s,[5] it has become common to refer to the grouping of Scripture, tradition, reason and experience in Wesley's theological method as the Wesleyan Quadrilateral. However, Methodist thought since Outler so latched on to the Quadrilateral as a rigid epistemological structure that Outler himself is reported to have regretted putting it forward.[6] The main problem with the image of the Quadrilateral is that it is static. Each component has a more or less independent vote concerning any item of data.[7] Wesley's own epistemology is far more dynamic, the way that contemporary science is understood to be dynamic. We do not expect that we will get all the right answers by simply making a good observation or putting together a sound syllogism. We expect our understanding to grow as we engage Scripture and experience in the light of reason and tradition. In the same way, the contemporary scientist engages experiments not simply to confirm what she already knows. The scientist also tries out hints and guesses to discover those places in which she still lacks understanding. Wesley's appreciation of this dynamic both distinguishes him from the more common scientific understanding of his day and makes his approach that much more relevant to our contemporary scene.

The roots of Wesley's "pre-modern" or "classical" approach to knowledge—to distinguish him from his Enlightenment contemporaries—can probably be found in his formation within the burgeoning

---

5. Albert Outler, *John Wesley* (New York: Oxford University Press, 1964).

6. Paul Wesley Chilcote, "Rethinking the Wesleyan Quadrilateral." *Good News Magazine* (http://www.goodnewsmag.org/magazine/JanuaryFebruary/jf05Quadrilateral.htm).

7. For example, Scott Jones's worries that experience might "vote against" Scripture (cf. *John Wesley's Conception and Use of Scripture* [Nashville: Kingswood, 1995] 31).

tradition of Aristotelian logic at Oxford as a student at Christ College. So well was he formed by this that he became Moderator of the academic debates at Lincoln College as a Fellow there after taking his masters degree. The Moderator job required a mastery of the various forms of logic and argumentation. Wesley extolled his own ability in logic (calling himself an expert[8]) and the importance of logic itself, placing knowledge of it "even necessary next, and in order to, the knowledge of Scripture itself"[9] and calling it "the gate" or "threshold" of all the other sciences.[10] He will explicitly own the implicit metaphysical assumptions that go along with Aristotelian logic, calling metaphysics the "second part" of logic. The metaphysical presumptions of logic are useful, Wesley says, "in order to clear our apprehension (without which it is impossible either to judge correctly, or to reason closely or conclusively) by ranging our ideas under general heads."[11] In other words, these ideas serve the *a priori* function of preparing our experience (our "apprehension" in Wesley's Aristotelian terminology) by helping us see what we can expect.

While Wesley generally appreciates John Locke's refutation of the rationalist position and his establishment of the empiricist one, Wesley does not appreciate Locke's dismissal of the *a prior* role that logic plays in experience. Throughout his *Remarks upon Mr. Locke's "Essay on Human Understanding,"* Wesley constantly attacks Locke when Locke attacks Aristotle. Wesley criticizes Locke for precisely those points at which Locke is trying to assert his form of empiricism over and against Aristotle's. For example, against Locke, Wesley firmly believes that things like "essences" and classifications of "genus" and "species" belong to reality itself, not to the human mind, and our *a priori* use of these concepts is what enables us to experience the world as it is.[12] That is, obviously, a much more confident approach to our knowledge of reality than either Polanyi or Lakatos will express two centuries later. Nevertheless, Wesley shares their methodological approach to knowledge

---

8. John Wesley, "Some Remarks on 'A Defense to the Preface of the Edinburgh Edition of Aspasio Vindicated'" §9, in *The Works of John Wesley*, ed. Thomas Jackson, 14 vols., CD-ROM edition (Franklin, TN: Providence House, 1994) 10:353; hereafter cited as (Jackson).

9. Wesley, "Address to the Clergy" §1.2 (Jackson 10:483).

10. Ibid., §2.1.5 (Jackson 10:491).

11. Ibid., §1.2 (Jackson 10:483).

12. Wesley, "Remarks Upon Mr. Locke's 'Essay on Human Understanding,'" ¶26 (Jackson 13:461).

combining deduction from first (or at least trusted) principles and induction from experience.

These trusted principles or affirmations about reality that we ourselves have not experienced—whether they concern God or the natural world—come to us in the form of tradition. Tradition represents the cumulative weight of the interpreted experiences of those who have come before, and they form the starting place of all explorations of knowledge—scientific or religious. All contemporary scientists must start out in school to learn the way their forbearers organized the world before they can challenge those systems of organization.[13] In the same way, religious folk absorb their basic understandings about God and God's interactions with the world from their religious ancestors. This makes tradition an inevitable part of any process of coming-to-knowledge, but it does not necessarily guarantee that it is a reliable. Just as the history of science reveals large shifts in the basic pattern by which we organize or world (from Newton to Quantum theory and relativity, for example), so, too, the religious frameworks by which one interprets one's religious life can also be challenged by experiences which cannot fit into them. Wesley's approach to tradition reveals this quite clearly.

Where Wesley will never cast any doubt on the truth of the basic principles of logic, his entire career could be seen as sorting the wheat from the chaff in terms of the tradition he had been handed. On the one hand, he seems compelled to ground his theological case for any doctrine or practice within tradition. So, for example, one of his first published works is a compendium of citations about the true nature of faith drawn from classical Anglican sources. He refers to Methodism as nothing other than the "plain, old religion of the Church of England."[14] On the other hand, his reading of Lord Peter King's account of the primitive church and Edward Stillingfleet's *Irenikon* convince him that some of the episcopal developments in the Church do not have so ancient a claim on tradition as they would wish.[15] This gives him "permission," as

13. Thomas Kuhn calls these "paradigms," and it is in the shift between paradigms that one can easily see that science is both impassioned and faith-based and not just dispassionate and objective as some would like to believe (*The Structure of Scientific Revolutions*, 3rd ed. [Chicago: University of Chicago Press, 1996]).

14. Wesley, *Journal* 16 October 1739 (Jackson 1:232).

15. "A Letter to the Rev. Mr. Clarke" [3 July 1756] (Jackson 13:211); "Letter to Dr. Coke, Mr. Asbury, and our Brethren in North America" [10 September 1784] (Jackson 13:251).

it were, to disregard some of them in order to ordain his own Methodist ministers for their work in Scotland or America. The authority of tradition is real, but must be "normed" by its interaction with other factors, as expressed in Wesley's famous quote that "we prove the doctrines we preach by Scripture and reason, and, if need be, by antiquity."[16]

There is a strong parallel here to the way science operates. The settled "paradigms" by which our knowledge is organized must be stable enough to endure attack by less adequate constructions (so astronomy is not likely to be taken over by astrology any time soon). But these paradigms are not so stable that they cannot be overturned when more adequate constructions come along.[17] In fact, good scientific traditions understand well the conditions under which they could be falsified. Many scientists would even suggest that a theory or tradition that does not supply conditions for its falsification cannot be considered a scientific theory at all.[18] Thus, in both theology and science, tradition is an argument, but it is one that can be overturned when a sufficient level of experience is against it.

There are core elements of any tradition, however, that function as if they were incapable of being overturned, a "Tradition" (capital "T") that none of its real adherents could imagine turning out to be false. These grounding traditions have what we might call a "canonical" status, and to overturn them is to deny the tradition outright and to "convert" from one stream of tradition into an entirely different one. For many in science, naturalism (either methodological or ontological) plays this

---

16. *A Farther Appeal to Men of Reason and Religion—Part III*, §3.28 (Jackson 8:233). This unequal treatment between "indubitable" sources like logic/reason or Scripture and "doubtable" sources like tradition or our own interpretation of our experience further complicate the picture of Wesley's religious epistemology as a static "quadrilateral," in which the four sides, however unequally weighted, are seen to function in the same way.

17. The helio-centric model of the solar system is again instructive. According to Archimedes, a Greek astronomer named Aristarchus proposed that the sun was really the center of the solar system back in the third century BC. But his model required that the universe be bigger (literally billions of miles across) than anyone was comfortable accepting at the time. The tradition of geo-centrism fit more of the known facts at the time and so the heliocentric paradigm was (some would say rightly) rejected, only to be resurrected 1,700 years later by Copernicus.

18. Good recent embodiments of this position can be found in Peter Woit, *Not Even Wrong* (New York: Basic, 2007) and Lee Smolin, *The Trouble With Physics* (New York: Mariner, 2007).

role.[19] To do "science," say some, one must assume that events have natural causes. One can be a good scientist and believe that Relativity or Quantum Theory might eventually be overtaken by other, better, theoretical constructions. However, to search for "supernatural causes" of natural events is to deny the core tradition of science and "convert" to some other way of organizing one's knowledge of the world. When confronted by an event that has no discernable cause, scientists as scientists are more likely to plead ignorance ("We just don't know how that works, yet.") than affirm a "supernatural intervention."

For Wesley, of course, the non-negotiable "canonical" core of the Christian tradition was found in the Scripture. Just as a form of naturalism prohibits certain kinds of explanations in advance (such as "God did it"), so, too, Wesley's affirmation of the absolute truth of Scripture functions in a determinative way over experience. It dictates in advance what kinds of things are—and are not—experience-able. As is true with logic, Wesley unashamedly assumes that the knowledge one gains from Scripture has an *a priori* role in shaping one's experience and preparing one to interpret it properly.

Returning to his interactions with Locke, we find Wesley refuting Locke's ideas on discontinuity of consciousness by asserting the religious doctrine of the soul. And Wesley will challenge Locke's dismissal of essences in reality by citing the Genesis account as proof that essences do exist.[20] His scriptural presuppositions will also ground his dismissal of certain experiential claims. such as John Hutchinson's scientific challenge to Newton, Captain Wilson's account of the virtuous but atheist natives of Palau, and even Count Zinzendorf's ideas about sin in believers,[21] among many examples that can be cited.

These *a priori* constructions that are applied to experience, however, are only half of the hermeneutical circle that drives Wesley's approach to knowledge and to theology. As we cycle from experience back to tradition and to Scripture, we find experience playing the

---

19. Another candidate for a functionally "canonical" scientific belief may a correspondence between mathematics and the physical world. If one surrenders that, it would be hard to do anything like science as it is conceived of today.

20. "Remarks Upon Mr. Locke's 'Essay on Human Understanding'" (Jackson 13: 458–59, 461).

21. *Journal* 31 July 1758 (Jackson 2:454), 1 December 1789 (Jackson 4:476), Sermon #13 "On Sin in Believers" §3.10 (Jackson 5:149).

normative role over what traditions endure and what interpretations of Scripture are appropriate. And so, just as in science, where experimentation can and does lead to changes in one's "research program" or "fiduciary framework," so, too, Wesley's engagement with the Christian life changes how he interprets Scripture. The easiest places to see this other side of his hermeneutical circle, the side where experience takes the most active role, are in his own coming to faith, his engagement with the Calvinists, and in his affirmations about Christian Perfection.

One of the better examples of the role experience plays in Wesley's hermeneutic is his encounter with Peter Böhler. When Wesley returns from Georgia, he is something of a broken man, having been disillusioned about the strength of his own faith and yearning for something more. His interactions with Böhler in the early part of 1738 revolve around the ideas of saving faith and instantaneous conversion. In Wesley's journal reflections on these events, he has this to say:

> When I met Peter Böhler again, he consented to put the dispute upon the issue which I desired, namely, Scripture and experience. I first consulted the Scripture. But when I set aside the glosses of men, and simply considered the words of God, comparing them together, endeavoring to illustrate the obscure by the plainer passages; I found they all made against me, and was forced to retreat to my last hold, "that experience would never agree with the *literal interpretation* of those scriptures. Nor could I therefore allow it to be true, till I found some living witnesses of it."[22]

Böhler does produce such living witnesses. And upon hearing them, Wesley writes, "I was now thoroughly convinced."[23] Whatever Wesley wanted to believe was true of Scripture, he found it impossible to argue with interpretations of Scripture that "proved true" in experience.

The same dynamic emerges in Wesley's understanding of the weight given to the doctrine of predestination. In the middle of his career, Wesley, reflecting on his early earnestness—an even vicious earnestness—against the idea, notes that he and his brother thought it "our duty to oppose Predestination with our whole strength, not as an opinion, but as a dangerous mistake . . . but still another fact stares me in the face. Mr. H— and Mr. N— hold this, yet I believe these have

22. *Journal* 24 May 1738 §12 (Jackson 1:102).
23. Ibid.

real Christian experience. But if so, this is only an opinion. It is not 'subversive' (here is clear proof to the contrary) 'of the very foundation of Christian experience.'"[24]

While Wesley will, after writing this, again take up theological arms against the noted proponent of predestination August Toplady, the quote still reveals something of Wesley's calmer reflection on how his experience with other Christians shifts the weight he gives to certain theological "opinions." The fact that there are people who are genuinely Christian and still hold the position of predestination is "clear proof" that it is not entirely the destructive opinion he thought it might be.

Even more clearly, in his *Plain Account of Christian Perfection*, Wesley demands that experience "verify" (or at least not falsify) his interpretation of Scripture for that interpretation to be valid. After adducing pages of Scriptural testimony for his doctrine of Christian Perfection, Wesley answers the question of why any further proof might be needed, seeing that Scripture seems to be so clear on the subject. His answer shows how much one's interpretation of Scripture is dependent upon one's experience. Wesley writes that "If I were convinced that none in England had attained what has been so clearly and strongly preached by such a number of Preachers, in so many places, and for so long a time, I should be clearly convinced that we had all mistaken the meaning of those scriptures; and, therefore, for the time to come, I too must teach that 'sin will remain till death.'"[25]

If Wesley means what he says here, experience is given an inescapable role of proving one's interpretation of Scripture. Just as Scripture provides a lens through which one interprets one's experience, so experience provides the lab in which one tests interpretations of Scripture. It is as if Wesley's ideas about Christian Holiness were a kind of Lakatosian "research program," a set of core affirmations that were made and acted upon to see what results such would bring. Wesley relies on experience to verify his claims. Of course, Wesley believes his doctrine to be amply verified by experience, but then perhaps that is why he held it until his death.

It is in the light of this mutual interaction between experience and Scripture that Wesley's interpretation of the doctrine of "spiritual

---

24. *Journal* 14 May 1765 (Jackson 3:212).
25. *Plain Account of Christian Perfection*, §19 (Jackson 11:406).

senses" must be understood. The idea, of course, is not Wesley's alone; it has deep roots within the Christian tradition. However, Wesley's appropriation of this concept has often been interpreted in a purely empiricist way, *a la* John Locke, in which the mind is said to receive data directly from God and independently of worldly experience or Scriptural affirmation.[26] The "spiritual senses," when tied closely to our experience of the world, could be seen as an independent criterion for truth. We may believe something on the basis of our "spiritual experience" regardless of its basis in tradition or reason or Scripture.

This would be nonsense for Wesley. As we have seen, experience does not function independently in Wesley any more than it does in science. It must be guided by and interpreted from within what one already believes to be true. Just as a scientist's interpretation of his experiments lies within the framework of his beliefs about, say, quantum theory, so Wesley's understanding of "spiritual senses" or "spiritual experience" is interpreted from within the framework of the ideas about spiritual reality that he grounds in Scripture. Even the very idea of "faith" as a kind of "supernatural sense" derives from Wesley's reading of Hebrews 11:1 (a favorite scripture passage of his, occurring over fifty times in his writings). When he describes what one "senses" through one's "spiritual senses," it is almost always couched in the language of Scripture.[27]

Wesley has a known aversion to enthusiasm as the belief that one receives independent data from one's spiritual experience,[28] a distrust of the Quaker idea of "inner light,"[29] and of the epistemic value of "spiritual impressions" in general. He tells the Methodist society at Fish-Ponds that spiritual impressions "were therefore not simply to be relied on,

26. So the opinions, among others of George Croft Cell, *The Rediscovery of John Wesley* (New York: Holt, 1935); J. C. Hindley, "The Philosophy of Enthusiasm: A Study in the Origins of 'Experimental Theology,'" *The London Quarterly and Holborn Review* 182 (1957) 99–210; Theodore Runyon, "A New Look at Experience," *The Drew Gateway* 57.3 (1988) 44–55; and Donald Thorsen, *The Wesleyan Quadrilateral* (Nappanee, IN: Evangel, 1990) 182–87.

27. Good examples of this can be found in the *Earnest Appeal to Men of Reason and Religion*, §6–7 (Jackson 9:4–5) and Sermon #113 "The Difference Between Walking by Faith, and Walking by Sight," §13 (Jackson 7:260).

28. Cf. Wesley's Sermon #7 "The Nature of Enthusiasm" (Jackson 5:467–78).

29. Cf. "A Letter to a Person Lately Joined with the People called Quakers [10 February 1748–49] (Jackson 10:178).

(any more than simply to be condemned,) but to be tried by a farther rule, to be brought to the only certain test, the Law and the Testimony."[30] The certainty does not come from the fact of the impressions but from the faith in Scripture.

Wesley's idea of "spiritual sense" is not an epistemic criterion but rather the vehicle by which the data of Scripture is made real in the life of the believer. Spiritual senses confirm and bring a level of assurance, and they are as trustworthy as the data from the senses. On the related question of "inward feelings," Wesley's responds to Dr. Rutherford's query by affirming a distinction between feeling and knowledge. One feels the fruit of the Spirit, but one only knows them as such because of the *a priori* role of Scripture: "Observe, what he inwardly feels is these fruits themselves: Whence they come, he learns from the Bible."[31]

Wesley's notion is like the novice chemistry student's first foray into the lab, after she has been told about these invisible entities called "ions." She has been told that she can mix two chemicals in a solution and that they will dissolve and reform into two other chemicals. Upon performing the "experiment," she can experience for herself what was predicted to have happened. She would be unlikely to come up the idea of "ions" on her own had she accidently put those two chemicals together and observed the result, but she might not also believe the idea of ions with the same force if she had never experienced their interaction for herself. The back and forth movement between *a priori* beliefs and their application in experience drives both empirical science and Wesley's approach to Christian theology.

Application

If, as we have hinted at in this cursory sketch, contemporary scientific method and Wesleyan theological method cohere in the way that they allow for empirical experience to challenge (or not) our construal of reality but also in the way that they demand some *a priori* construal in the first place, some intriguing implications arise from this. We will content ourselves with noting two of them.

First, if both theology and science proceed in much the same way, important conversations between these two disciplines need not end

---

30. *Journal* 22 June 1739 (Jackson 1:206).
31. *A Letter to the Rev. Dr. Rutherford* [28 March 1768] §3.1 (Jackson 14:354).

in "he said, she said" impasses. One can in both instances appeal to experience to solve the disputes—though, of course, the differing presumptions that each discipline brings to the table must be recognized. Take the matter of the interpretation of Genesis 1 and 2. If experience is the arena in which we test our understanding of Scripture in the arena of holiness, the same should be said of our understanding of Scripture's account of creation. This need not be confined to issues like the fossil record or carbon dating; it could also include the question of whether believers' other "experiences" of the working of God are best understood, for instance, as instantaneous and immediate or as progressive and gradual. The theological intuition of how God tends to work in one area might give us the frame of understanding properly to expect how God might work in other areas.

Of course, common inductions of our experience are not merely challenges to some understandings of religion—they are also challenges to blind dogmatisms in science. Those, for example, who want to make a moral issue against religious belief—and claim that no one should believe anything for which they do not have sufficient evidence[32]—should be aware of how contrary that kind of rigid evidentialism is to the experience of most people.

A second implication concerns the comfortable home theology and science could both have together in a Christian university setting. If strong commonalities of method exist between them and they are both working on a common body of truth, then, as both Cardinal Newman and the First Vatican Council observed more than 100 years ago, we should be patient with apparently discrepancies between the claims of both disciplines. It might be that the jury is still out and that not enough experience is available to determine between competing interpretive claims. We have neither a completed science nor a perfect interpretation of Scripture. Given that, many conflicts between science and religion are unnecessary. Many conflicts deal with impasses for which there is not yet enough information to solve. Scientists and theologians approach the world differently, but we can agree that it is the same world of experience they both approach.

There will, of course, continue to be conflicts between understandings purportedly rooted in science and understandings offered in the

---

32. William Clifford is the "usual suspect" here (cf. his "Ethics of Belief" in *Ethics of Belief and Other Essays* [Amhurst NY: Prometheus] 1999).

name of religion. Given that there is faith involved in both disciplines, this should come as no surprise. However, the force with which those conflicts play themselves out can be lessened if each discipline is aware of its own interplay between affirmation and experience. The common "rules of engagement," so to speak, between these two mean that we can afford to be generous and tolerant, knowing that poor ideas—of either religious or scientific origin—will eventually prove themselves false in the ebb and flow of believing and living.

7

How the Discoveries of Science and Archaeology Shift Interpretations of Genesis

Robert D. Branson

The interpretation of Genesis 1–11 has become a contentious issue. It is contentious not only in the church but also in the political and educational arenas of our country. The focal point of the debate has been particularly the creation narratives. But the entire "pre-history" material of the Bible has drawn criticism and fierce defense.

An historical approach to interpreting the narratives has been a leading influence in the modern era. Many church leaders have taken a strong stand defending the essential historicity of the stories, believing that any other interpretation moves toward falsifying the accounts and thus casting doubt on the reliability of Scripture. However, continual pressure from the discoveries and theories of science raise questions about the adequacy of a historical-literal interpretation. Archaeological finds in the ancient Middle East (ANE) have helped us understand better the general culture of which ancient Israel was a part. Science and archeology now challenge the hegemony of the historical interpretation.

The purpose of this paper is not to suggest that we need a new approach to interpreting Genesis 1–11. My purpose is to recognize that a new paradigm—to borrow a term from Thomas Kuhn—of interpretation has already arisen in biblical studies. And this new paradigm can be more fruitful for reconciling conflicts between science and creation stories of Genesis.

If "outside" influences such as science and archaeology lead us to a new understanding of these theologically important passages, how does that shift affect a Wesleyan understanding of the authority and inspiration of Scripture? Wesleyan theologians from the nineteent century, such as Watson, William Burt Pope, and Miley, and from the twentieth, such as A. M. Hills, Byrum, H. Orton Wiley, Kenneth Grider, and H. Ray Dunning have advocated a dynamical/dynamic theory of inspiration. While emphasizing the work of the Holy Spirit in guiding the persons who recoded Scripture, the dynamic theory of inspiration "preserves the scriptural truth that God speaks through human agencies," says H. Orton Wiley. The dynamic theory of inspiration "insists that the agent is not reduced to a mere passive instrument."[1] William Burt Pope noted that "the precise relation of the human to the Divine is a problem which has engaged much attention, and has not yet been, though it may yet be, adequately solved."[2] It might be doubted that we will ever adequately understand the mystery of the Divine-human interaction in the process of producing the Bible, any more than we will adequately understand the mystery of the Incarnation. However, Wesleyan theologians have not been afraid to face the facts of science and archaeology as they bear on the process of inspiration.

I proceed in this paper by first analyzing Kuhn's concept of a paradigm shift as an adaptable model to understand what has been happening in how Genesis 1–11 is understood. I briefly examine some aspects of the theological/biblical conflict produced by the Copernican scientific revolution as an example of a paradigm shift caused by outside influences. I describe a paradigm that has proven inadequate for the interpretation of Genesis 1–11 and what influences have forced a change of interpretation. Finally, I look at how the new paradigm fits with the Wesleyan approach to inspiration.

Thomas Kuhn's book *The Structure of Scientific Revolutions* was one of the pivotal works in the shift from the modern to the post-modern age.

1. H. Orton Wiley, *Christian Theology*, 3 vols. (Kansas City, MO: Beacon Hill, 1941) 1:176.

2. William Burt Pope, *A Compendium of Christian Theology*, 3 vols., 2nd ed. (London: Wesleyan-Methodist Book Room, 1880) 1:175.

As an historian of science, Kuhn noted that "some accepted examples of actual scientific practice—law, theory, application, and instrumentation together—provide models from which spring particular coherent traditions of scientific research."[3] These "coherent traditions," which he labeled "paradigms," are perpetuated by being taught to succeeding generations of students. Paradigms provide the students and practicing scientists with the understanding of the procedures of science.

The practice of science also at times produces anomalies that a reigning paradigm cannot incorporate adequately.[4] Eventually, the anomalies accumulate to the extent that a new theory is offered, usually by a younger member of the scientific society, to incorporate the data. By such means, a paradigm shift takes place, and the criteria for "determining the legitimacy both of problems and of proposed solutions" changes.[5] Kuhn found that paradigms not only provided the practical and intellectual environment with which to practice science, but they also prejudiced the outcome of what scientists were expecting in experiments. This finding along with the admission that theories are "simply man-made interpretations,"[6] helped to shatter modernity's image of the objective scientific observer.

Kuhn was aware that paradigm shifts had social, political and even theological ramifications. We will examine shortly perhaps the most famous paradigm shift, the Copernican theory of the universe, to see how it impacted our understanding of the Bible. The mechanics of scientific revolutions as Kuhn identified them are peculiar to science itself. But other fields also develop paradigms, sometimes called worldviews. The paradigms of other fields are supported by a mass of factual details, accepted theories, and essential presuppositions. Educational institutions guide the students into acceptable practices and procedures of their chosen disciplines and thus perpetuate the paradigms to succeeding generations. When anomalies within the discipline or pressures from outside demonstrate the inadequacies of paradigms, new paradigms arise. Such paradigm shifts have previously occurred in biblical studies.

---

3. Thomas Kuhn, *The Structure of Scientific Revolutions* (Chicago: University of Chicago Press, 1962) 10.

4. Ibid., 52–53.

5. Ibid., 108.

6. Ibid., 126.

The advent of the Copernican understanding of the universe is an example of a paradigm shift that arose due to "new" knowledge made available by another discipline. On March 5, 1616 and in response to Galileo, the Congregation of the Index condemned

> the Pythagorean doctrine concerning the mobility of the earth and the immobility of the sun, which Nicolas Copernicus, *De revolutionibus orbium coelstium* . . . taught, and which is false and altogether incompatible with divine Scripture . . . ; therefore, in order that an opinion ruinous to Catholic truth not creep further in this manner, the Sacred Congregation decrees that the said Nicolas Copernicus, *De revolutionibus orgim* . . . be suspended until corrected.[7]

The moving hand behind the ruling was that of Roberto Bellarmino (1542–1621), who sent to Galileo a warning that same spring about his teaching as fact that the earth moved. It would not be until 1633 that Galileo would be condemned. The conflict was not so much about the facts of science as between an "unproven" theory and the authority of the Church and Scripture. The Copernican theory was accepted by many, although not because it could be proven. It was not until 1830 that scientific evidence of the "annual parallax" became available. Rather, Copernicus's theory provided "a coherent, integrated view" for science.[8] Bellarmino argued that because the Holy Spirit inspired the Scriptures, the Bible could not be false. And because the Church is not an institution of men, but of God, it cannot err in its teaching.[9] Both Scripture (Ps 93:1) and the Church taught that the earth does not move, therefore, the Copernican theory is false.

Often over looked in this debate is that the concept of the universe popular in the seventeenth century was not based on biblical descriptions. It was based on the theory of Claudius Ptolemy (c. AD 100–170), which placed the earth at the center of the universe and around which the moon, sun, planets, and stars rotated. In the biblical/Mesopotamian view, earth is a ball with water above and below it. A solid dome above

---

7. Richard S. Westfall, "The Trial of Galileo: Bellarmino, Galileo, and the Clash of Two Worlds" (paper presented for the 1988 Gross Memorial Lecture, Valparaiso, IN) 1.

8. Owen Gingerich, "Space, Time, and Beyond: The Place of God in the Cosmos" (paper presented for the 1992 Gross Memorial Lecture at Valparaiso University, Valparaiso, IN) 9.

9. Westfall, "Trial of Galileo," 5–6.

(Gen 1:6, 7, 8, 14, 15, 17; Ps 19:2; Ezek 1: 22, 23, 25; Dan 12:3) separates the waters, and on that dome is hung the sun, moon and stars.[10]

Ultimately, the clash between the Church and science was over two paradigms. The Church held that the biblical description of the physical universe was inerrant. This is not to say that there have not been others in the history of the Church who have interpreted the Scriptures in other ways. But during the sixteenth and seventeenth centuries, a view of the universe was supported by a paradigm drawn from the Scriptures and the teachings of the Church. And a paradigm shift occurred because of information drawn from a scientific source: astronomy.

In the modern era, interpretations of Genesis 1–11 (particularly the first three chapters) have become the focal point of debate. The paradigm out of which many contemporary people interpret these chapters is an historical paradigm. That is, many people believe the Genesis chapters give us an accurate account of what actually happened. This practice of taking Genesis as historical and literal was present in the Christian tradition prior to the contemporary period. Josephus, for instance, recounted the early chapters of the Bible as history, adding many details from oral traditions or his own suppositions as he wrote.[11] John Calvin also considered Genesis as historically accurate. He titled his discussion of creation, "The History of the Creation of the World." The accuracy of the accounts was guaranteed, said Calvin, when Moses wrote down "facts which the fathers had delivered as from hand to hand, through a long succession of years, to their children." To those who wondered how such facts could be available given that no human witnesses were present for much of the creation, Calvin responded that "no sane person doubts that Adam was well-instructed (by God?), respecting them all."[12] This paradigmatic framework is very much with us today.

The term "history" has various connotations and has been used with different meanings at different times. While the modern historian seeks objective records and multiple sources to reconstruct a reliable history, such procedural understandings cannot always be attributed to a writer who lived prior to the modern age. The term "history" is often used

---

10. See illustration in Robert D. Branson, Jim Edlin, and Timothy M. Green, *Discovering the Old Testament: Story and Faith* (Kansas City: Beacon Hill, 2003) 65.

11. Josephus *Ant.* 1:2–75.

12. Jean Calvin, *Commentaries on the First Book of Moses Called Genesis*, 45 vols., trans. John King (Grand Rapids: Eerdmans, 1948) 1:57–59.

to describe events that actually occurred or persons who actually lived, even if there is no sufficient modern evidence to prove this. Terrence Fretheim recognizes this distinction when he writes that "while it is not possible to determine whether the women and men of Genesis were actual historical persons, it seems reasonable to claim that the narratives carry some authentic memories of Israel's pre-exodus heritage."[13]

The movement generally identified as "scientific creationism" has tried to enlist a type of science to combat the theory of evolution. Howard Van Till criticizes the scientific analysis by those committed to scientific creationism as functioning "to diminish the demand for both craft competence and professional integrity and to disable the generally accepted epistemic value system."[14] What is driving those committed to scientific creationism is not science, but the belief that the account of creation in Genesis is history. Henry Morris, a primary force behind creation science says that "the creation chapters of Genesis are marvelous and accurate accounts of the actual events of the primeval history of the universe."[15] In response to the question of how these accounts were preserved for posterity, Morris argues:

> In accord with the common practice of ancient times, records and narratives were written down on tables of stone and then handed down from family to family, perhaps finally, to be placed in a library or public storehouse of some sort. It seems most reasonable to believe that the original records of Genesis were written down by eyewitnesses and handed down through the line of patriarchs, from Adam through Noah and Abraham and finally to Moses.[16]

Bert Thompson is another representative of the creation science movement who maintains the historicity of the Genesis narrative. "It is our contention that the material in Genesis 1–11 is historically true," says Thompson "and that it represents believable, literal history that is 'correct in substance.'"[17] Thompson goes on to attack the theory of

---

13. Terence E. Fretheim, "The Book of Genesis," in *New Interpreter's Bible*, 12 vols. (Nashville: Abingdon, 1994) 1:327.

14. Howard J. Van Till, Davis A. Young, and Clarence Menninga, *Science Held Hostage* (Downers Grove, IL: Intervarsity, 1988) 45.

15. Henry M. Morris, *Scientific Creationism* (Forest Green, AR: Master, 1974) 203.

16. Ibid., 205.

17. Bert Thompson, *Creation Compromises* (Montgomery, AL: Apologetics, 1995) 96.

evolution, stating that "science has not proven evolution true. Nor will it ever, for such a task falls far beyond the scope of the scientific method."[18] What undergirds the arguments of both Morris and Thompson is the modernist acceptance that historicity equals truth and, because the Bible is inspired, it is true. Therefore, the accounts of Genesis must be historical. Divine inspiration becomes the guarantor of the Bible's historicity.

The typical response by contemporary biblical scholars to this kind of argument is to say that Genesis offers a literary narrative. As such, Genesis is inspired by God but not of necessity historically accurate. The truth of Genesis can be theological without that truth aligning with contemporary science.

Not all persons who maintain the historicity of Genesis 1–11 are part of the creation science movement. Many from various fields of study accept the essential historicity of these chapters. Astronomer Owen Gingerich suggests that the theory of the "Big Bang" beginning of the universe posits "some mysterious prior state that can be traced back to within a split second of an apparent time zero." Since our universe apparently had a beginning and thus a history, "this view is surprisingly consonant with the Biblical [sic] narrative, which is fundamentally a historical vision of the world."[19] Regardless of whether one is part of the scientific creation movement or just accepts that Genesis 1–11 is a historical account, what is being accepted is a paradigm that is basically in conflict not only with science, but also what has become known in the last one hundred fifty years about the cultural background of Israel in general and Genesis 1–11 specifically. The continuing advance of knowledge both in disciplines of science such as geology,[20] biology,[21] genetics,[22] and astronomy[23] and in our understanding of the

---

18. Ibid., 102.

19. Gingrich, "Space, Time, and Beyond," 17.

20. Davis A Young, *Christianity and the Age of the Earth* (Grand Rapids: Zondervan, 1982).

21. Richard G. Colling, *Random Designer* (Bourbonnais, IL: Browning, 2004).

22. Darrell R. Falk, *Coming to Peace With Science* (Downers Grove, IL: Inter Varsity, 2004).

23. Howard J. Van Till, "The Scientific Investigation of Cosmic History," *Portraits of Creation*, Howard J. Van Till, ed. (Grand Rapids: Eerdmans, 1990) 83–125.

Bible's cultural backgrounds evident in recent archaeology make history as the interpretive paradigm untenable.

While Genesis 1–11 has been read as history, the ANE accounts of creation and theogony fall into the literary category of mythology. The Exodus event so impacted the Israelite way of conceptualizing their relationship with God that they eventually rejected mythological approaches. According to Old Testament scholar, Dennis Bratcher, "the two opposing categories for Israel (to use a more modern mode of thought) are not 'history' and 'fiction' (history being that which can be verified by data and fiction that which does not correspond to verifiable data and therefore is historically untrue) but rather 'history' and 'myth.'" Israel told its stories in the form of "existential human experience" rather than cosmic clashes among the gods. Stories were related "in historical terms of human actions and interactions with God within human existence." The story tellers drew upon the ANE mythological imagery but "historicized those images into a narrative about human experience."[24]

When George Smith published in 1876 *The Chaldean Account of Genesis*, he began a paradigm shift in our understanding of Genesis 1–11. As more texts from the ANE have become available, more parallels between them and biblical accounts have become obvious. Some interpreters emphasized the similarities in the materials, and others the differences. Simon Parker offers a middle ground when he argues that "a just comparison gives due weight to both commonalities and differences and seeks to explain both—as respectively part of the common culture Israel shared with its neighbors and antecedents, or as part of the particular culture or sub-culture of the individual work—or indeed of the creativity of its author(s)."[25]

Our perspective can deepen if we compare the Mesopotamian cultural backgrounds of Genesis 1–11, specifically the creation account of Genesis 1, the Garden incident (2–3), the genealogy of chapter 5, and the flood narrative (6–9). These comparisons are not new and can be found in many scholarly works on scripture. Kenton L. Sparks argues, for instance, "that the Priestly Writer was an avid student of ancient texts and that his anthology of Israelite tradition was deliberately

---

24. See Bratcher's work on this and similar issues at http://www.crivoice.org.

25. Simon B. Parker, "The Ancient Near Eastern Literary Background of the Old Testament" in *New Interpreter's Bible*, 12 vols. (Nashville: Abingdon, 1994) 1:234.

shaped to follow patterns and motifs found in Mesopotamian literature."[26] By reviewing the literary parallels, it will become apparent that we should read Genesis 1–11 for theological insight not historical facts. Of course, caution here is required. The exuberant mistakes of scholars who tried to show literary dependence between biblical accounts and Mesopotamian documents, from such as Ebla, are all too familiar.[27]

The theological independence of Israel is certainly evident in the creation narrative of Genesis 1. There is only one God, and God is separate from and not part of the created order. Even the physical elements are demythologized. For example the sun (Hebrew *shemesh*) is referred to as the "greater light" (v 16), lest the reader think of the sun god Shamash.[27] The structure of the universe, however, with its solid dome holding back the waters above, the flat earth, and the sun, moon, stars and planets all occupying the underside of dome, corresponds to the ANE cosmic geography.[28] E. A. Speiser notes seven items in Genesis 1 which are in identical sequence with Enuma Elish: existence of primeval chaos, creation of light, the firmament, the dry land, the luminaries, humanity, and finally the gods/God rests.[29] The odds of two documents coming up independently with seven items in the exact same order are 5040 to 1. Although Sparks wants to argue that the Priestly writer drew directly from Enuma Elish,[30] most scholars suggest that the writer rather drew from the common cultural pattern of creation.[31]

The early history of humanity was viewed in antiquity as a golden age when humans lived in an idyllic setting. Humans had special relationships with deities and lived extremely long lives. The biblical account conforms to this general pattern. Adam and Eve lived in a garden paradise where God met with them. The life spans of early humans are reduced in four stages: prior to the flood the longest lives; after the flood

26. Kenton L. Sparks, "Enuma Elish and Priestly Mimesis: Elite Emulation in Nascent Judaism," *JBL* 126:4 (2007) 626.

27. Gerhard Hasel, "The Polemic Nature of the Genesis Cosmology," *Evangelical Quarterly* 2 (1974) 89.

28. John H. Walton, *Ancient Near Eastern Thought and the Old Testament* (Grand Rapids: Baker Academic, 2006) 165–78.

29. E. A. Speiser, *Genesis*, in *The Anchor Bible* (New York: Doubleday, 1964) 10.

30. Sparks, "Enuma Elish," 631.

31. John H. Walton, *Ancient Israelite Literature in Its Cultural Context* (Grand Rapids: Zondervan, 1989) 37. See also his conclusion comparing Genesis 1 with Atrahasis, 40.

a general reduction from 600 years for Shem to 148 for Nahor; from Abraham to Moses a range from 200 to 100 years, and after Moses life spans typical of present day norms.[32] This view of a descent of humanity from paradise to present day conflicts with scientific views of ascent from simple forms of life to more complex. The stories of Genesis 2–11 probably originated separately, each having its own motif but drawing on the general ANE culture when told by tribal story tellers. Through a complex process, the stories were brought together to make a fairly unified narrative to describe the ancient "history" of the world and Israel. This helps explains the awkwardness of some of the stories that produce those common questions like, where did Cain get his wife? Or, if Cain and Abel were the first children of Adam and Eve, of whom did Cain have to be afraid when God cursed him?[33] This compiling of disparate stores into a longer account has a parallel in the origin of the Gilgamish epic. Eight independent Sumarian stories were compiled by an Old Babylonian author/editor in the early second millennium to make a coherent narrative.[34]

There are several accounts of the creation of humanity in the ANE, and the Israelite accounts (1:26–23; 2:4—3:24) are distinctive when compared to Mesopotamian stories. For example, in Genesis humanity is monogenesis rather than polygenesis. Humanity is also the pinnacle of creation, rather than an afterthought. Humanity is created to rule instead of serve.[35] In the garden story, a secondary theme intrudes at the beginning and end (2:9; 3:22). This theme addresses the quest for eternal life, or to put it negatively, why do we have to die? There is no indication in the text that humanity was created immortal. The couple had access to the tree of life, and that tree is what conveyed immortality. Humans were cast out of the garden lest after sinning they might eat of the tree and gain immortality. The quest for immortality was also a theme in ANE myth and ritual (see both the Gilgamish Epic and the

---

32. J. Maxwell Miller and John H. Hayes, *A History of Ancient Israel and Judah* (Philadelphia: Westminster, 1986) 58–60.

33. Nahum M. Sarna, *Understanding Genesis: The Heritage of Biblical Israel* (New York: Schocken, 1974) 29.

34. Lawson G. Stone, "From Tribal Confederation to Monarchic State: The Editorial Perspective of the Book of Judges" (PhD diss., Yale University: 1987) 173–87.

35. Walton, *Ancient Near Eastern Thought*, 27–30.

Adapa Story).³⁶ In the biblical story, the quest for immortality forms part of the backdrop waiting to come to the fore. The various accounts, both biblical and non-biblical, are consistent at this point: immortality is removed from humanity's grasp. Death awaits all.

Science has placed in great doubt the historicity of the Adam and Eve narrative. Anthropological and genetic studies place the origin of our species much earlier than previously thought. Sometime between 160,000 to 100,000 years ago, our ancestors appeared in Africa.³⁷ About 45,000 years ago we developed spoken language.³⁸ Such extended time periods make it difficult to accept the story of an idyllic setting situated in the recent past and inhabited by an original couple from whom all humanity descended.

In Genesis 5, we have the genealogical record of ten generations that stretches from Adam to Noah. The list has often been compared to the Sumerian King list, which records the reigns of eight kings from five cities who ruled for a total of 241,200 years prior to the flood. The longest reigns were by Alalgar of Eridu (36,000 years) and En-mem-gal-Anna of Bad-tibira (43,200 years). Even granting that the scribes may have used a base 6 system of counting, the numbers are unbelievably high. After the flood, the Sumerian numbers decrease to normal lengths.³⁹ Old Testament scholar, Claus Westermann, reviews the theories of direct dependence of one document on the other and concludes that both documents "are a reference to the generally widespread view that the life-span of the primeval ancestors was longer than the present life-span. . . . This may well have been a generally known motif."⁴⁰ Finally, the similarities and differences between the flood narrative (6:1—9:17) and the flood accounts in the Gilgamish Epic and Atrahasis Epic are well known.

The theological sophistication of the Genesis account that weaves together human culpability, divine justice executed by one God, and

---

36. Sarna, *Understanding Genesis*, 25.

37. David L. Wilcox, "Establishing Adam: Recent Evidences for a Late-Date Adam," *Communication* 1 (2004) 49–54.

38. "Linguists Seek a Time When We Spoke as One," *Christian Science Monitor* (19 July 2007).

39. "The Sumerian King List," A. Leo Oppenheim, trans. (ANET, 265–66).

40. Claus Westermann, *Genesis 1–11: A Commentary*, 3 vols. (Minneapolis: Augsburg, 1974) 1:353.

covenantal promise argues for a development later than its ANE counterparts. There is, however, a "material identity of the tale in the two versions," as Eugene Fisher puts it. As an appendix to his article Fisher lists twenty-four points of comparison between the two versions.[41] The story line, even to the detail of the sending forth the birds, argues for an awareness of cultural influence. Stories were told and retold over the centuries until adapted by a writer as a vehicle for Israelite theology.

The attempt to prove from the biblical account that there was a universal flood within recent history responsible for laying down the fossil records is impossible to sustain. The sedimentary rock record has been shown by radiometric dating methods to have a high antiquity. Although these methods have been assailed by young-earth creationists, they have proven scientifically valid.[42] There is no geological record of a world-wide flood, and no archaeologist has reported evidence of a more localized one that would float a boat to the top of mountains (Gen 7:19—8:4). The historicity of such a flood must be given up. At the conclusion of his book on the various interpretations of the biblical flood account, geologist Davis Young argues that "the extrabiblical data pertaining to the flood have been pushing the church to develop a better approach to the flood story and indeed to all the early chapters of Genesis." The extrabiblical evidence includes, 1) "the failure after several centuries of effort to locate physical remnants of the biblical deluge," 2) the evidence that the geological structures of the earth have been laid down over extensive periods of time, 3) the view that the flood's effects were confined only to the globe's surface features cannot be sustained, 4) and "a variety of biogeographical evidence . . . counts conclusively against such an event," such as the lack of evidence "to indicate that human or animal populations were ever disrupted by a catastrophic global flood at any point in the past." Davis summarily concludes: "I submit that there is something inherently flawed in any hermeneutic that prevents us from reading God's handiwork properly and that repeatedly puts us at odds with the established conclusions of a scientific community that is composed not just of opponents of Christianity but also of confessing Christians."[43]

41. Eugene Fisher, "Gilgamesh and Genesis: The Flood Story in Context," *CBQ* 32 (1970) 392–403.

42. Young, *Christianity*, 93–116.

43. Davis A. Young, *The Biblical Flood: A Case Study of the Church's Response to Extrabiblical Evidence* (Grand Rapids: Eerdmans, 1995) 93–116.

While a segment of the Church still clings to inadequate hermeneutical approaches to interpreting Genesis 1–11, I want to suggest that the discipline of biblical studies as a whole has already understood the implications of the readings of the ANE culture and the findings of the scientific community. A paradigm shift has already taken place in biblical studies. While a few scholars may suggest some historical background to the narratives—such as a local flood forming the basis of what grew as the story tellers embellished the tale to be the account of a worldwide catastrophe—none would argue that the narratives are history in the modern sense of that term. Biblical scholars see the biblical materials as the product of Israelite theologians drawing from cultural materials for distinctive theological insights into the nature of God, his governance of the world, and his movements toward judgment and redemption.

Wesleyan biblical scholars of the early twentieth century approached Genesis as an historical document. Most of those working in the latter part of the century have recognized that such an approach is inadequate. They accept the findings of science and archaeology and interpret the texts as theological writings set within an ANE cultural framework. Does such a shift in interpretation undermine Wesleyan theology, particularly its understanding of inspiration? Fundamental to Wesleyan theology is the belief that the Scriptures have been inspired by God and are foundational for theology. Two questions need to be asked. What has been our historic understanding of inspiration? Is it flexible enough to incorporate new approaches to interpreting Genesis?

The dynamic theory of inspiration, in which God and humans cooperate in the writing of the Bible, has been the standard approach to biblical inspiration in the Wesleyan tradition. W. B. Pope (1822–1903), a British Methodist writing in the 1870's, produced a three volume systematic theology that set a precedent for this theory. Pope maintained a dynamical theory of inspiration, and he argued that the Spirit "acted upon and through the faculties of the inspired person." Pope identifies the Bible as "a Divine-human collection of documents: the precise relation of the human to the Divine is a problem which has engaged much attention, and has not yet been, though it may yet be, adequately solved." As to the authority of the Bible, he says that "plenary inspiration makes Holy Scripture the absolute and final authority, all-sufficient as the supreme Standard of Faith, Directory of Morals, and Charter of Privileges to the Church of God. Of course, the Book of Divine revelations cannot contain anything untrue, but its infallibility is by itself especially connected with religious truth."[44] As to infallibility, he seemingly contradictorily says that "sometimes (the biblical writers) have to register facts, or supposed facts, which they gather from public records, sometimes to record traditions, legends, current opinions, or uninspired predictions handed down by tradition: in these cases they are only witness of what they found."[45] As to creation, Pope allowed for an interpretation of "day" to be an extended period of time for the creation of the physical universe,[46] but he rejected the concept of Darwinian evolution.[47]

John Miley (1813–1895) taught at the newly established Methodist school of Drew University. In an appendix to his two-volume theology, Miley also maintained the dynamical view of inspiration in which God used human instrumentality in recording "divine truth" but did not over ride their consciousness or personalities. This accounts for variations, said Miley, "of which there are many, (but which) are quite indifferent to a real and sufficient inspiration."[48] He argued that Moses gave an historical account of creation, but Miley was sensitive to the problems that geology had raised about the age of the earth. He gave several options for correlating the two, opting finally for an interpretation given by Augustine and Thomas Aquinas that the first three days of creation were extended periods of time.[49]

A.M. Hills (1848–1935), the first president of Olivet Nazarene University, also accepted the dynamical view of inspiration. He rejected a verbal theory of inspiration.[50] Hills's view of inspiration was wide enough to recognize that Scripture contains error and is not infallible in every aspect. Hills said that "those who maintain that we must accept every statement of Scripture, or none of it, should consider that no doctrine more surely makes skeptics." And again, "in spite of all discrepancies, and disagreements, and errors, and minor inaccuracies, the

44. Pope, *A Compendium*, 1:174–75.
45. Ibid., 1:172.
46. Ibid., 1:398.
47. Ibid., 1:403ff.
48. John Miley, *Systematic Theology*, 2 vols. (New York: Eaton and Mains, 1894) 2:485.
49. Ibid., 1:298–308.
50. A. M. Hills, *Fundamental Christian Theology*, 2 vols. (Pasadena: C. J. Kinne, 1931) 1:123–127.

Bible still remains God's inspired and infallible book. But *infallible for what?* . . . It infallibly guides all honest, and willing and seeking souls, to Christ, to holiness, and to heaven."[51] Hills adopted an expanded time sequence in Genesis 1 to accommodate the findings of geology, and he was even willing to accept a theory of theistic evolution. But Hills rejected biological evolution as espoused by Darwin, whom he considered the author of "fascinating fiction."[52]

Russell R. Byrum (1889–1980), instructor at the Anderson Bible School and Seminary and today known as Anderson University, also understood inspiration as involving "both the human and the divine element in the production of the Bible." Byrum appears to have been influenced by theologians A. H. Strong and Charles Hodge in the formation of his ideas, even to the accepting that the original manuscripts (the autographs) as infallible. However, Byrum was willing to consider that the Bible contained errors, but he thought those errors were limited to the Bible's "references to history and science," not "its moral and religious teaching." The errors might pertain to secular matters, but "the inspiration of its religious message would not necessarily be affected."[53] Concerning creation, Byrum held that the Mosaic account of Genesis 1 is an accurate history.[54] But he also thought that the "days" may be interpreted as extended periods of time to correlate with the findings of geology. He notes that

> it is a distinct advantage to religion to show, if it can be done, that the Bible narrative is not inconsistent with the claims of science. It is improper to debar the student of science from faith in the inspired record by hedging it around with human interpretations that are not required by internal facts of the Bible. And it is never right so to interpret the Bible that it contradicts certainly known facts of nature.[55]

As to evolution, Byrum repudiated "every form of evolution as the method of divine creation."[56]

51. Ibid., 1:134.
52. Ibid., 1:262–72.
53. Russell R. Byrum, *Christian Theology* (Anderson, IN: Warner, 1925) 169–76.
54. Ibid., 235.
55. Ibid., 237.
56. Ibid., 253. A revised edition of Byrum's work appeared in 1982. That edition eliminated out-dated material but holds essentially the same positions Byrum originally

Writing in the same theological movement, Gilbert W. Stafford, another Anderson University School of Theology theologian, took a more community approach to the understanding of the inspiration of the Bible. The Scriptures are those that are "experienced by the church at large as being inspired by God," says Stafford. The Bible is "accepted by the church at large as being sacred writings." Its purpose is primarily "instructive for salvation," and it is useful for "instructing, judging, aligning, and shaping the people of God."[57] Stafford adopted a more irenic approach by seeing the similarities in views of inspiration rather than their differences.[58]

Phyllis Bird has argued that in the modern era, "the evangelical or conservative wing of Protestantism" has continued a discussion on the authority of the Bible. Outside this orbit, however, the issue has been "ignored or obscured."[59] This may explain why it is difficult to find a discussion of inspiration by theologians in some of the Wesleyan denominations. Biblical inspiration has continued to be a topic of discussion, however, among theologians in the Church of the Nazarene.

Prominent early Church of the Nazarene theologian, H. Orton Wiley, in agreement with Pope and Miley, maintained a dynamical theory of inspiration. Wiley said that the "the Bible becomes the infallible Word of God, the authoritative rule of faith and practice in the Church."[60] Church of the Nazarene scholar, S. S. White, also accepted the dynamic theory of inspiration and viewed the Bible as "an infallible rule of faith and practice."[61]

A later twentieth-century theologian, H. Ray Dunning, accepts the dynamical theory of inspiration. But Dunning sees the inspiration

---

laid out. Concerning errors in scripture, a brief section has been added to explain that what some might consider moral errors are more appropriately identified as a lack of understanding the differences between Western and Oriental cultures (Russell R. Byrum, *Christian Theology*, revised ed., Arlo F. Newell, ed. [Anderson, IN: Warner, 1982] 133). Of greater note is the toning down the position that the Genesis record is accurate history. Only once does the section refer to "the historic nature of the record" (189). Byrum's original rejection of all forms of evolution is retained.

57. Gilbert W. Stafford, *Theology for Disciples* (Anderson, IN: Warner, 1996) 52.

58. Ibid., 46–49.

59. Phyllis A. Bird, "The Authority of the Bible" in *New Interpreter's Bible*, 12 vols. (Nashville: Abingdon, 1994) 1:34.

60. Wiley, *Christian Theology*, 1:171, 176–77.

61. S. S. White, *Essential Christian Beliefs* (Kansas City, MO: Beacon Hill, 1942) 92.

residing in the writer not the text. Such a theory "implies the historical character of the biblical language." Dunning means not that the Bible is strictly history, but that words "are historically conditioned by the writer's intellectual, cultural, and societal milieu." Dunning takes into account the discoveries of archaeology and recognizes that the writers were influenced by the surrounding cultures. For example, while Israel maintained its distinctive theological presuppositions, it borrowed worship and ritual forms from the Canaanite culture. This leads Dunning to restrict the authority of the Bible to its "soteriological aspects."[62]

Another contemporary Church of the Nazarene theologian, J. Kenneth Grider, also accepted the dynamic theory of inspiration. Grider maintained that "Scripture is inerrant on doctrine and practice." He allowed that "it might contain errors in the areas of mathematics, science, of such like," yet he maintained "the doctrine of a racial fall through a historical Adam."[63]

We can summarize by saying that Wesleyan theologians have maintained a dynamical/dynamic view of inspiration that incorporates both the Spirit's guidance and human limitations, including cultural perspectives. Absolute infallibility or inerrancy has been rejected. Some theologians readily admit that the Bible contains errors in the areas of history, science, and mathematics. The Scriptures, however, are viewed as infallible in the areas of salvation, faith, and practice. By acknowledging that the Bible is incarnational, being generated by both the Creator and creatures, Wesleyans leave room to acknowledge the impact that the ANE culture had upon the writers. The Bible is accepted as a book of theology/religion that contains many types of literature and is highly accurate in many of its details. But the Bible's authority is limited to its message of redemption and matters of faith and practice.

Concluding Remarks

A paradigm shift has occurred concerning how we should understand Genesis 1–11. In biblical studies, this paradigm shift is complete. Biblical scholars agree that the Israelite writers were inheritors of the

---

62. H. Ray Dunning, *Grace, Faith, and Holiness* (Kansas City, MO: Beacon Hill, 1988) 70–76.

63. J. Kenneth Grider, *A Wesleyan-Holiness Theology* (Kansas City, MO: Beacon Hill, 1994) 65–75.

Mesopotamian understanding of the "origins" of the world and the early "history" of humanity. The writers of Genesis used that cultural background as a vehicle for their distinctive theological understanding of God's creative activities and humanity's theological privilege and corruption.

This perspective requires an adjustment in how we interpret biblical material. We should give up a strictly historical approach to understanding the first chapters of Genesis for one that is literary and theological. Such an approach is not contrary to a Wesleyan understanding of inspiration, because Wesleyan scholars have typically taken into account the cultural background and human limitations of the writers of Scripture. This paradigm shift in interpreting Genesis allows science to speak about vast time spans and complex processes of development without being in conflict with the message of Scripture. Wesleyans maintain that the Bible is infallible in its teachings on faith (what we are to believe) and practice (how we are to live).

8

Rooting Evolution in Grace

Rebecca J. Flietstra

Modern biology and Christian belief are often portrayed as antithetical. This is particularly true of creation and evolution. Supporters of evolutionary theory typically claim that the evolutionary process—indeed, all of life—is rooted in, and formed by, selfish competition. According to this paradigm, all purported expressions of love (including the concept of a God who expresses love) and self-sacrifice exist as a delusion. These are simply means to gain advantage. Many Christians, in response, claim that *evolution* is the delusion. They argue that a bloody and cruel process could never be used by a loving Creator.

For those of us who both believe in a Creator God and accept evolutionary theory, the stark options currently getting attention are discouraging. Instead of choosing sides, we seek to find compatibilities and to build bridges between our faith commitments and our scientific paradigms. Much of this bridge building has focused on re-statements of creation theology. While this work has been invaluable, it has also been criticized for forcing theology to always follow biology's lead. In this paper, I look at both theology and biology. I propose ways we might think about evolutionary theory that might be more compatible with Christian belief.

Darwin's Five Theories

Before discussing how we might re-frame evolutionary theory in light of Christian belief, we should first look at how evolution is commonly presented. Ernst Mayr, a zoologist who was instrumental in the development of neo-Darwinism, effectively argued that Darwin's "one long argument" was actually a combination of five different theories:

1. Evolution as such
2. Common descent
3. Multiplication of species
4. Gradualism
5. Natural selection

In the 1800s, these theories—while overlapping—could be distinguished from each other and separately considered. Each could be individually accepted or rejected. For example, one of Darwin's contemporaries, Jean Baptiste Lamarck, would have recognized a gradual change in species, but utterly rejected common descent, multiplication of species, and natural selection. Today, biochemist and Intelligent Design advocate Michael Behe accepts common descent, but appears to reject gradualism—at least for some species, some of the time.

These theories are fairly basic, but it is worth taking the time to describe each of them briefly. Here is what Mayr said about each:

1) *Evolution as such.* This is the theory that the world is neither constant nor recently created nor perpetually cycling but rather is steadily changing and that organisms are transformed in time.

2) *Common descent.* This is the theory that every group of organisms descended from a common ancestor and that all groups of organisms, including animals, plants and microorganisms, ultimately go back to a single origin of life on earth.

3) *Multiplication of species.* This theory explains the origin of the enormous organic diversity. It postulates that species multiply, either by splitting into daughter species or by "budding," that is, by the establishment of geographically isolated founder populations that evolve into new species.

4) *Gradualism.* According to this theory, evolutionary change takes place through the gradual change of populations and not

by the sudden (saltational) production of new individuals that represent a new type.

5) *Natural selection.* According to this theory, evolutionary change comes about through the abundant production of genetic variation in every generation. The relatively few individuals who survive, owing to a particularly well-adapted combination of inheritable characters, give rise to the next generation.[1]

Evolution as Such and Gradualism

While strict, six-day creationists would object to all five of these theories, some of these elicit more of a "visceral" response than others. To some extent, "evolution as such" and "gradualism" are not as problematic as the others theories. Certainly the word "evolution" itself can raise the blood pressure of many "Bible-believing" Christians. But the idea that the world has changed over time, especially if all the biological change has been gradual, seems fairly reasonable. Creationists, for example, readily acknowledge that all the various breeds of dog have gradually risen over time with selective breeding. Even more broadly, many creationists readily accept the changes that would have been necessary after Noah's Flood in order to produce the variants we see around the globe. For example, they would argue that a single pair of bears would have produced offspring as diverse as polar bears, sun bears, and grizzlies.

The big objection is the length of time required for significant changes in living organisms. For someone who insists on a literalistic reading of scripture,[2] the age of the earth and the universe is automatically limited to a few thousand years—a fraction of the billions of years

---

1. Ernst Mayr, *One Long Argument: Charles Darwin and the Genesis of Modern Evolutionary Thought* (Cambridge, MA: Harvard University Press, 1991) 36–37.

2. For example, Creationist Henry Morris claimed that there is only one true reading of Scripture, one that involves no interpretation: "Only the doctrine of verbal inerrancy adequately expresses the true nature of Biblical inspiration. This warning . . . stress the necessity of literal interpretation. Actually, a literal interpretation is not an interpretation at all, for it takes the words at face value, assuming that the Holy Spirit (using the thoughts and abilities of the human writer whose words He inspired) was able to say exactly what He meant today. Any kind of allegorical or figurative interpretation of those words (unless directly indicated in the context) assumes that the interpreter knows better than the Holy Spirit what He should be saying, and such an attitude is presumptuous, if not blasphemous" (Henry Morris, *The Defender's Study Bible* [Grand Rapids: World Bible, 1995] 1468).

required by evolutionary theories. Even beyond this matter of fact insistence, however, there is also a sense that excess time is wasteful. Henry Morris wrote, or instance, argued that "evolution is inconsistent with God's omnipotence; since He has all power, He is capable of creating the universe in an instant, rather than having to stretch it out over aeons of time.[3]" Morris also said that "evolution is inconsistent with God's purposiveness. If God's purpose was the creation and redemption of man, as theistic evolutionists presumably believe, it seems incomprehensible that He would waste billions of years in aimless evolutionary meandering before getting to the point.[4]"

Many secular scientists agree with Morris about what the time issue must mean for theology. But they argue that the vast time proves that there is no Creator who might have a purpose for this universe. Atheistic scientists are likely to argue that human existence—indeed the entire history of terrestrial life—is merely an inconsequential blip in the time-line of the universe.

I will confess that I once found Morris's arguments convincing. For the first seventeen years of my life, I identified myself as a creationist—more by default than out of any conviction. In the absence of any other evidence, I simply assumed that young-earth creationism was the only Christian option.

My world changed when I was exposed to evolutionary theory during my freshman year at a Christian college. I found myself not only convinced by the scientific arguments but also amazed by their simultaneous simplicity and complexity. I discovered that my acceptance of evolutionary theory did challenge my beliefs—but in unexpected ways. Although I had always been taught about God's loving patience, for instance, my belief in a God who had created everything in six days had prevented me from fully recognizing God's patience. The God of a six-day creation could speak and instantly get the results he wanted. Such a God certainly must find my own repeated attempts at obedience frustrating. But a God who could "waste" billions and billions of years on an evolving creation, *that* God most certainly had plenty of patience for my own slow journey. Scripture also suggests that God prefers to add rather than to subtract time:

---

3. Henry M. Morris, *Scientific Creationism* (Green Forest, AZ: Master, 1985) 219.
4. Ibid.

> But do not forget this one thing, dear friends: With the Lord a day is like a thousand years, and a thousand years are like a day. The Lord is not slow in keeping his promise, as some understand slowness. He is patient with you, not wanting anyone to perish, but everyone to come to repentance. (2 Pet 3:8–9)

One could argue that the time required by evolution reveals, rather than conceals, a God of grace.

God's patient grace also suggests the "otherness" of God. If God spoke every detail of every event in creation, the universe would exist only as an extension of God. Without freedom to grow and develop, creation as creation cannot exist. God's grace suggests a different kind of purpose than the one Morris describes.

Common Descent and Multiplication of Species

The second set of theories—common descent and multiplication of species—also might teach us something theological. Young-earth creationists object this set of ideas, because they claim the ideas directly contradict scripture. According to their reading of Genesis, all creatures were created as distinct kinds with defined limits, limits that remove any possibility of macroevolution. Morris, for instance, argues that "the Scriptures are very clear in their teaching that God created all things as he wanted them to be, each with its own particular structure, according to His own sovereign purposes . . . Even though there may be uncertainty as to what is meant by 'kind' (Hebrew *min*), it is obvious that the word does have a definite and fixed meaning. One 'kind' could not transform itself into another 'kind.'"[5] Young-earth creationists often also cite 1 Corinthians 15: 38–39: "But God gives it a body as he has determined, and to each kind of seed he gives its own body. All flesh is not the same: Humans have one kind of flesh, animals have another, birds another and fish another."

When young-earth creationists describe the repopulating of the earth after the Flood, they speak of an original pair of dogs that produced all the members of the "dog kind:" wolves, foxes, coyotes, dogs, etc. This belief appears to coincide with common sense. Plants and animals are presented to us in categories. Even young children can distinguish be-

---

5. Ibid., 216–17.

tween members of the cat family and members of the dog family. We look around the world and see "clumps" not "transitional species."

The boundary around the human kind is particularly high and unbreachable, according to young-earth creationists. Unlike the other kinds, the human kind contains only one species. Within this species, all persons are commonly descended from Adam and Even—and that's as far as common descent extends. Rejecting common descent protects humankind from being related to chimpanzees, whales, oak trees, and pond scum. It also apparently protects our special status as bearers of the image of God. Morris argues that "man was not only created in God's spiritual image; he was also made in God's physical image. His body was specifically planned to be most suited for the divine fellowship (erect posture, upward-gazing countenance, brain and tongue designed for articulating symbolic speech—none of which are shared by the animals)."[6]

Contemporary science and theology undermines the young-earth creationist argument about radical human uniqueness. Every time we draw a line between humans and the other animals, another study nudges or blurs that line. And theologians such as Jürgen Moltmann argue that image bearing cannot be summarized by a list of characteristics that distinguish humans from other primates:

> It is not the spirituality of men and women, and not what distinguishes them from animals, which makes them God's image on earth. They are his image in their whole and particular bodily existence. It contradicts belief in creation if we define the human being's essential quality, and what corresponds to God in him, by subtracting the animal and then regarding what is left as something on its own.[7]

Image bearing is our vocation, our calling, based on our relationship with God, and not on any innate special status or features. A sharp boundary between humans and the rest of creation may not be doing us any favors. This line attempts to place us alongside God, separated from the rest of creation. But the line should be placed between God and all of creation—with humans rightly recognized as created and not

---

6. Henry Morris, *The Defender's Study Bible*, note on Genesis 1:26.

7. Jürgen Moltmann, *God in Creation: A New Theology of Creation and the Spirit of God*, trans. Margaret Kohl (Minneapolis: Fortress, 1993) 245.

divine. Image-bearing viewed in this way offers us the grace that comes from not having to seek and defend our status.

Common descent also helps us recognize the grace of relationship. The old gospel song may say "the world is not my home," but common descent tells us otherwise. Young-earth creationists place value on humans, because humans are all commonly descended from Adam and Eve. As a Christian who accepts evolutionary theory, I place value on all living organisms, not simply because we are all created, but also because we share a common genetic heritage. In other words, affirming common descent can help us realize the intrinsic value of all creation, not just human creatures.

Natural Selection

The most difficult theory to reconcile with Christian belief—and, actually, for even many non-fundamentalist Christians and non-Christians to accept—is the theory of natural selection. Natural selection on a small scale may be readily accepted, and may indeed feel like common sense. But natural selection as the driving force, as the foundation for evolution, repulses people. The theory of natural selection appears to be ugly and evil, describing a process centered on death and struggle, rather than on goodness and love. For many, such a process would not only make humans and the rest of creation essentially evil, but it would also reveal either an unloving God or no God at all.

Both young-earth creationists and atheistic scientists can sound as if they agree on the idea that natural selection undermines the idea that God is a loving Creator. For instance, Henry Morris has written:

> Evolution is inconsistent with God's nature of love. The supposed fact of evolution is best evidenced by the fossils, which eloquently speak of a harsh world, filled with storm and upheaval, disease and famine, struggle for existence and violent death. The accepted mechanism for inducing evolution is overpopulation and a natural selection through extermination of the weak and unfit. A loving God would surely have been more considerate of His creatures than this.[8]

Atheistic evolutionist, Richard Dawkins, writes words that support some of what Morris argues:

8. Morris, *Scientific Creationism*, 219.

> If you look at the way natural selection works, it seems to follow that anything that has evolved by natural selection should be selfish. Therefore we must expect that when we go and look at the behaviour of baboons, humans, and all other living creatures, we shall find it to be selfish.[9]

Among all the objections to evolutionary theory, this one—the juxtaposition of a loving God over against a bloodthirsty process—probably packs the greatest emotional punch.

In devising his theory of natural selection, Charles Darwin drew on the economic writings of Rev. Thomas R. Malthus, as found in *An Essay on the Principle of Population*. This extended essay argued that all living species exhibit reproductive capacities far beyond what can be supported by their environment. Rather than respond to these limits by self-limiting the number of offspring, "the superabundant effects are repressed afterwards by want of room and nourishment."[10] Both Charles Darwin[11] and Alfred Russell Wallace[12] found in Malthus' writings a possible mechanism for the evolution and origin of different species. That is, the resulting competition for scarce resources leads to a "struggle for existence,"[13] a struggle that favors those who are best adapted for their current social and physical environment.[14] Such individuals can subsequently pass on their particular traits to future generations.[15] This competition is particularly "severe between the individuals of the same species, for they frequent the same districts, require the same food, and are exposed to the same dangers."[16]

---

9. Richard Dawkins, *The Selfish Gene*, 2nd ed. (Oxford: Oxford University Press, 1989) 4.

10. Thomas R. Malthus, *An Essay on the Principle of Population*, reprint of the 7th ed., with introd. by T. H. Hollingsworth (London: Dent, 1973) 6.

11. Charles Darwin, *The Autobiography of Charles Darwin and Selected Letters*, ed. Francis Darwin (New York: Dover, 1958) 42–43.

12. Alfred Russel Wallace, *My Life: A Record of Events and Opinions*, reprint (New York: Dodd, Mead, 1905; New York: AMS, 1974) 361–62.

13. The phrase "struggle for existence" is the title of the third chapter in Charles Darwin's *On the Origin of Species*. He uses this phrase, along with "struggle for life," repeatedly in this chapter and throughout his book.

14. Charles Darwin, *The Origin of Species*, reprint of the 1st ed., with introduction by J. W. Burrow (London: Murray, 1859; New York: Penguin, 1968) 115, 119.

15. Ibid., 115.

16. Ibid., 126.

Since Darwin's day, harsh struggle and competition have been increasingly used to explain *all* life processes, including the very origin and existence of living beings. Thus even before the first cells arose out of the RNA soup, individual RNA strands competed with each other for nucleotide bases, energy and space. The genes descended from this prebiotic struggle eventually developed larger structures—first single cells and then multicellular bodies—that enabled them to compete better against rival genes. Prey began to struggle with predator, cells struggled with viruses, and bodies struggled against parasites.

Yet the greatest struggles exist within a species. This intra-species struggle is not just for space and food and against danger. Competition appears in even the most intimate relationships. Not only do males and females compete *for* mates, but they also compete *with* their mates. Not only do individuals struggle to produce and raise to maturity more offspring than their neighbors, but they also compete with their own offspring.[17] Fetuses seek to exploit the resources of the pregnant mother; the bodies of pregnant females battle to maintain some resources for their own strength. Postnatally, parents invest in offspring only as much as necessary, reserving resources for future offspring. Correspondingly older siblings pit themselves against younger siblings, and younger against older, trying to dominate the time, energy and protection of their mutual parents.

It appears difficult to imagine how we could ever think positively about natural selection or see God's grace in it. But part of the answer to how we can reconcile God's grace and natural selection is the discovery that natural selection has more to it than competition. Generally when I teach evolutionary theory, I break down the process of natural selection into three steps:

1. Individuals of a species vary; some of these variations are inherited.
2. More individuals within each species are produced than will live to grow up and to reproduce.
3. Individuals with certain traits are more likely to survive and to reproduce than those with other traits.

---

17. Robert L. Trivers, "Parent-Offspring Conflict," *American Zoologist* 14 (1974) 249–64.

Put in these terms, natural selection almost appears as common sense. Further, the competitive aspect of natural selection doesn't seem as blatant in this summary. This summary can also help us notice that natural selection is not just about a battle for survival and mates, but it is also about diversity and abundance.

Diversity and Abundance

First, natural selection depends on differences, on diversity within the local population. We tend to take this diversity for granted, and we also tend to think of variety as a good thing. But this is actually a radical way of viewing species. A more common way to understand species is to establish an archetype—an ideal—for that species. Individuals are then compared with this ideal, with any differences viewed as a deficiency. This is comparable to how dog breeds are rated in dog shows.

This is still how many creationists view species. For them, all mutations are viewed as harmful and/or as losses of information. To the extent that natural selection is accepted, it is understood as a conservative process—one that decreases variations and maintains the species already present. In contrast, the theory of natural selection can help us recognize the value of diversity. Diversity, here, is not an afterthought or a problem. Diversity is fundamental to evolution.

Second, natural selection requires abundance. "Abundance" is not a term typically associated with natural selection. Instead—citing Morris again—natural selection is a "random, wasteful, inefficient trial-and-error charade" that entails the "suffering and death of multitudes of innocent animals."[18] Such wastefulness appears difficult to reconcile with a good and gracious God. But part of this difficulty might be resolved by choosing to use a term other than "wasteful." "Wasteful" is a pejorative term, one that connotes squandering, misusing, and devaluation. But what one person might consider wasteful, another might more positively describe as lavish, prodigal, and abundant.[19]

At the heart of creation lies God's promise of abundant life. God does not begrudge life, miserly doling it out to a select few individual

---

18. Henry M. Morris, "Recent Creation is a Vital Doctrine," *Impact* 132 (June 1984). http://icr.org/pubs/imp/imp-132.htm.

19. Think of the Jesus' answer to Peter's question on forgiveness (Matt 18:21–35), the miracle at Cana where Jesus turned water into wine (John 2:1–11), or the story of Mary's anointing of Jesus' feet with an expensive perfume (John 12:1–8).

organisms or species. God showers life widely throughout the creation. The first blessing of creation called the animals to "be fruitful and multiply and fill the waters in the seas, and let birds multiply on the earth."[20] Later in Genesis, God promises Abraham, "I will make your offspring like the dust of the earth; so that if one can count the dust of the earth, your offspring also can be counted."[21] The promise of abundant life plays an even more central role in the New Testament. The gospels, epistles, and book of Revelation all portray the coming kingdom as a prodigious feast, abundantly open to all the peoples and nations. The parable of the prodigal son describes a younger son as a profligate wastrel. But the true prodigal of the story is the father, for the son eventually runs out of resources, while the father is the one who continues to love and give without measure.[22] Our God is a God of excess, of overflowing cups and bountiful grace.

At the same time, abundance and waste aren't merely synonyms or different ways of describing the same thing. Waste and abundance aren't equals. Instead, waste (like selfishness) is a derived property, one that depends on the prior existence of abundance. In the case of evolution, "waste" follows life's *over*abundance. As Thomas Malthus observed, populations increase geometrically such that even a small growth rate can, over time, cause the population's size to skyrocket. Even without predation or disease, abundantly fertile species will unavoidably reach limits as they run out of resources.[23]

Christians can understand this process as the inevitable result of God's blessings to creation. God's first blessing to creation was fruitfulness, the promise of abundant offspring. This abundance was gifted to a creation that, by definition, is limited. As can be said of humans—"Even free of sin, we would still be embodied selves, with inevitable limits"[24]—so we can recognize that the entire creation necessarily has a limited existence. God, the divine Creator of the universe, could not

20. Gen 1:22.

21. Gen 13:16.

22 Aelred R. Rosser, *Workbook for Lectors and Gospel Readers 2004, United States Edition* (Chicago: Liturgy Training, 2003) 93–96 (3rd Sunday of Lent); see also, Henri J. M. Nouwen, *The Return of the Prodigal Son* (New York: Doubleday, 1992).

23. Thomas R. Malthus, *An Essay on the Principle of Population*, reprint of the 7th ed., with introduction by T. H. Hollingsworth (London: Dent, 1973) 6.

24. William C. Placher, *Narratives of a Vulnerable God: Christ, Theology, and Scripture* (Louisville: Westminster John Knox, 1994) 71.

and cannot create a limitless creation. Creating a world without limits requires creating another deity—an utter impossibility. Nor does it seem within God's character to have created a world of underabundant life. A world of little fertility would not have hit its limits quite as quickly. But it would also have been a world of caution and constraint, where limits would prevent and eliminate abundance, rather than follow behind.

Living Selves

Finally, even if the third aspect of natural selection—individuals with certain traits are more likely to survive and to reproduce than those with other traits—is recognized as an inevitably selfish step, we still need to acknowledge that selfishness itself is a derived trait, dependent on selfhood. Competition may indeed drive natural selection at times, but this competition, this selfishness, requires the previous, underlying existence of cooperation. Life is not essentially selfish—even if selfishness is common. Life is essentially cooperative. Simply put, selfhood is more fundamental than selfishness.

To be a self is to have life. Nothing that lives does not have a self; every being that can be termed a self must be (or must have been) alive. From both a theological perspective and a biological perspective, life can be considered a fundamental good. Certainly this good can be misused and otherwise perverted, but at its core, life is a good. A living self should properly seek (consciously or unconsciously) a continued existence and should pursue abundant life (in terms of longevity and/or offspring). These pursuits are good goals, affirmed in the opening chapters of Genesis: "be fruitful and multiply."

The algorithm of natural selection[25] similarly begins with abundance. Natural selection also inevitably involves competition and selfish behaviors, but these are derived aspects of the pursuit of abundant life. Thus we could envision how the goals of abundant life could be pursued without struggle or competition: under conditions of abundant resources, in an environment devoid of predators or disease. Even if those conditions do not currently exist (and even if they have never existed[26]), we can still recognize that the abundance of life always pre-

---

25. Daniel C. Dennett, *Darwin's Dangerous Idea: Evolution and the Meanings of Life* (New York: Simon & Schuster, 1995) 48–60.

26. It is theoretically possible that the very first cells (or cell-like beings) did not

cedes competitive struggles. In other words, life could theoretically exist without competition, but competition inherently depends on the existence of life.

Because life is essentially good, the pursuit of life—whether exhibited as a desire to stay alive or to produce offspring can also be considered basically good.[27] Self-interest can certainly lead to selfishness, but the two should never be confused. Self-interest is a normal, necessary aspect of selfhood. A healthy organism that failed to flee danger, to seek food, or to pursue appropriate reproductive options would not be classified as "self-sacrificial." Such an organism would be "self-less" in the worst sense of that term. A self-less human does not typically make a good friend. A person who does not maintain a self cannot share with another self or subsequently offer up any self as a sacrifice for another.

Living organisms, by definition, are cooperative units that seek a continued, abundant existence. Some of that cooperation and abundance may ultimately involve some competition and selfishness, but the latter are always subservient to the former. We might not see the origin of new species without competition, but we would not see life without cooperation.

Interestingly, all the great transitions of biological history involve a greater level of cooperativeness—the origin of cells, the formation of symbiotic relationships that then produced eukaryotic cells, the generation of multicellular organisms, the origin of sexual reproduction. At each level of life, we see cooperation. Living selves are composed of smaller components that must work together for life to arise and continue. Each cell consists of different structures that must successfully interact in order to maintain homeostasis. As living organisms have become more complex, the level of cooperation also increased. Multicellular organisms are composed of numerous specialized and highly interdependent cells. Members of sexually-reproducing species must, at a minimum, cooperate during fertilization. Species with vulnerable, slowly-developing young must cooperatively care for those offspring.

---

have predator/prey relationships or diseases. They might also have had abundant resources that could have initially limited competition.

27. Of course, like all created goods, life can be idolized: pursued for the wrong reasons or maintained at the expense of other goods. This concession does not mean that life no longer is essentially good, but that its living out can sometimes be unhealthy or even evil.

Conclusion

In this paper I have not intended to sound overly optimistic or naive. Life's history certainly is littered with death—and most of it has not been of the "peaceful" variety. Evolution and natural selection certainly entail brutal competition, and I don't want to in any way diminish the pain and suffering that shapes life even today. I simply want to suggest an alternative paradigm for understanding natural selection and life's long history on earth. The alternative I have suggested is a paradigm that fits well with a vision of a life-giving God of grace and the general theory of evolution.

9

On Giving Intelligent Design Theorists What They Say They Want

W. Christopher Stewart

Since the early 1990s, the debate about the meaning and significance of Intelligent Design Theory continues to widen. The debate is found in magazines, journals, books, conferences, blogs, listserves, dining rooms, hotel lobbies, bus queues, school board meetings, classrooms, courtrooms, television, and other public forums, and it draws more and more voices into the often heated and too frequently unenlightening conversation. Intelligent Design Theory is currently, for better or worse, a major focal point in what Steve Fuller in his recent book-length contribution to the scuffle aptly describes as "the signature intellectual struggle of the modern era," namely, the relationship between science and religion.[1] Even a casual observer of the imbroglio cannot help but notice that the issues involved here reach across multiple academic disciplines and are often exceedingly complicated, historically and conceptually. The stakes in the debate, though often overstated, are nonetheless significant enough (at least for *western* culture) to be worthy of the attention it continues to receive from some of our best

---

1. Steve Fuller, *Science vs Religion: Intelligent Design and the Problem of Evolution* (Malden, MA: Polity, 2007) 1.

minds and policy-makers, though not in every instance with equally constructive results.

At this stage of the game, so much has been spoken and written on the subject of Intelligent Design Theory and the Movement with which it is often associated, that one is tempted (and as you're about to discover one often gives in to the temptation) to repeat the famous lament commonly applied to U.S. Congressional debates. A. C. Grayling recently attributed the lament's origin to a Hungarian parliamentarian who rose to his feet in the midst of a lengthy National Assembly debate to point out that "everything has been said, but not everyone has said it." Very little of what I have to say here has not been said or at least intimated by someone else, though it is perhaps fair to say that not everyone has *heard* it, and some have presumably stopped *listening*.

Nevertheless, given the ways that the debate swirling around Intelligent Design has evolved (if you'll pardon the expression), it would be helpful at this juncture to reinforce the distinctions between three distinct agendas associated with Intelligent Design these days, and to attempt to clarify the relationships between them. That more and more speakers and authors are separating these agendas and beginning to apply criteria appropriate to each agenda individually seems to me to be a development worth encouraging. To begin, I want to *distinguish* between these three agendas, *summarize* what ID theorists say they want with respect to each of them, and say a bit about whether and how to give it to them. With respect to the latter, I want to focus a little more closely on one of these agendas and consider whether with respect to that agenda ID theorists *should* want what they say they want. I will indicate why I suspect they already have (in principle at least, if not in fact) everything they should want, or at least everything worth having. I'll suggest why I think it is unreasonable (and unscientific) to deny Intelligent Design theorists the part of what they say they want that they are perfectly entitled to want. I'll also comment on the nature of some of the *connections* between the three distinct agendas currently associated with Intelligent Design. I close with a few remarks locating (in broad strokes) the Wesleyan tradition with respect to each of these agendas, comparing its aims and methods in each case (broadly construed, and with some specific references to its founder) with those of ID theorists.

What Intelligent Design Theorists Say They Want

First, a few caveats. In talking about "what Intelligent Design theorists say they want," I realize (as you should also) that I'm not always referring to the same people. Intelligent Design is, like the Catholic Church, New York City, the two major American political parties, and other complex social phenomena, *a big tent*. Not all of the people eager to associate themselves with it are in complete agreement with everything everyone else is saying or doing. Nor is it appropriate to describe everyone associated with Intelligent Design as some sort of *theorist*. It's not even the case that all friends of ID are participating in each of the three principal agendas associated with Intelligent Design at the present time. (In fact, it may be that there is only *one* person who is doing so, but even that could presumably be debated.)

The three distinct agendas associated with Intelligent Design at the present moment have to do with science, apologetics, and the reform of Western society. By "science" I simply mean the social and collaborative efforts of hundreds of thousands of people around the world to understand, predict the future course of, and sometimes control the natural world. Efforts to do this involve collecting data about natural processes, theorizing about them, and then collecting more data or performing experiments the results of which are subsequently sifted and used to extend, confirm, refine, and sometimes falsify (or at least discredit) our theories about those processes (ourselves included). In this context, ID represents itself as a "constructive scientific project" that aspires to produce empirically adequate and intellectually satisfying scientific theories. Beyond this, ID theorists anticipate a major conceptual revolution in science as design theory expands its reach from biology and cosmology to encompass and transform the rest of the sciences, displacing (methodological) naturalism with design theory as "the dominant perspective in science."[2] It is "high time," writes Kenneth Poppe in his book, *Reclaiming Science from Darwinism* (2006), "that science make a clean break with natural evolution."[3]

---

2. Here I am quoting from the so-called "Wedge" document." This document is posted on a number of websites, including the website of The Center for Science & Culture, where you can find "the exact original document in question" as well as the Discovery Institute's response to charges regarding the "Wedge" document: "The 'Wedge Document': 'So What?'" (www.discovery.org/a/2101).

3. Kenneth Poppe, *Reclaiming Science From Darwinism* (Eugene, OR: Harvest, 2006) 183.

By "apologetics" I mean any attempt to influence via reasoning (rather than force) the choices people make between specific articulations of alternative and competing worldviews. In the West, there are principally two worldview traditions that compete for our allegiance. Both have been around for a long time, and there are no indications that either is going to fade from the scene any time soon. These two worldview traditions are theism and naturalism.[4]

In the context of apologetics, ID theorists want a defeater for naturalism. By "defeater," I don't just mean a black-eye or a bump on the head but a knockout punch. ID theorists are enthused by the discovery of what appear to be (and ID theorists claim to be in fact) natural phenomena that defy explanation entirely in terms of natural laws (or "nomic regularities") working on material bodies. The usual suspects here are that the universe appears to be "fine-tuned" to support life (at least as we know it), and the existence of biological structures whose complexity is *"specified"* or *demonstrably "irreducible"* to or *not explainable in terms of* natural causes (in this case the neo-Darwinian triumvirate of biological reproduction, random genetic mutation, and natural selection), at least in the absence of intelligent design. By using science to support belief in an intelligent Creator and undercut atheistic materialism, ID theorists see themselves as turning the tables on naturalism. "Naturalism" is an ideology that ID advocates regard as having received a lot of undeserved credibility over the past several decades from what they consider bad science (chiefly Neo-Darwinian evolutionary theory), which bad science in turn draws life-support more from "dogmatic philosophy" than "the weight of evidence." ID theorists are fond of characterizing evolution as itself a religion that requires more faith to believe than God creating.

Third, by the reform of Western society, I mean the "cultural renaissance"[5] ID advocates anticipate once modern Western society is fully released from the shackles of naturalism. Even after the defeat of

---

4. I refer to worldview "traditions" because, as most readers will be aware, there is more than one way to express each of these points of view. Theism, for example, includes Islamic and Jewish perspectives as well as Christian ones. I ignore pantheism here, not because it is unimportant or not worth considering, but simply because it does not exert much of an attractive force on most Westerners, at least not in comparison with theism and naturalism.

5. William A. Dembski, *The Design Revolution* (Downers Grove, IL: InterVarsity, 2004) 307.

naturalism, or as ID theorists and others sometimes call it, "scientific materialism," there are still its destructive moral, cultural, and political legacies. Here I refer to the sweeping socio-political (and scientific) agenda laid out in, among other places, the notorious "Wedge document." In this context, Intelligent Design again bears a slight resemblance (albeit in reverse) to some of the more radical strains of socialism that sprang up in the first half of the nineteenth century, many of which virulently attacked religion as at best a flight of wishful thinking and at worst an elaborate and deceptive conspiracy or "opiate" used to oppress the masses. Intelligent Design, of course, sees atheistic naturalism as the modern oppressor, no longer associated merely with the radical fringe of Western society, but dominating if not completely controlling its major institutions (not unlike the way religion, specifically Christianity, dominated them in nineteenth century Europe), from science and the media to education and government. Given this state of affairs, some of its advocates see ID as a tool to renew and invigorate Western culture, and perhaps at the same time help prevent non-Western cultures eager to appropriate the benefits of Western science and technology (if not Western values) from repeating our mistakes vis-à-vis naturalism.

William Dembski argues in *The Design Revolution* (2004) that challenging what Phillip Johnson calls "the modernist monopoly on science" is, in effect, to drive a wedge between "science as an empirical enterprise that goes where the evidence leads" and "science as applied materialist philosophy that maintains its materialism regardless of the evidence."[6] Although he now thinks that the wedge metaphor has outlived its utility, and with the appearance of books such as Barbara Forrest and Paul Gross's *Creationism's Trojan Horse: The Wedge of Intelligent Design* (2004)[7] has even become a liability, Dembski nonetheless explains the promise of Intelligent Design in these terms: "Pounding the wedge at that point of weakness is supposed to invigorate science, renew culture, and liberate society from the miasma of materialism and naturalism."[8]

---

6. Ibid.

7. Barbara Forrest and Paul Gross, *Creationism's Trojan Horse: The Wedge of Intelligent Design* (Oxford: Oxford University Press, 2004).

8. Dembski, *Design Revolution*, 307.

On Giving Intelligent Design Theorists What They Say They Want

Let us start with Intelligent Design's goal of reforming and reinvigorating Western society and culture, about which I don't actually have a lot to say. It is this aspect of ID's three-fold agenda that foes of Intelligent Design seem to consider the most alarming, even dangerous. The reference to a Trojan Horse in the title of Forrest and Gross's book pretty much says it all. There are some significant differences between Intelligent Design as it is being advanced by the likes of Michael Behe, William Dembski, and others, ID in all its forms is widely perceived to be religiously motivated through and through. Its opponents take this to be sufficient reason to exclude it from the public sphere.

A lot could be said here, but it is not my main concern in this essay. I will say, however, that although there's no denying that Intelligent Design theory is powerfully appealing to many self-identified religious fundamentalists and political conservatives, that by itself is insufficient reason to dismiss ID as a theoretical orientation for the sciences. ID theorists are as entitled as anyone to attempt to reform Western society and culture, by any legally and ethically permissible means available to them. Along the same lines, the non-theist Steve Fuller sees the ACLU's efforts to drive a wedge between the teaching of science and theology in the 1920s as "morally equivalent" to (and far more successful than) the Discovery Institute's efforts thus far to drive a wedge between the teaching of science and what Fuller describes as "the anti-theology prejudice euphemistically called 'methodological naturalism.'"[9]

Dembski suggests in *The Design Revolution* that in order for Intelligent Design to succeed as "a cultural and political enterprise," it must also succeed as "a scientific enterprise." The latter is, he thinks, logically if not temporally prior to the former.[10] This connection requires closer consideration than I have time for here, but it seems to me that the legitimacy or effectiveness of the Intelligent Design Movement's efforts to deploy the theistic worldview to address what it takes to be a wide range of social and political evils does not depend in any way on the success of Intelligent Design as a scientific project. Indeed, it seems to me that Christian theists have been engaged in similar efforts to improve human

---

9. Fuller, *Science vs Religion*, 123–24.
10. Dembski, *Design Revolution*, 308–9.

society for centuries without any evident reinforcement from "theistic science." But perhaps I am not quite understanding Dembski's point.

I want to turn next to a few considerations in connection with ID's efforts in the context of apologetics, or the choice between competing worldviews. Design or "teleological" arguments for the existence of God have been around for a long time. One of the more interesting claims associated with Intelligent Design theory in its most recent manifestation is associated with the work of William Dembski. In a series of books (and numerous articles) beginning with *The Design Inference* in 1998,[11] Dembski has developed what he calls an "explanatory filter" capable (he thinks) of detecting the presence of a kind of complexity ("specified complexity") that cannot be explained either by chance or by laws working on antecedent conditions. By default, therefore, we are compelled to attribute the complex event or state of affairs in question to design. Besides the intricacies of his argument (for those with an appetite for detail), what's novel and exciting (if not entirely convincing to everyone) about what Dembski is up to here is the case he is making for the *empirical detectability* of intelligent design.

Design inferences of this sort have always been loosely based on experience. What's so impressive about Dembski's formulation is both its precision and the alleged force of the design inference. ID's ability to deliver a knockout punch to naturalism depends on our ability to detect design empirically in something like the way Dembski describes, namely, as the only possible (or at least only plausible) explanation of the facts, which while just shy of "logical demonstration," nonetheless achieves a "statistical justification so compelling as to demand assent" from rational individuals.[12] Students of the history of the philosophy of science will recognize this as an ideal that goes all the way back to Aristotle, for whom science is "demonstrative" in the sense of delivering us "proofs" of what must be so and cannot be otherwise with respect to the natural world. Nowadays, any scientific claim purporting to describe what must be so and cannot possibly (or even plausibly) be otherwise runs counter on the face of it to the widespread conviction that for any given body of observational data there will always be an

---

11. William A. Dembski, *The Design Inference: Eliminating Chance through Small Probabilities* (Cambridge: Cambridge University Press, 1998).

12. Dembski, *Intelligent Design: The Bridge Between Science & Theology* (Downers Grove, IL: InterVarsity, 1999) 149.

indefinite number of theories or hypotheses capable of explaining the data (though perhaps only a handful of live ones). We are never in a position to rule out empirically the very possibility of an alternative explanation of any given event or state of affairs. This predicament is rooted in the "underdetermination of theory by data" and "fallibilism" so familiar to post-positivistic philosophy of science.

But apart from swimming upstream against the current of contemporary philosophy of science, Dembski's design inference faces other problems that *limit* without *completely undermining* its utility in the struggle to defeat naturalism as a worldview. As Loren Haarsma has pointed out in the American Scientific Affiliation journal, when scientists are faced with some puzzling event, they ultimately arrive at one of three conclusions: either the event is fully explainable, partially explainable, or unexplainable via known natural mechanisms. Intelligent Design theorists (like Dembski) claim to be in a position to rule out the possibility that an as-yet unknown natural cause is responsible for the event. Haarsma points out that although Intelligent Design advocates are *doing science* when they try to show that some phenomenon is unexplainable in the above sense (even on a narrow definition of science as tightly focused on (a) identifying the most effective methods for learning about nature and (b) figuring out what we learn about nature when we apply them), it is nonetheless flawed as a *scientific* conclusion based on *empirical* considerations. Ruling out the possibility that there exists an as-yet unknown natural law responsible for the event is at least partially based on considerations that are (as Haarsma notes) "philosophical, historical, and religious" (that is to say, not strictly speaking "scientific").[13]

In another essay from the pages of the American Scientific Affiliation's journal, Howard Van Till makes the even stronger point that Intelligent Design's success as a naturalism defeater is "impossible to achieve by ID's scientific strategy." It is impossible largely due to the fact that in the case of the alleged "specified complexity" of the bacterial flagellum, "the probability that the *E. coli* bacterium could have become equipped with a flagellum by the joint effect of *all* natural causes" (including both known and unknown causes) "cannot be computed by anyone [. . .] who has less than a complete knowledge of the universe's formational

---

13. Loren Haarsma, "Is Intelligent Design 'Scientific'?" *Perspectives on Science and Christian Faith* 59 (2007) 56–57.

economy,"[14] which pretty much rules out everyone, with the possible exception of God.[15]

Van Till concedes, of course, that in the face of a biotic system or other state of affairs that is unexplainable via known natural mechanisms, it is *logically permissible* to insist that its appearance requires at least one instance of non-natural action. But mere logical permissibility is hardly what is needed to defeat naturalism.[16] In addition, Michael Murray argues that even when we are confronted with a case in which the earmarks of intelligent design are clear (such as, in Murray's example, winning five straight hands of poker with a hand of four aces dealt from a freshly opened pack of preshuffled cards), it is not possible *by empirical means* to distinguish between the two ways in which intelligent design might have secured this result: intervention and deck-stacking. With respect to the natural world, Murray is also skeptical of our ability to decide between intervention and deck-staking by *philosophical* means, citing the arguments of Christian philosophers on both sides of this debate. The obvious point is that if we only have access to the *outcome* of the poker games, we're not in a position to determine whether the cheating involved intervention (like an ace up the sleeve) or somehow stacking the deck ahead of time. In the latter case, moreover, the fact that none of the rules of poker were violated from the start of the game (which Murray dubs "methodological rule-following") would not undercut what he calls "the cheating inference." Likewise, given that we are without any way to rule out by empirical means the possibility of intelligent design via deck-stacking, contrary to the opinion of ID advocates such as Behe and Johnson that (as Behe

---

14. By which phrase he means the sum total of "all of the physical resources, all of the formational capabilities, and all of the structural and functional potentialities needed for the natural formation of every kind of structure, system, and organism that has appeared in the universe's formational history."

15. Howard J. Van Till, "Is the ID Movement Capable of Defeating Naturalism? A Response to Madden and Discher," *Perspectives on Science and the Christian Faith* 56 (2004) 294.

16. As a side note, this is very similar to the way Aquinas handled the alleged "demonstration" that the world is eternal. Aquinas both insisted that the eternity of the world had not in fact been demonstrated, by Aristotle or anyone else, and at the same time conceded that neither could it be "demonstrated" that the world was created. Both options were therefore live possibilities from a logical or strictly philosophical point of view, even if only one of them comported with revealed theology.

puts it) "if a biological structure can be explained in terms of natural laws, then we cannot conclude that it was designed,"¹⁷ design inferences can still be warranted even when "the designed outcomes can be [fully] explained by appeal to the regular operations of the laws of nature."¹⁸

The significance for Murray's point that success at explaining an event in terms of nomic regularities does not trump design explanations is that the apologetics agenda of Intelligent Design does not in fact depend (at least not entirely) on design being empirically detectable, let alone empirically demonstrable, even if ID's ability to deliver a knockout punch to naturalism does. There are, as Murray himself notes, "less bold" versions of Intelligent Design that do not purport to provide scientific explanations that compete with methodologically natural ones. These less bold versions nevertheless argue that the current scientific evidence *strongly suggests* that our ability to arrive at a *complete* explanation of natural phenomena is, in the final analysis, *likely* to demand that we take Intelligent Design seriously.¹⁹ Many (maybe most) ID theorists will probably find this more modest and highly qualified conclusion less than fully satisfying, but it nonetheless makes a helpful contribution to the aims of theistic (or at least deistic) apologetics. The

17. Michael J. Behe, *Darwin's Black Box: The Biochemical Challenge to Evolution* (New York: Free, 1996) 203.

18. Michael J. Murray, "Natural Providence (Or Design Trouble)," *Faith and Philosophy* 20 (2003) 316.

19. Robert O'Connor concludes a carefully argued essay challenging the novelty claims of contemporary ID theory on a similar note. He argues that whereas appeal to design is not *necessary* to account for the sort of very remarkable phenomena upon which inferences to intelligent design tend to be based in the literature (such as the famous bacterial flagellum), intelligent design nevertheless represents "a rationally warranted, philosophically viable interpretation" of such phenomena (not to mention the cosmos as a whole), and as such "an empirically informed, discriminating choice" for anyone seeking an explanation of information-rich systems "in terms of the intentional and transcendent choice of a personal agent." Like Van Till and Murray, O'Connor contends that we are not, nor can we ever be, in a position to establish conclusively by empirical means when we are confronted with a significant quantitative increase in "complex specified information" (CSI) within any given time interval. Nor are we able to demonstrate empirically that the quantity of information present in some phenomenon must ultimately have been introduced by a source "external to the natural system itself." However reasonable it might be to suppose that a given natural system "might not always have contained the level of CSI detectable at any given point," such a conjecture "takes one well beyond the limits of empirical inquiry." See O'Connor's "Old Wine in New Wineskins," in *God and Design: The Teleological Argument and Modern Science*, ed. Neil A. Manson (New York: Routledge, 2003) 66–87.

design inference may not be demonstrative, but it's pretty darn good, maybe even compelling.[20]

Even without Dembski's explanatory filter or Behe's "irreducible" complexity, it is fair to say that Intelligent Design remains an effective tool for natural theology or "contending for the faith," as Dembski puts it.[21] Rather than join the battle for inclusion of references to the direct and immediate activity of a divine agent in explanations of human experience at a point internal to the natural sciences, we should seek to do so on a different level. In the final analysis, the criteria of adequacy with respect to the choice of a worldview are much broader and less well-defined than any internal to either science or theology. And these critera encompass both what you might call intellectual adequacy on the one hand (a matter of such factors as explanatory power and logical consistency), and existential or practical adequacy on the other (a matter of satisfying the needs and aspirations of human persons).

Turning to Intelligent Design's scientific aspirations, I think it is fair to say that most of the debate about ID has focused on its claim to scientific legitimacy. Opponents of ID have deployed a number of strategies to deny ID scientific credentials, such as citing its alleged religious motivation, untestability, and unfalsifiability. ID theorists strenuously deny each of these allegations. What about falsifiablity? Is ID falsifiable? In *The Design Revolution*, Dembski rightly insists that although a scientific refutation of Intelligent Design would not necessarily undermine belief in intelligent design of the deck-stacking variety, ID is in principle as falsifiable as any other scientific standpoint:

> If complex biological systems like the bacterial flagellum could be explicitly shown to result from material mechanisms (like the Darwinian mechanism), it would not follow as a logical entailment that the intelligent design of life is false in the sense of being necessarily untrue. One could, for instance, argue that a designer had designed the laws of physics and chemistry so

---

20. Note the recent and celebrated "conversion" of the arch-atheist Antony Flew on the basis of the scientific evidence for intelligent design, though Flew seems to prefer the phrase "Aristotelean deism" to describe his present position vis-à-vis the existence of God. See Mark Oppenheimer, "The Turning of an Atheist," *The New York Times Magazine* (4 November 2007) 37–41.

21. Dembski, "The Task of Apologetics," in *Unapologetic Apologetics: Meeting the Challenges of Theological Studies*, eds. William A. Dembski and Jay Wesley Richards (Downers Grove, IL: InterVarsity, 2001) 31.

that life would emerge by means of the Darwinian mechanism. In that case intelligent design would not, strictly speaking, be falsified. Biologists, however, would rightly discard it as superfluous.[22]

With regard to the superfluity of Intelligent Design in the event that the cosmic designer turns out to be a cosmic deck-stacker, I want to say "not so fast."

In science, testability has to do with a given theory's ability to make contact with the natural world in very specific and rule-governed ways. "At the heart of testability," continues Dembski,

> is the idea that our scientific theories must make contact with and be sensitive to what's happening in nature. What's happening in nature must be able to affect our scientific theories not only in form and content but also in how much credence we attach to or withhold from them. For a theory to be immune to evidence from nature is a sure sign that we are not dealing with a scientific theory.[23]

Whether a theory is or can be made testable or not isn't something to be decided *a priori* or overnight. It is a pragmatic question that often takes quite a bit of time to sort out.

Some of the *a priori* claims about ID's alleged untestability are buttressed by the *a posteriori* observation that ID has yet to produce a single, testable prediction in any scientific context in which it has been deployed. Here I think we need to clarify what sort of role Intelligent Design theory is perfectly entitled to play in science, and just what sort of theory it is or can become. Although once again a lot could be said here, I want to point in a direction that does not seem to me to be getting quite the attention it deserves. In a pair of essays on whether or not worldviews have in fact and should be allowed to shape science, Stephen Wykstra makes a number of helpful distinctions between various levels of scientific change and different sorts of scientific theories, which do not each possess the same degree of "empirical import" or cash value. Just below the level of worldviews in Wykstra's hierarchy are a variety of "guiding commitments" of an ontological, methodological, or axiological sort. These commitments are very general claims about

---

22. Dembski, *Design Revolution*, 281.
23. Ibid., 280.

the world that are broad enough to be shared by programs in different branches of science, yet not specific enough to be empirically testable. They are also not static, but arrived at and refined via trial-and-error, generally over long periods of time. They are also "metascientific" or "extra-empirical" in the sense that they themselves are not explanatory hypotheses per se, from which we can deduce specific *empirical* consequences, but rather quite general claims about the world that guide scientists in the process of formulating the explanatory hypotheses that we typically have in mind when we use the word "theory."[24]

Below the level of guiding commitments, then, are the *theories* with which science "achieves its distinctive aims of getting insight into the world." At this level, Wykstra further distinguishes between "core theories" and more specific "determinate theories." A core theory is a comparatively vague basic idea, such as "the wave theory of light," or "the theory of evolution," or "the kinetic theory of heat." It is only when a core theory is rendered more specific by being conjoined with a network of subsidiary "specifying claims" that it becomes sufficiently "determinate" to gain "empirical import" and thereby become empirically testable. Moreover, core theories can be "fleshed out" by different scientists into distinct and competing determinate theories, at which level we adjudicate between these rivals by deducing empirical consequences that can either be satisfied or disappointed by the course of experience (either via the collection of more data or the performance of experiments).[25]

I suggest (without really developing or illustrating the suggestion in much detail) that Intelligent Design is or can be at best a "core theory" and at worst a "guiding commitment" in science. This may or may not be less than what ID theorists really want, but it seems to me to be all that they should want, and all they really need (at least with respect to their scientific aspirations). There *are* no, and never *have been* any, good scientific reasons to deny them this role, which amounts to less that of an explanatory hypothesis per se than an explanatory hypothesis generator. That ID has in fact played such a role in the history of modern

---

24. Stephen J. Wykstra, "Have Worldviews Shaped Science? A Reply to Brooke," in *Facets of Faith and Science. Volume I: Historiography and Modes of Interaction*, ed. J. M. van der Meer (Landham, MD: The Pascal Centre for Advanced Studies in Faith and Science/University Press of America, 1996) 91–111.

25. Ibid., 98–99.

science is hard to dispute—some would say impossible to dispute (citing examples from the work of scientists like Newton, Faraday, and Mendel). As Del Ratzsch and others point out, a design outlook at the extra-empirical guiding commitment level might well lead one to exploit analogies to agent products (such as machines and art) as guides to theorizing. A design outlook might also "generate expectations of finding deeper patterns underlying cases of apparent randomness," or promote a willingness to allow "reductionist philosophical dictates to be challengeable in suitable empirical situations, should suitable empirical situations ever arise," and thus advance the aims of science more effectively than an outlook resigned to a view of nature as entirely devoid of thought and mind.[26]

Critics of Intelligent Design might well concede all of this and still ask, "Where's the beef? Where are the empirically testable determinate theories spawned by ID? When will ID cease to be a promissorial outline of a scientific research program and begin to produce some novel empirical results?"[27] At this point, ID advocates and sympathizers, such as sociologist of science Steve Fuller, urge patience.[28] Fuller reminds us

---

26. Del Ratzsch, *Nature, Design and Science* (Albany: State University of New York, 2001) 142.

27. Philip Kitcher poses this particular question ("Where's the Beef?") as a way of highlighting what he sees as the non-existent explanatory advantages of direct appeals to interventionist ("hands-on Creator") models of ID (which he dubs "neo-creo") with respect to the extant empirical data in the biological and earth sciences. Indeed, he is keen to point out the explanatory disadvantages of interventionism. While he is cognizant of the existence of deck-stacking models of ID (on which the Creator is imagined to "set things up and let them unfold by natural processes"), he does not consider the prospect that a design stance might have heuristic pay-offs as a guiding commitment or core theory over and against alternative standpoints from which to generate testable (non-interventionist) determinate theories that could improve our explanatory grip on the relevant phenomena. As a guiding commitment or core theory, the explanatory power of ID would be indirect at best. Direct explanatory appeals would be made (as in prior examples of religious worldviews shaping scientific theorizing) to determinate theories inspired by the design standpoint, themselves devoid of direct interventionist references or any other obvious "theological resonances." See Kitcher's "Born-Again Creationism," in *Intelligent Design Creationism and Its Critics: Philosophical, Theological, and Scientific Perspectives*, ed. Robert T. Pennock (Cambridge: The MIT Press, 2001) 257–87, esp. 281–87.

28. Fuller, whom I mentioned earlier, actually testified as an expert witness on behalf of the defense in *Kitzmiller v. Dover Area School District* in the fall of 2005. In both his expert witness statement and his testimony on the stand, he emphasized that the heuristic potential of Intelligent Design in what philosophers of science refer to as

that at the beginning of the twentieth century, fifty years after *Origin* and a quarter-century before the re-discovery of Mendelian genetics, the main supporters of Darwinism were located outside the universities and even outside the lab-based biological sciences. Biologists struggled to identify a plausible underlying causal mechanism responsible for "the striking patterns of common descent and differential evolution" that Darwin had described, at which time the theory was being kept in the public eye in part by what Fuller refers to as "congenial ideological currents," among them "eugenics and scientific racism."[29]

Refusal to support (or in some circles to forbid scientists from even mentioning without condemnation) research that departs from the mainstream of scientific orthodoxy at any given moment can be bad for what Charles Sanders Peirce dubbed "the economy of science." The central problem of the economy of science is "how with a given expenditure of money, time, and energy, to obtain the most valuable addition to our knowledge."[30] Whereas, in many cases, work that diverges sufficiently from the settled opinions of "the great body of scientific men" (not to mention women) ought to be, and indeed generally is, regarded with suspicion and tends "of itself to argue incompetence,"[31] Peirce also recognized the potential economic advantages[32] (in select cases) of encouraging small groups of researchers to explore paths that deviate from more familiar lines of scientific investigation. Although it does not appear to most detached observers that Intelligent Design Theory has developed sufficiently to merit significant attention as an alternative scientific research program in any field of science, complete with discrete, distinctive, and empirically testable implications (and some doubt that it will *ever* do so), there is little reason at this stage to rule out the possibility that it might do so on a limited scale with respect to particular

---

"the context of discovery," together with ID's unflinching commitment to the justification of its knowledge claims in terms of laboratory experiments and probability theory without references to divine agency, make ID unquestionably scientific.

29. Fuller, *Science vs Religion*, 122–23.

30. C. S. Peirce, *Writings of Charles Sanders Peirce: A Chronological Edition*, Vol. 4., eds. Max Fisch et. al. (Bloomington: Indiana University Press, 1989) 72.

31. C. S. Peirce, *Collected Papers of Charles Sanders Peirce*, Vol. 1, eds. Charles Hartshorne and Paul Weiss (Cambridge, MA: Belknap, 1931) paragraph 32.

32. By "economic advantages," Peirce means the likelihood of producing the most rapid advancement of science at the least cost over the long run.

scientific problems at some point in the future. Given that there is reason to doubt that Intelligent Design Theory will ever enter into science as anything more than a core theory or guiding commitment, as distinct from an empirically falsifiable explanatory hypothesis about some specific natural phenomenon, however, it is not clear in what sense ID *per se* could ever become a specific target of research funding.

ID's heuristic potential (in the context of science) does not depend in any way on our ability to produce good, non-question-begging empirical evidence for intelligent design. In the context of discovery, it is permissible to *assume* a design outlook and approach the business of formulating testable determinate theories from that perspective. Only its value as a naturalism defeater (in the context of apologetics) requires that intelligent design be empirically detectable. Michael Murray characterizes the suggestion that ID "might provide a useful background assumption when we are theorizing" as possibly a "last ditch" effort to avoid the conclusion that ID is "helpful natural theology but useless science."[33] He admits to difficulty knowing just what to make of this suggestion *a priori*. I am saying that it is *impossible* to make *anything* of this suggestion *a priori*, and that the proof, as the saying goes, is in the pudding. Now and at every point in the past, the same goes for any of the guiding assumptions that have been operative in the history of our efforts to comprehend the natural world.

Intelligent Design and the Wesleyan Tradition

In the final section of this essay, I'd like to offer a few remarks that I hope will contribute in some small, preliminary way to the conversation Randy Maddox and others have initiated about how the characteristic convictions and concerns of the Wesleyan tradition (broadly understood to include the religious movement associated with its eponymous founder and the theological tradition that continues to inform it) might inform Christian engagement with the natural sciences.[34] Specifically, I will comment briefly on the Wesleyan theological tradition's connections to each of the three broad agendas associated with Intelligent

---

33. Murray, "Natural Providence," 321.

34. See, for example, chapter 1 above by Randy L. Maddox, "John Wesley's Precedent for Theological Engagement with the Natural Sciences."

Design, comparing its aims and methods in each case with those typically associated with ID.

I begin with ID's goal of reforming and reinvigorating Western society and culture. Although the Wesleyan tradition identifies strongly with ID's aims in this respect, it differs quite sharply (by and large) with respect to the means employed to achieve these aims. Following the example of its founder, the Wesleyan tradition at its best has maintained a broad and deep commitment to social justice and the reform of society. In his life and ministry, John Wesley (1703–1791) modeled close relationships between evangelical conversion, personal piety and social action. He was among the first prominent churchmen to take a public stand against slavery, and he applied his considerable organizational skills to the amelioration of a wide range of other social evils. His interest in literacy and education expressed itself tangibly in his efforts to raise standards of learning for clergy as well as laity, and he arranged for the publication and sale of affordable books on a many different topics (including natural philosophy). Wesley was also zealous in his efforts on behalf of the "working poor," insisting on the responsibility of Christians to provide material relief to the impoverished in the form of food or clothing as needed, meaningful work, and assistance to debtors thrown into prison. Moreover, Wesley's interest in medicine (including his enthusiasm for the medical uses of electricity[35]) reflected his appreciation for the practical application of early modern science to the improvement of the human condition.

For Wesley and his followers, however, the pursuit of social transformation across a wide front, although religiously motivated, is neither as polemical nor as politicized as that typically associated with the Intelligent Design Movement. The emphasis in the Wesleyan tradition has always been on practical theology and personal piety rather than theological systems or rational apologetics, expressing itself directly in entrepeneurial social action unmediated (though not necessarily so) by political entanglements. By contrast, Intelligent Design theorists tend to draw close connections between intellectual conversion (from one or another variety of naturalism to theism) together with the control of existing social institutions and the reform of society. As I noted earlier, ID theorists tend to view social evils as ultimately rooted in Western

---

35. John Wesley, *Primitive Physick: Or, An Easy and Natural Method of Curing Most Diseases* (London: J. Palmar, 1751).

society's enslavement to a naturalistic worldview, rather than (in the case of Wesley) spiritual rebellion from God on a personal level. ID's strategy, accordingly, is to destroy the epistemic credentials of naturalism as a worldview before dealing with "its destructive moral, cultural and political legacies" (though, as I pointed out, Dembski insists that this is a logical if not temporal ordering of priorities). By contrast, Wesley begins with individual spiritual transformation via reception of the gospel in repentance and faith and proceeds from there to the gradual transformation of the understanding, guided by both the rejuvenated natural and the newly awakened spiritual senses. The drive to improve society, although aided and abetted by the fruits of understanding (as in the case of Wesley's interest in applied science, especially in the context of medicine), flows from spiritual rebirth rather than cognitive realignment.

The legitimacy and success of our collective efforts to improve society does not depend, as ID theorists often suggest, on the success of any attendant intellectual or scientific enterprise. And this leads us back to ID's agenda in the context of apologetics, which boils down to its efforts to deliver a knockout punch to atheistic naturalism. ID's deployment of science as a weapon against naturalism contrasts sharply with Wesley's approach to the relevance of the sciences for theology and the choice between competing worldviews. That Wesley placed a high value on the Christian being conversant with the deliverances of the sciences is nowhere more clearly manifest than in his *Survey of the Wisdom of God and Creation, Or a Compendium of Natural Philosophy*. First published in 1763, this popular summary of the sciences of his day went through several editions, ending with the final (posthumous) revision of 1842.

One of the more interesting features of Wesley's *Survey* (for my purposes) is the fact that he edited out the references to atheism contained in his sources. For example, as Maddox has noted, one of Wesley's sources was William Derham's *Astro-Theology*, which is sprinkled with passages such as the following:

> That the observations of the Psalmist is agreeable to experience, is manifest from the deductions which all nations have made from God's works, particularly from those of the heavens; namely, that there is a God; and that such as have pretended to

atheism and have deduced God's works from chance, etc., are singular and monstrous in their opinions.[36]

Later Derham wonders whether "there by any found among rational beings so stupid, so vile, so infatuated with their vices as to deny these works [in this case the sun and moon] to be God's and ascribe them to a *necessity of nature*, or indeed a mere *nothing*, namely *chance*!"[37] Neither of these passages made it into Wesley's *Survey*. Unlike Derham, after a discussion of the ratios of the distances between the planets (to which Johannes Kepler had attached great significance in his 1596 *Mysterium Cosmographicum*), rather than asking whether we can "without great violence to reason, imagine this to be any other than the work of God?" Wesley omits this question and simply interprets these proportions as evidence of God's concern for order and life.[38] Likewise, instead of seeing in the annual motions of the planets a "clear manifestation of the [existence of the] great Creator," Wesley sees instead a "clear manifestation of the Creator's wisdom."[39]

Recent studies of the context of Wesley's *Survey* stress the fact that for much of the eighteenth century "natural philosophy" was suffused with theological overtones. Its most fundamental purpose was to exhibit the power, wisdom, and goodness of God as manifested in God's creation in the service of a direct assault on the arguments of atheists. Although Wesley's *Survey* heartily embraces the former, it is unusual for its day in its reluctance to leverage these efforts to mount a straightforward refutation of atheism.[40] To do so would have been

36. William Derham, *Astro-Theology; or, A Demonstration of the Being and Attributes of God, from a Survey of the Heavens* (London: William Innys, 1715) 2–3.

37. Ibid., 196–97 (emphasis in the original).

38. The relevant passages here are *Astro-Theology*, 59 and *Survey*, 3:308.

39. In this case, the relevant passages are *Astro-Theology*, 84 and *Survey*: 3:310. For the details of each of these illustrations I am indebted to Maddox.

40. Laura Bartels Felleman, "John Wesley's *Survey of the Wisdom of God in Creation*: A Methodological Inquiry," *Perspectives on Science and the Christian Faith* 58 (March 2006) 68–73. Felleman's essay provides a helpful summary of the contextual studies to which I allude, in particular: Andrew Cunningham and Perry Williams, "De-Centering the 'Big Picture': *The Origins of Modern Science* and the Modern Origins of Science," *British Journal for the History of Science* 2 (1993) 407–32; Cunningham, "Getting the Game Right: Some Plain Words on the Identity and Invention of Science," *Studies in the History and Philosophy of Science* 19 (1988) 365–89; and Cunningham, "How the *Principia* Got Its Name; or, Taking Natural Philosophy Seriously," *History of Science* 29 (1991) 377–92.

inconsistent with Wesley's religious epistemology, according to which drawing inferences about God from the works of God may well draw a person's mind upward to God, but cannot compel the atheist due to the fact that prior to salvation the atheist's spiritual senses are closed, making it impossible for the atheist accurately to discern God's nature, the knowledge of which arises via personal acquaintance rather than by logical inference.[41]

Wesley's rhetorical strategy contrasts sharply with that of Intelligent Design theorists. Wesley was careful not to overestimate the epistemic force of theistic arguments drawn from our experience of the natural world. Indeed, the whole tone of his *Survey* was to illuminate *who* God is rather than to establish *that* God is. By contrast, Intelligent Design theory inverts these priorities. According to Dembski, as "a robust program of scientific research" (rather than an "underdeveloped philosophical intuition"), intelligent design is "more powerful" than natural theology in the force of its conclusions in that it points to natural phenomena "that can be adequately explained *only* by recourse to intelligent causes" (italics added), and at the same time "more modest" in that it is "under no obligation to speculate about the nature, moral character or purposes of any designing intelligence it happens to infer" (which he suggests is a matter best left to theologians).[42] As such, ID has much more in common with the strident and often dismissive (of the atheist's stubborn resistance to logic and empirical evidence) evidentialist apologetics from which Wesley shies away in the *Survey*, and which is more typical of the natural theology of his time. Wesley's aims in his *Survey* rather more reflect the tone of pre-modern natural theology, which sought rather to strengthen and refine religious faith rather than compel assent from non-believers.[43]

Deism was the prevailing response of religiously-inclined intellectuals to the self-contained, Newtonian clockwork universe during the

---

41. I owe this point about Wesley's rhetorical strategy vis-à-vis atheism to Felleman, who pointed it out to me in correspondence. She discusses the point in greater detail in a (thus far) unpublished section of "The Evidence of Things Not Seen: John Wesley's Use of Natural Philosophy" (PhD dissertation, Drew University, 2004).

42. Dembski, *Intelligent Design: The Bridge Between Science & Theology*, 107.

43. I owe this point to Maddox, who also cites in this regard Nicholas Woltersorff's "The Migration of Theistic Arguments: From Natural Theology to Evidentialist Apologetics," in *Rationality, Religious Belief, and Moral Commitment*, ed. R. Audi & W. Wainwright (Ithaca, NY: Cornell University Press, 1986) 38–81.

century that produced John Wesley. According to deism, God ceased to have any further involvement with after creating it. God ceased to be affected in any way either by the ongoing course of nature or human affairs generally. It was against deism rather than atheism that Wesley directed most of his arguments. Against the deists, Wesley insisted that God is both present and active in the universe, not merely to maintain it in existence and (as Newton famously suggested) intervene from time to time to restore lost momentum or preserve the order of the planets, but down to the lowliest detail, there being nothing "so small or insignificant in the sight of man, as not to be an object of the care and providence of God."[44]

Wesley's approach to the relevance of the natural sciences for theology is closer to what John Polkinghorne calls "the new natural theology," which is modest about both its relationship to science (abandoning all attempts to give theological answers to scientific questions) and also about its relationship to the total body of theological opinion (at best culminating in "a rather etiolated concept of God, such as the Architect of the Universe or the Great Mathematician").[45] The new natural theology forswears all attempts to "prove" God's existence on pain of irrationality. The truth about theism is not that it is "logically inevitable" but rather that "it gives us the deepest and most satisfying *insight* into the way the world is."[46]

Finally, with respect to ID's scientific aspirations, I'm not sure there is anything distinctively Wesleyan in my suggestions thus far, following Wykstra and Ratzsch, about the proper way to think about the relationship between theology or worldviews and science. Wykstra and Ratzsch themselves quite clearly see what they are doing as developing a "pluralist" and "integrationsist" conception of science rooted in the work of the Reformed theologian and politician Abraham Kuyper. They resist the "segregationist" impulses of people who sympathize with what John Hedley Brooke calls "that most familiar stance among modern scientists" that "in the practice of science and in the construction of scientific knowledge," religious outlooks "should be kept at arm's length

---

44. John Wesley, quoted in John C. English, "John Wesley and Isaac Newton's 'System of the World'" *Proceedings of the Wesley Historical Society* 48 (1991) 75.

45. John Polkinghorne, "Where is Natural Theology Today?" *Science and Christian Belief* 18 (2006) 171–72.

46. Ibid., 171.

from scientific theorizing."⁴⁷ On the supposition that all truth is God's truth, there is no reason to think that Wesleyans (and everyone else, for that matter) shouldn't simply help themselves to their insights.

Perhaps there is reason to think, however, that those who identify more closely with the Wesleyan tradition might well contribute something distinctive to these discussions. For example, although he himself inclines to the Leibnizian deck-stacking model of design, Murray appropriately concedes that "universe creation and providential superintending of universes are tricky businesses," and suggests that open theists might have more reasons than others to suspect that "perhaps no set of natural entities and powers could [or *would*], through deck-stacking, bring off everything God intended for his creation to accomplish."⁴⁸

Deck-stackers and their critics (chiefly ID theorists) agree *that* life and the universe were designed by an intelligence, but disagree about *how* the design of life and the universe was (or is) being accomplished. At issue here is how best to conceive of God's action in the world in relation to the picture of the inner workings of the cosmos emerging from the natural sciences at any given point in time. This is a particularly interesting and vexed question, and the object of some of the most fascinating and creative thinking over the past couple of decades along the interface between theology and science. Deck-stackers prefer to think of the design of nature as front-loaded at the beginning of the universe in such a way that it is not necessary to suppose that anything be added subsequently from outside the system of nature to explain how the universe came to be the way it is (after its inception) or predict the way it's likely to go in the future. Dembski dismisses front-loading as tantamount to deism. He (rightly) criticizes the deistic approach to divine action as a philosophically and theologically "unsatisfactory halfway house between theism [...] and naturalism."⁴⁹

As an alternative to front-loaded design, Dembski suggests what he calls "interactive design," according to which design is introduced

---

47. John Hedley Brooke, "Religious Belief and the Natural Sciences: Mapping the Historical Landscape," in *Facets of Faith and Science. Volume I: Historiography and Modes of Interaction*, ed. J. M. van der Meer (Lanham, MD: The Pascal Centre for Advanced Studies in Faith and Science/University Press of America, 1996) 1.

48. Murray, "Natural Providence," 324.

49. Dembski, *No Free Lunch: Why Specified Complexity Cannot Be Purchased Without Intelligence* (Lanham, MD: Rowman & Littlefield, 2002) 344.

"by imparting information over the course of natural history."[50] According to Dembski, the "bare possibility" of front-loaded design is not enough to recommend it over and against interactive design, except in the absence of "empirical grounds" supporting the latter. Of course, such grounds to warrant interactive design are precisely what Intelligent Design theorists claim to possess—a claim hotly disputed by critics. But even without an empirical means to establish conclusively *that* information has been imparted into the world subsequent to its origin (even if we remain in the dark about *how* "unembodied designers" imparted the information), Dembski can find no reason to suppose that the design of the universe must be front-loaded. But this is a much stronger claim than deck-stackers typically make. It's not that the design of the universe *must* be front-loaded, but rather that we are in fact (again contrary to the claims of ID theorists) without a reliable empirical means to determine otherwise. As Owen Gingerich reminds us, just as it is "beyond the capability of science" to settle the dispute between atheistic and theistic evolution, it seems likewise to be beyond the empirical methods of science to settle the dispute between front-loaded and interactive design, leaving the matter to be resolved on the basis of other, non-scientific (i.e., theological or philosophical) considerations.[51]

The real target of Dembski's response to front-loaders is mechanism or reductive physicalism. The key question is whether or not it is appropriate (or even permissible) to construe the course of nature as *guided* in some way. Mechanists or reductive physicalists insist that it need not, is not, and furthermore cannot be so. Random variation and natural selection are entirely sufficient by themselves to explain the origin and course of development of life.[52] Theists of all stripes are

50. Ibid.

51. Owen Gingerich, *God's Universe* (Cambridge: Harvard University Press, 2006) 69.

52. In *The Edge of Evolution: The Search for the Limits of Darwinism* (New York: Free, 2007), Michael Behe associates this viewpoint with "Darwinism," which he opposes to any alternative according to which, at the very least, "after its initiation, the universe unfolded [without interference] exclusively by the intended playing out of natural laws" from initial conditions established to ensure particular outcomes, such as life, adding that "the purposeful design of life is [...] fully compatible with the idea of universal common descent." Behe presents an "extended fine-tuning" view of divine action that is both distinct (he thinks) from theistic evolution and does not require any "active meddling with nature." It simply requires "that the agent who caused the

united in their opposition to mechanism, although they disagree about the best way to conceive of the manner in which God both maintains and guides natural processes. In a concise but very helpful survey of the landscape of opinion regarding divine action in the universe, Nancey Murphy divides the mainstream of modern theologically orthodox alternatives to deism into two camps: interventionism (according to which God sometimes acts in violation of the laws of nature, which makes conflicts between theological and scientific explanations inevitable an ineliminable) and immanentism (according to which God is the immanent but noninterfering ground of nature, which effectively eliminates the possibility of conflict between theological and scientific explanations, and with it the prospect of any meaningful consonance between these two worlds of discourse).[53] In Murphy's terms, the goal is to locate a noninterventionist alternative to interactive design that avoids these extremes, evades the pitfalls of deism, and preserves (in some measure) the "informationally open" world preferred by the theist (in contrast to the "informationally closed" world preferred by the deist, and of course naturalism).[54]

As Murphy notes in her survey, the frontiers of physics have pushed us well beyond the clockwork universe from which deism seemed to many (and still seems to some) the only scientifically respectable response. Physics opens up novel options for understanding divine action and steering us on a course between interventionism (where she locates ID) and immanentism. Polkinghorne, for example, interprets "chaotic unpredictability [at the sub-atomic level] as a sign of ontological openness."[55] To regard the future as thus "open" (metaphysically speaking) does not demand that we abandon the principle of sufficient reason, but only that we concede "that the portfolio of causes that bring about the future is not limited solely to the description offered by a methodologically reductionist [bottom-up] physics and framed only in terms of the

---

universe was able to specify from the start not only laws, but much more." See *The Edge of Evolution*, 229–32.

53. Nancey Murphy, "Science, Divine Action, and the Intelligent Design Movement: A Defense of Theistic Evolution," in *Intelligent Design: William A. Dembski & Michael Ruse in Dialogue*, ed. Robert B. Stewart (Minneapolis: Fortress, 2007) 154–65.

54. Dembski, *No Free Lunch*, 344.

55. Polkinghorne, *Exploring Reality: The Intertwining of Science and Religion* (New Haven: Yale University Press, 2005) 35.

exchange of energy between constituents." If we broaden our concept of causal influence far enough to include "holistic effects of an informational, or pattern-forming kind," the result is a more open-ended, top-down form of causality he calls "active information."[56] Polkinghorne suggests that such an enrichment of the concept of information opens the door to "a physical world within whose open grain it would be fully conceivable that the God who is that world's Creator is providentially at work though the input of active information into its unfolding history, in a manner that operates non-interventionally within the grain of nature, rather than interventionally against it."[57]

Polkinghorne's proposals are strongly suggestive of open theism, beside which his approach to "the causal nexus of the world" seems entirely congenial. In point of fact, Polkinghorne has publicly extolled the promise of open theology in connection with our overall understanding of the natural world. Instead of conceiving of the world as "ready-made" (borrowing a phrase from Charles Kingsley), Polkinghorne interprets open theology to be advancing a picture of the world as "an unfolding process" that creatively balances "chance and necessity at the edge of chaos."[58] A robust expression of the Wesleyan theological tradition, open and relational theology has developed over the past two decades as a more biblically, intellectually and existentially satisfying (at least in the minds of its defenders) alternative to both classical theism (whose impassive deity bears a striking resemblance to that of deism) and process theism (a variety of immanentism according to which God non-coercively seeks to persuade his creatures simply by providing them with an initial aim and direction).

56. Ibid.

57. Ibid., 36. Another approach to divine action in tune with contemporary physics that also represents a non-deistic alternative to interventionism and immanentism is that of Robert J. Russell, which Murphy dubs "QDA" ("quantum divine action"), according to which God's acts in the natural world by determining otherwise indeterminate processes, but "only in such a way that does not override the intrinsic behavior of the various creatures he has made." See Murphy, "Science, Divine Action, and the Intelligent Design Movement," 162–65. Also see Russell, "Quantum Physics in Philosophical and Theological Perspective," in Russell, William R. Stoeger, S.J., and George V. Coyne, S.J., editors, *Physics, Philosophy, and Theology: A Common Quest for Understanding* (Vatican City State: Vatican Observatory Press, 1988) 343–74.

58. See Polkinghorne, "The Promise of Open Theology" www.enc.edu/history/ot/Polkinghorne_lecture.html.

It is not my intention here to give a full account of the resources of open and relational theology in its engagement with the natural sciences, as important as this project is for the future of the religion and science dialogue, but rather simply to note its affinity with the sort of non-interventionist approaches to divine action sketched by contemporary scientist-theologians such as Polkinghorne.[59] To cite just one example, Clark Pinnock maintains that the open view of God sees the world as "a subtle and supple place [. . .] where not everything would be predictable and where novelties can happen." The open view of God regards the world as "self-making" to a large degree, replete with "places of openness for God to move about in and previously unheard of ways of understanding how God influences the world" (thanks to such features as quantum indeterminacy, randomness and uncertainty).[60]

To return finally to Murray's question about whether open theists have more reasons than others to doubt that any set of natural entities and powers "could, through deck-stacking, bring off everything God intended for his creatures to accomplish," proposals such as Polkinghorne's and the very broad comments of open theists on the subject of divine action in the natural world seem to suggest that they do not, at least not obviously. It is perfectly conceivable that, unless one is inclined to insist *a priori* that every instance of divine action represents an influence from outside the system of nature, at least with respect to God's providential governance of nature (e.g., to ensure particular outcomes, such as the origin and development of life), open theism may be perfectly compatible with the idea that the actual *design* of nature is entirely front-loaded.[61] But these are deep waters, and as Polkinghorne

---

59. For detailed discussions of the lineaments of open theism, consider the following: David Basinger, William Hasker, Clark Pinnock, Richard Rice, and John Sanders, *The Openness of God: A Biblical Challenge to the Traditional Understanding of God* (Downers Grove,IL: InterVarsity, 1994); John Sanders, *The God Who Risks: A Theology of Providence* (Downers Grove, IL: InterVarsity, 1998); Clark Pinnock, *Most Moved Mover: A Theology of God's Openness* (Grand Rapids: Baker, 2001).

60. Pinnock, *Most Moved Mover*, 129–31.

61. Though I don't have space to develop it properly here, it's worth considering in this context Simon Conway Morris's observation that "Life is [. . .] pervaded by inherencies, by which I mean that much of the template of complex life is assembled long before the structures themselves evolve [. . .]. Following on, we can also see that, far from being a contingent muddle, life is pervaded with directionality; by no means everything is possible, but what is possible will evolve repeatedly." From the prevalence of evolutionary convergence (that is, evolutionary development along independent

himself exhorts us to bear in mind, the fresh approaches to divine action in the natural world that are now being stimulated by the leading edge of contemporary particle physics "remain largely hopes for future understanding." It's worth observing, however, that in light of these developments open theists seems to be well placed to inform our thinking about the God-creation relationship as what Polkinghorne calls our "fragmented knowledge of the causal structure of physical reality" continues to expand and deepen.[62]

Conclusion

The proper aim with respect to theology and science is, as Ernan McMullin has urged, "consonance without direct implication."[63] There is little reason to object to any notion of science (or for that matter theology) that, as Van Till says, locates it "within the framework of [our efforts to construct] an all-encompassing, biblically informed, theistic worldview that does indeed draw from *all* that we know about God, his creation and his revelation."[64] Intelligent Design theorists regard the success of ID's scientific aspirations as the linchpin in its wider agenda to undermine naturalism and address what they take to be its deleterious effects on society and culture (though not necessarily in that order). As I've tried to suggest, I'm not sure why this need be the case. Although there is little doubt that design-argument-based apologetics has received a major shot in the arm from contemporary ID theory,

---

lines) in such complex systems as the camera-eye, large brains (in the cases of *Homo erectus* and dolphins), and culture, Morris agrees with those who conclude on the basis of such evidence (and more besides) that "short of utter devastation, such as might be inflicted by a supernova exploding nearby, the emergence of various biological properties during the course of evolution is virtually guaranteed," and "that if the biology of form is constrained, then, no matter how far away [...] other] worlds might be, there too will be humanoids." See Morris, "The Paradoxes of Evolution: Inevitable Humans in a Lonely Universe?" in *God and Design: The Teleological Argument and Modern Science*, ed. Neil A. Manson (New York: Routledge, 2003) 329–47. Morris's argument is developed in greater detail in his *Life's Solution: Inevitable Humans in a Lonely Universe* (Cambridge: Cambridge University Press, 1993).

62. Polkinghorne, *Exploring Reality*, 37.

63. Ernan McMullin, "How Should Cosmology Relate to Theology?" in *The Sciences and Theology in the Twentieth Century*, ed. Arthur Peacocke (Notre Dame: University of Notre Dame Press, 1981) 17.

64. Howard Van Till, "When Faith and Reason Cooperate," *Christian Scholar's Review* (September 1991) 45.

it has been a legitimate and successful enterprise ever since Aquinas made it one his five ways to demonstrate the existence of God, and even a good while before that. Furthermore, even in a world without "specified" or "irreducible" complexity, design-inspired efforts to ameliorate social evils and reinvigorate culture on the part of advocates of one of the many articulations of theism around, whether haredic, masortic, Sunni, Shiite, Wesleyan, Pentecostal, Reformed, Catholic, Anglican, Lutheran, or what have you, remain both a going concern and a moral imperative.[65]

---

65. Thanks are due to my colleague, John Tyson, who reviewed sections of this chapter and made several very helpful suggestions.

10

Attachment, Spiritual Formation, and Wesleyan Communities

Sarah DeBoard Marion and Warren S. Brown

Introduction

In August of 2007, Bill Hybels, head pastor of the Willow Creek church network, announced at his annual Leadership Summit that he had recently received "the biggest wakeup call of his adult life."[1] Results from a recent survey conducted by his executive pastor Greg Hawkins shocked him when they revealed that the many church programs and activities were not "feeding" the most committed Christians in the congregation. Individuals who described themselves as "committed" or "centered" on Christ reported that they were not growing closer to Christ, although they were participating in church programs. Those who were exploring Christianity or early in their Christian growth reported feeling the most satisfied with what they were getting from church. Thus, the programs of the church were fostering the spiritual formation of seekers and early Christians, but not more committed Christians.

---

1 Bill Hybels, video of address to the Willow Creek Leadership Summit (Fall 2007): www.reveal.com.

After analyzing the research findings, Hybels came out publicly that he "got it wrong." He and his associates then came up with a solution to this problem, which was to intervene with individuals as they begin to enter a more "committed" phase in their relationship with Christ. At this phase of their faith journey, the Willow Creek pastoral staff would help individuals create customized personal spiritual growth plans to help them become "self-feeders" rather than relying on the church to feed them spiritually.

While the results of this large survey are interesting, what is more striking for the purposes of this paper is the response of Hybels and Hawkins. The assumption made in this solution is that the reason that individuals weren't growing in their faith was that they weren't spending enough time *alone* with God.

In this paper, we wish to propose a different solution. We will argue that spiritual maturation occurs primarily through interpersonal interaction occurring in small, more interdependent groups. Spiritual formation is neither primarily a solo process, nor does it primarily occur in large groups.

We will first present arguments from developmental psychology and theories of psychotherapeutic change. We will describe how the most powerful change occurring in psychotherapeutic contexts occurs as a direct result of the interpersonal relationship between therapist and client. This process can be modeled by attachment theory in developmental psychology. Within this discussion, we will explore research regarding the nature of the basic processes that underlie the formation of human attachments. One of these processes is the tendency to imitate another person's behavior, a skill that is present at birth and forms the basis for establishing reciprocal interactions with other human beings. We will also present evidence from the neurodevelopment literature suggesting that the brain is a self-organizing system which becomes organized via its history of interactions within the social environment. Second, we will discuss human change and flourishing as they relate to interdependence using the work of Alasdair MacIntyre and Friedrich Schleiermacher. Finally, we will discuss how Wesleyan practices provide a necessary corrective to the problems facing congregations today. We particularly focus on church size, and the inherent limitation of large groups in fostering the close human interactions and interdependence that is required for spiritual development and change.

Factors in Change

Brad Strawn and Warren Brown[2] highlight the contribution cognitive psychology makes to our understanding of Wesleyan practices and the ongoing, relationally-mediated grace that transforms one's "tempers" or disposition. They highlight the cognitive psychology literature showing that our actions are not often under conscious control, but are instead mediated through unconscious automatic mechanisms. These mechanisms are acquired by procedural learning and manifest themselves in behaviors typically not modulated by consciousness or will. Strawn and Brown also show how contemporary psychoanalysis may offer a particular form of relational grace to individuals who seek psychological healing—that is, transformation of their habits and tempers.

It is important to add to this work by identifying how psychological theories and practice may apply outside the formal therapeutic context. We believe there are factors that promote or set the stage for development and change within everyday social contexts, including early and often reciprocal attachment relationships, imitation of other persons, and social-context-dependent neurobiological organization of the self.

IMITATION

Andrew Meltzoff and others argue that infants come hardwired with the mechanisms needed for attachment. The mechanism is the inherent tendency to imitate.[3]

Termed the "like me" developmental framework, Meltzoff theorizes that infants engage in "bidirectional learning effects," in which they both learn behavior by observing the action of others and learn the action of others through their own behavior. Perception and production of behavior have a reciprocal influence on one another. This lays the foundation of an infant's ability to develop a view that another person is like him or herself with similar thoughts and feelings.

---

2. Brad Strawn and Warren Brown, "Wesleyan Theology through the Eyes of Cognitive Psychology and Psychotherapy," *Journal of Psychology and Christianity* 23 (2004) 121–29.

3. Andrew Meltzoff and Jean Decety, "What Imitation Tells Us about Social Cognition: A Rapprochement between Developmental Psychology and Cognitive Neuroscience," *Phil Trans. Royal Society of London* B 358 (2003) 491–500. Andrew Meltzoff, "The 'Like Me' Framework for Recognizing and Becoming an Intentional Agent," *Acta Psychologica* 124 (2007) 26–43.

The "like me" framework has three components or stages: early *action representation* leads to *first person experience*, which leads to *understanding other minds*. Meltzoff's early research established that within an hour of birth infants begin to imitate the facial expressions they observe. The "acts seen" and "acts done" in this scenario are coded together in the brain and are therefore tightly linked to one another. While the infant does not see his or her own behavior (facial expressions), there are links to the observed behavior through proprioception. This dual coding—*action representation* of observed and imitated behavior—lays the groundwork for an infant to be able to link *first-person experiences* (such as desire for a certain toy just out of reach) with bodily signs of longing (in the face and the body). Finally, when the infant observes others acting or looking similar to the map of their first-person experience, he or she can properly attribute to that person the same internal state previously felt.

The "like me" framework provides infants with the early tools needed to form a mature understanding that others are intentional agents like themselves. Even very young infants pay closer attention to an adult who is imitating their moves vs. imitating another baby's gestures. At just over a year, they begin to modify their facial expressions to test whether an adult is really imitating them or not, showing that the relationship is being considered in a more abstract manner. This is the beginning of a "theory of mind."

This theoretical framework has been supported by the discovery of "mirror neurons" in the motor cortex of higher primates, including humans. These neurons in the *motor* cortex are activated during *observation* of actions. Work by Jean Decety and others has further indicated that, in humans, there is a top-down effect of observed intention on the motor system, such that observing another with the intention to act looks neurologically more like performing the act itself than simple observation. Meltzoff recognizes, however, that the idea that we have mirror neurons does not provide the whole answer to becoming a mature intentional agent and acquiring a theory of mind. In his words,

> Persons are more than dynamic bags of skin that I can imitate and which imitate me. In the mature adult notion, persons have internal mental states—such as beliefs, goals and intentions—that predict and explain human actions. . . . the adult human framework is not simply one of resonance. We are able to rec-

ognize that everyone does not share our own desires, emotions, intentions and beliefs. To become a sophisticated mentalizer one needs to analyze both the similarities and differences between one's own states and those of others. That is what makes us human.[4]

For human beings to become adults capable of continued maturation in understanding and wisdom, they first need to develop the mental capacity to think about the parallels between their own thoughts and actions and those of others. Meltzoff's work provides evidence for a mimetic system which is online early in life and provides the grounding for this capacity.

The question now becomes, "how do such capacities develop most fully in the human organism?" The answer comes in two parts. First, capacities for social understanding and adequate social behavior develop through a process of self-organization based upon complex interactions with the environment. Second, this happens in the context of relationship, at first in the context of the attachment relationship with a primary caregiver (most often a mother), and then in the context of other attachment relationships.

Neurodevelopment—Self-Organizing from Experience

"How do we become the complex interactive humans that we are?" Steven Quartz and Terrence Sejnowski pose this more general question through a series of more specific questions: "How do neural mechanisms participate in, or underlie, cognitive development? In what ways do cognitive and neural processes interact during development, and what are the consequences of this interaction for theories of learning? In short, how is the mind built from the developing brain?"[5] Their answer comes out in the form of a neural constructivist manifesto in which they argue convincingly that cognitive development takes place in humans through complex interaction with the environment, such that interactions with the physical and social environment fundamentally change the learner at a neuron level. In a sense, they are answering the question of nature or nurture by demolishing the question. The human

---

4. Ibid., 495, 498.

5. Steven Quartz and Terrence Sejnowski, "The Neural Basis of Cognitive Development: A Constructivist Manifesto," *Behavioral and Brain Sciences* 20 (1997) 537–96.

organism is neither fixed at birth with certain qualities via genetic endowment, nor is it a *tabula rasa* to be shaped entirely at the whim of the environment. Rather, the human mind is a true interactive emergent. Within certain minimal genetic constraints, the brain is largely a self-organizing system.

For example, Jerome Kagan has shown that every baby is born with a given temperament, which by 4 months can be characterized as primarily "inhibited" (20% of infants) or "bold/fearless" (40%) with the rest showing a mix of the two styles. However, Quartz and Sejnowski point out that by the age of four years only 10% of children show these extremes in temperament. Thus being born "*some* way" does not equal being born "*that* way." [6] Even more striking is some emerging work by Stephen Suomi,[7] who bred rhesus macaques to be primarily inhibited (fearful) or bold in temperament, all the while tracking their behavior and biochemistry. He later placed the fearful/inhibited macaques in a cage with uninhibited, nurturing foster mothers and watched as the animals became less fearful and less "ramped up" physiologically, with a parallel reduction in adrenaline levels and stress hormones like cortisol. Quartz and Sejnowski conclude that "it takes a long time to build your personality and the flexible behavior it allows."[8]

For our purposes, given this emphasis on the impact on brain development of the ongoing reciprocal interactions with one's social environment and culture, it is critical to establish the possibility for *ongoing* change beyond early childhood. Just how long does it take for personality to become fixed? Does it ever become fixed? Quartz and Sejnowski answer a resounding "no," that in fact personality is an "open program" in the way that some computer super-games have been created to learn game knowledge as they play.

> Open programs have the advantage of shaping personality for changing and unanticipated roles. . . . This powerful feature is the hallmark of the human mental flexibility at the core of cul-

---

6. Steven Quartz and Terrence Sejnowski, *Liars, Lovers and Heroes: What the New Brain Science Reveals about How We Become Who We Are* (New York: Quill, 2002) 128.

7. M. Champoux, A. Bennett, C. Shannon, J. D. Higley, K. P. Lesch, and S. J. Suomi, "Serotonin Transporter Gene Polymorphism, Differential Early Rearing, and Behavior in Rhesus Monkey Neonates," *Molecular Psychiatry* 7 (2002) 1058–63.

8. Quartz and Sejnowski, *Liars, Lovers, and Heroes*, 130.

tural biology. Slowly, as you experience your world over many years, out of the partnership between your anchoring internal guidance system and your user's guide to life emerges an intellectual coup: the impressive flexibility that allows you both to reshape your world and to respond to its personality-shaping contexts.[9]

Quartz and Sejnowski extend this "open program" quality to constructs we typically view as fixed, such as intelligence. They also extend this quality across the lifespan. And there is proof: compared with 50-year-olds, the dendrites or tree-like branches of 80-year olds have been found to be 35% *more* complex.[10] They go on to develop five elements that predict successful, flexible brain aging: 1) stimulation, 2) novelty, 3) family and social context, 4) a positive self-model, and 5) exercise. For our present purposes, we wish to particularly highlight the family and social context with attachment (which we will cover next) being the glue that binds persons together in formative social groupings.

Attachment Theory and Ongoing Mechanisms of Change

Attachment theory has become increasingly woven into the fabric of psychoanalytic thinking and, more generally, how psychologists view human development. Attachment theory was originally conceived and promoted by John Bowlby as a way to account for evolutionary advantages of the infant–mother dyad. This theory also explains how the quality of our earliest relationships set the stage for the remainder of our development—adequate and secure nurturing tends to promote confident, emotionally resilient adults who have faith in their own ability to love and be loved. Adults whose early attachments are insecure have increased difficulties regulating emotions and relating to others. And while the infant–mother dyad generally receives the most attention, L. A. Sroufe and others have shown that larger, systemic influences are

---

9. Ibid., 130.

10. S. J. Buell and P. D. Coleman, "Quantitative Evidence for Selective Dendritic Growth in Normal Human Aging but Not in Senile Dementia," *Brain Research* 214 (1981) 23–41.

also important and can alter for good or ill the person's "working model" of relationships.[11]

Allen Schore has lately recast attachment theory in terms of the neurobiological regulation and dysregulation of affect, arguing that individuals who have experienced consistently good attachment relationships will have a more resilient neurobiological system for regulating positive and negative emotional states.[12] Schore argues that attachment experiences are processed and stored in the implicit memory system generally found in the non-dominant right hemisphere. The representations that are encoded endure in memory as a network of cognitive and emotional memories that continue to shape expectations and behavior in later relationships. J. M. Siegal[13] has also demonstrated that emotional resilience, cognitive abilities, and behavioral flexibility are associated with the development of a secure attachment style.

Most importantly for our present argument, Sable[14] discusses the ways in which attachment theory continues to be relevant for adults in both traditionally therapeutic and non-therapeutic contexts. Within the context of psychotherapy, Sable and other authors highlight the positive aspects of the attachment relationship that develops between therapist and client. Attachment theory helps to frame the relationship between therapist and client as the primary mode of change. The therapist is a "secure base" from which the client can explore often frightening and intense emotional experiences, and which can help regulate the client's positive and negative effect. As long ago as 1940, Fairnbairn discussed therapeutic relationships as ongoing experiences of "genuine emotional contact."[15] The relationships that develop

11. L. A. Sroufe, B. Egeland, and E. Carlson, "Placing Early Attachment Experiences in Developmental Context: The Minnesota Longitudinal Study," in *Attachment from Infancy to Adulthood: The Major Longitudinal Studies*, ed. K. E. Grossman, K. Grossmann, and E. Waters (New York: Guildford, 2005) 48–70.

12. A. Schore, *Affect Regulation and the Origin of the Self: The Neurobiology of Emotional Development* (Hillsdale, NJ: Lawrance Erlbaum, 1994).

13. J. M. Siegal, "An Interpersonal Neurobiology of Psychotherapy: The Developing Mind and the Resolution of Trauma," in *Healing Trauma*, ed. M. F. Solomon and D. J. Siegel (New York: Norton, 2003) 1–56.

14. P. Sable, "Accentuating the positive in adult attachments," in *Attachment & Human Development*, 361–74.

15. W. R. D. Fairnbairn, "Schizoid factors in the personality," in *Psychoanalytic Studies of the Personality* (London: Tavistock, 1940) 3–27.

between therapists and clients have been described as "unique relationships" that are "co-created over time, are emotionally significant, and have their own specific 'ways of being together.'"

While there is clearly something unique about the attachment relationship that develops between therapist and client, attachment theory also applies to other forms of interpersonal relationships. When thinking about the formative aspects of attachments outside the therapy room, it is important to identify the parameters of such a relationship. It would not be feasible or even desirable to develop a meaningful attachment relationship with every person you encounter. Can formative attachment relationships occur within the context of a church? If so, under what circumstances?

As a way of providing some initial reflections in this regard, it is useful to contrast this more common form of attachment relationship with parental or therapeutic relationships. Unlike parenting and therapy, everyday adult attachment relationships would not focus on a need for training or amelioration of pathology. They would also not be one-sided. That is, neither member of the dyad has professional or parental authority over the other—they are equal participators in the relationship. Thus, as partners in the relationship they are equally accountable to one another. However, similar to good parenting or good therapy, it should be a secure relationship in which one can feel safe to express ideas, opinions, and genuine affect (both positive and negative), and have them respectfully and compassionately responded to and regulated (in a limited way) by the other person.

Thus far we have noted: 1) the power of imitation of other persons in cognitive and social development; 2) the self-organizing nature of the brain in development and throughout life; and 3) the formative power of interhuman attachment both in and out of a traditional therapeutic context. However, how does all of this connect more directly with Christian formation—for example, with Willow Creek and the obstacles churches face in terms of faith development and growth? We posit that ongoing transformative experiences leading to spiritual maturity function in the same way that our earliest development occurs, and that change occurs in the unusual context of therapy—that is, based upon the formative power of attachment relationships. We turn next to the work of MacIntyre and Schleirmacher to think about how interdependence can enhance human development and flourishing within larger social contexts.

Human Interactions and Human Formation

Philosopher Alasdair MacIntyre, in his book titled *Dependent Rational Animals: Why Human Beings Need the Virtues*,[16] has given a good account of the importance of interpersonal interactions in human flourishing. This title, *Dependent Rational Animals*, is quite explicit regarding MacIntyre's views. "Animals" refers to MacIntyre's view of humankind as continuous with the animal world, as well as his view of the embodiment of our essential humanness. "Rational" expresses MacIntyre's understanding of the critical role of practical reasoning in fostering human flourishing. This form of rationality is not limited to the conscious, problem-solving rationality of classical philosophy. Rather, the rationality referred to here is more like common everyday wisdom. In the end, the goal of human development for MacIntyre is to become rational in the sense of being an "independent practical reasoner." We read MacIntyre as pointing to something that is not unlike the sort of spiritual maturity and wisdom that the church seeks to promote (and for which there seemed to have been little evidence in the Willow Creek survey). However, the critical step in becoming an independent practical reasoner is, for MacIntyre, development of the virtue of "acknowledged dependence" (thus, the designation of humans as "*dependent* rational animals").

MacIntyre's main point is that only those persons who are continually able to acknowledge and function within their dependence on others are successful in becoming truly effective independent practical reasoners. MacIntyre argues that "the acquisition of the necessary virtues, skills, and self-knowledge is something that we in key part owe to those particular others on whom we have had to depend." This dependence is most formative for children (within the context of parent-child attachments), but it continues throughout life in particular forms of social attachments. "For we continue to the end of our lives to need others to sustain us in our practical reasoning," says MacIntyre. We are particularly dependent on others for continued self-knowledge, and help with both mental and moral errors. "From both types of mistake the best protections are friendship and collegiality."[17]

---

16. Alasdair MacIntyre, *Dependent Rational Animals: Why Human Beings Need the Virtues* (Chicago: Open Court, 1999).

17. Ibid., 96.

Thus, we take from MacIntyre the idea that formation in the virtues of life generally—and Christian life specifically (that is, Wesley's "holy affections and tempers")—is dependent on relationships with other persons. Those other persons may be a family when we are young children, a wider range of adult mentors during adolescences, or a network of Christian colleagues within the church throughout adult years.

Eighteenth century theologian, Friedrich Schleiermacher, provides us with further guidance on the development of virtues, tempers, and Christian habits within the context of groups such as the church. Schleiermacher deals with the issue of how we might learn to be a person whose life includes compassion, particularly habits of benevolence on behalf of the poor. The problem is that neither contemplation of one's own privileged status nor reflection on one's moral obligations elicit sentiments in any of us sufficient to give rise to meaningful benevolent actions. Schleiermacher felt that the binding power of pure obligation is insufficient. However, the solution for Schleiermacher was through the combination of "sociable connections" and small-group action. Compared to individual action, the small-group mode not only has the benefit of being more effective, but simultaneously "strengthens the intensity of the sentiments of those performing the benevolent actions."[18] Within groups of persons engaging in such action, there is reciprocal strengthening of benevolent and compassionate affections and sentiments.

According to Schleiermacher, an important new dimension comes into play in group activity. Theologian Michael Welker describes this process: "Complex and strengthening sentiments arise in me when my action is embedded in an interconnection with the action of other human beings, strengthening this interconnection and being strengthened by it."[19] It is likely that reciprocal *imitation* is one key factor—we learn by observing and imitating one another. Schleiermacher helps us to understand the role and power of smaller groups, with their more intense "sociable connections" (or attachments) and the opportunity afforded to grow by imitation of one another. Further, we begin to see how understanding these influences can contribute to the church's attempt to enhance the spiritual formation of people.

18. Ibid., 173.
19. Ibid.

Group Size and Human Formation

What we believe is implied by the views of MacIntyre and Schleiermacher is a theory of human maturation and spiritual formation that is focused on top-down influences from groups to persons. These ideas are resonant with what is implied by the social-context-based self-organization of the brain during child development. Meltzoff's research shows that the abilities necessary for allowing the formative influence of interpersonal imitation are present in humans from birth. When observing the actions of others, our own actions are specifically primed for imitation (by mirror neuron activity). Quartz and Sejnowski highlight well the self-organizing aspect of the human brain, and the necessary interactions that must take place between the environment and the person for human systems to come "on line." The social environment has a life-long impact on the brain and its behavioral products. Attachment theory focuses us on the formative power of close, dyadic interpersonal relationships. In this light, we suggest that networks of dyadic attachment form the bonds (the "sociable connections") that allow small-group networks to form, and to exert a formative influence on individuals within groups toward becoming independent practical reasoners, and within the church, becoming spiritually mature persons.

However, can we find any help in clarifying the dimensionality of "small" when it comes to human groups? What size group would allow for sufficient interpersonal attachment to be formative? What size would be able to sustain the "sociable connections" of Schleiermacher and allow for formation of mature and wise persons (that is, "independent practical reasoners") through the inter-dependency championed by MacIntyre?

Here we believe help is provided by the work of British Anthropologist Robin Dunbar and his famous Dunbar Number. Dunbar was interested in the relationship between the maximum size of cohesive groups (as indicated by stable relationships over time) and the size of the brain. He did field observations of 36 primate species and compared the average size of stable groups to their average brain size. He then used regression analysis to project this relationship onto human groups. The regression predicted that human groups of 147.8 persons would be able to maintain stable relationships over time—so the Dunbar Number was set at 150 persons. As Dunbar wrote, ". . . there is a cognitive limit to the number of individuals with whom any one person can maintain stable relationships . . . [and] this limit is a direct function of relative neocortex size."[20] Thus, human group sizes exceeding the Dunbar Number—150 persons—have too many people involved for maintaining stable relationships over time.

Of course, as with all such formulas, things are not quite that simple. Sustaining stable relationships within a group of 150 persons would demand considerable effort. The effort would require something like 42% of one's time spent in the human equivalent of ape social grooming—very close forms of interpersonal contact that form and maintain sociable connections. For this reason, the maximum group size depends, according to Dunbar, on the degree of social dispersal. Human groups that are dispersed will meet less often, and so the group size will need to be smaller than 150 for sufficient opportunity for maintaining stable relationships.

A great deal of work has been done on group sizes with respect to social networks as they occur in the cyber space of the Worldwide Web. The focus here is the capacity of persons to track nodes (other people) in an interactive web network. One commentator has suggested the following relationships between group-size and the level of network meshing:[21]

- 12 is the average capacity to track nodes in a totally meshed network
- 50 is the average capacity to track nodes in an optimally meshed network
- 150 is the average capacity to track nodes in a sub-optimally meshed network

Here again we see that the group size that is optimal for maintaining stable relationships depends also on the nature of the network and its demand for enmeshment among its members.

---

20. As quoted by Christopher Allen on "Life with Alacrity," www.lifewithalacrity.com/2004/03/the dunbar numb.html.

21. From Ton Zijlstra, www.zylstra.org/blog/archives/001183.html.

Revisiting the Church of Wesley

Viewing human formation and change through the lens of interpersonal attachments and group-to-person influence suggests why a church like Willow Creek is finding less Christian growth and personal change than they would have liked to see. Perhaps when churches such as this gather, there are simply too many people in the room. Maybe the focus on numerical growth championed by the "church growth movement" (for which our institution, Fuller Theological Seminary, must take some responsibility) has misunderstood the nature of the church and spiritual formation.

It is obvious to most that Wesley's organization of members into classes, bands, and societies was an important contributor to the growth of Methodism. These groupings set persons within consistent smallgroups which had the expressed mission of encouraging the spiritual growth of each member, as well as creating a context for ministry to the poor, the ill, and those in prison. As Wesley famously said,

> The gospel of Christ knows no religion, but social; no holiness but social holiness… I mean not only that it cannot subsist so well, but that it cannot subsist at all without society, without living and conversing with [others].[22]

The ideas we have presented in this paper suggest why Wesley's form of organization of the church was so powerful, and why it should not to be considered antiquated and merely of historical interest.

One problem, of course, is that the societies that surround the church in the modern Western world are often highly dispersed, offering rather restricted opportunities for interaction. Our lives are considerably more dispersed than the towns and villages of Wesley's late 18th Century England. However, this makes the demand to consider seriously the social structure of the church even more important. If attachment and sociable connections are, in fact, important in spiritual formation, we need to re-think seriously the size structuring of the church. This does not necessarily require formally breaking up large churches. The problem is not simple, therefore, neither is the solution. What it does require is to find creative, and perhaps unique, ways of being together that will foster meaningful and reciprocal attachment

---

22. As quoted by Randy L. Maddox, *Responsible Grace: John Wesley's Practical Theology* (Nashville: Kingswood, 1994) 209.

relationships and interconnected social networks that are stable over time. To use a truly Wesleyan notion, the church needs to find ways of being *eclesiola* ("little church") within *ecclesia* ("large church") through relational means of grace.

Contributors

Robert D. Branson (PhD, Boston University) is retired Professor of Bible, Olivet Nazarene University, Bourbonnais, Illinois

Warren S. Brown (PhD, University of Southern California) is Professor of Psychology, School of Psychology, Fuller Theological Seminary, Pasadena, California

Timothy J. Crutcher (PhD/STD, Catholic University of Louvain) is Associate Professor of Church History and Theology, Southern Nazarene University, Bethany, Oklahoma

Laura Bartels Felleman (PhD, Drew University) is Assistant Professor of Wesleyan Studies, Memphis Theological Seminary, Memphis, Tennessee

Rebecca J. Flietstra (PhD, University of Kansas Medical Center) is Professor of Mammalian Physiology at Point Loma Nazarene University, San Diego, California

John W. Haas Jr. (PhD, University of Delaware) is Emeritus Professor of Chemistry, Gordon College, Wenham, Massachusetts

Michael Lodahl (PhD, Emory University) is Professor of Theology & World Religions at Point Loma Nazarene University, San Diego, California

Randy L. Maddox (PhD, Emory University) is Professor of Theology and Wesleyan Studies, Divinity School, Duke University

Sarah DeBoard Marion (PhD, Fuller Theological Seminary) is Assistant Professor of Psychology at the Graduate School of Psychology, Fuller Theological Seminary, Pasadena, California

Contributors

Jürgen Moltmann (PhD, University of Göttingen) is Professor of Systematic Theology Emeritus in the Protestant Faculty of the University, Tübingen, Germany

Thomas Jay Oord (PhD, Claremont Graduate University) is Professor of Theology and Philosophy, Northwest Nazarene University, Nampa, Idaho

Marc Otto (MA, Point Loma Nazarene University) is Administrative Pastor at San Diego First Church of the Nazarene, San Diego, California

W. Christopher Stewart (PhD, University of Notre Dame) is Professor of Philosophy, Houghton College, Houghton, New York

Index

Abel, 147
Abraham, 143, 147, 166
absolute, 131
Adam, 143, 146–48, 154, 161–62
adapa story, 148
aesthetics, ix
affection, 63
Africa, 148
agriculture, 55
AIDS, 118
air, 19
Alalgar of Eridu, 148
Allen, Christopher, 210
Ancient Middle East (ANE), 138, 145, 147, 149–50, 154
angel(s), 30, 75
Anglicanism, 17, 31, 40–41, 47, 61, 69, 71–72, 85–87, 129
animal, 92, 104, 106, 149, 157, 160–61, 165, 107
animal, dependent rational, 207
animal psychology, 41
animal spirits, 41
animal suffering, 29
annihilation, 28, 118
anthropocentrism, 34–35, 108
anthropology, 117, 148
Anthony, Abbot, 110
anti-atheism, 78
anti-newtonian system of scriptural science, 49
antiscience, 41, 43, 56

apocalypse, 115
apices, (Medium of Letters), 110
apologetics, 23, 47, 176, 179, 187, 196
Aquinas, Thomas, 116, 151, 178
Arbuthnot, John, 39
archaeology, 138–39, 145, 149, 154
Archimedes, 130
architecture of the universe, 190
Arianism, 80
arithmetic, 10
Aristarchus, 130
Aristotle, 10, 12, 41, 62, 66, 123, 125–26, 178
aristotelian principle/causes/method, 62, 66–67, 72, 83, 97, 128, 180
art, 10, 183
Ashworth, William B., 12
Asia, 117
assurance, 76
Atrahasis Epic, 148
astro-Theology, 18, 21–22
astrology, 114, 130
astronomy, 10, 26, 44, 51, 125, 142
astronomer, 11, 86, 144
atheism, 43, 58–59, 62, 65, 73, 77–80, 83, 85, 90, 96–97, 99, 101, 187–89
atonement, 42
Audi, R., 17
Augustine, 42, 110, 117, 151
Averroes, Islamic Philosopher, 111
axioms, 63, 181

216 Index

Babylonia, 147
Bacon, Francis, 5, 11, 33, 35–36, 40, 42, 55, 85–86, 108, 124
bacterium, 177
Baker, Frank, 8, 38
Barber, Frank Louis, 5
Barbour, Ian, 85, 96–97
Basinger, David, 195
Baxter, Richard, 18, 69
Behe, Michael, 175, 178–80, 192
Bennett, A., 203
Bentley, Richard, 48
Bethlehem, 98
biblical criticism, 42
biblical witness, 68, 111, 121
biochemistry, 157
biogeography, 149
Big Bang, 112, 144
biology, xii, 44, 84, 144, 156, 167, 172, 181
Bird, Phyllis A., 153
Black, Jeremy, 15
bleaching, 55
blessing, 166
blood of transfusions, 55
Body, 54–55, 66, 109, 116
Böhler, Peter, 132
Böhme, Gernot, 112
Böhme, Jakob, 113
Bonhoeffer, Detrich, 119
Bowby, John, 204
Bloch, Ernest, 108
body-soul connection, 79
Bonnet, Charles, 5, 30, 38
Bowler, Peter J., 7, 9
Boyle, Robert, 6, 25, 40, 48–49
Brahe, Tyco, 126
Brain, 32, 67, 79, 112, 199, 201–2, 204, 209
Branson, Robert D., xii, 142
Brantley, Richard E., 40
Bratcher, Dennis, 145
Bray, Thomas, 39
Brooke, John Hedley, 17, 23, 41, 190–91

Brown, James Robert, 9
Brown, Warren S., xiii, 33, 200
Brown(e), Peter, 39–40, 63–65, 67, 69–70, 73, 97, 102
Buckley, Michael, 23
Buddeus, Johann Franz, 19, 84
Buell, S. J., 204
Bultmann, Rudolf, 115
Burke, James G., 39
Burnet, Gilbert, 65–66
Burnet, Thomas, 43
Butler, Bishop Joseph, 39, 48
Butterfield, Herbert, 9
Byrom, John, 31
Byrum, Russel R., 139, 152

Cain, 147
Calvin, Jean, 142
Calvin, John, 142
Calvinism, 132
Cannite, 154
capitalism, 34
Cappadicians, 110
Cartesian, 41
catholic spirit, 24–25
Catholicism, 61–62, 66, 71, 74, 76, 86, 141, 172
celestial being, 29
cell, 108, 164
Cell, Eukaryotic, 168
cell-like beings, 167
Cell, George Croft, 134
certainty, 59
chain of being(s), 29, 38, 45
chain (or scale) of being, 41
chain of nature, 89
Chalmers, A. F., 9
Chambers, 43
Champoux, M., 203
chaos, 118–19, 121, 146, 194
chemical, production of, 55
Chemistry, 135
Cheyne, George, 29, 39, 77–78
Cheyne, John, 41

Chilcote, Paul Wesley, 27, 127
Chillingsworth, William, 24, 61
Chit-Chat Club, 4
Christ, 75–76, 115–16
Christian System/Tradition, 55, 109, 115, 131, 134, 156
Christianity, 42, 47, 82, 111–12
Church of England, 129
Church of God, 150
civic society, 17
civilization, 116
Clarke-Leibnitz Controversy, 38
classical, 127, 194
Clayton, Philip, xi
Clifford, William, 136
Clutterback, Richard, 99
cognitive realignment, 187
Coleman, P. D., 204
Coleman, William, 34
collegiality, 207
Collier, Wilbur, 5
Colling, Richard R., 144
colonialism, 108
comet, 41
common descent, 157, 160, 162, 184
common experience, 69
common law, 66
common sense, 24, 49, 160, 165
Complex Specified Information (CSI), 179
conscience, 74, 76
consciousness, 200
conservatism, 57
contemplation, 22
contextuality, 27
conversion, 132, 186
conviction(s), 22–23, 34, 66, 76, 79, 82, 159, 176
Copernicus, Nicolas, 97, 126, 130, 139–41
corruption, 155
cosmic designer, 181
cosmic renewal, 28, 121
cosmos, 12–13, 109, 112, 115–16, 141, 191

cosmology (cosmological), 7, 13, 19, 26
Coulson, Charles, xi
Cowper, William, 39
Coyne, George V., 194
creation, 34–36, 44–45, 49, 55, 58, 65–66, 78, 83, 85, 88–89, 93, 95, 97, 102–5, 109–10, 116–20, 136, 138, 142, 144–47, 151, 156, 159–60, 162, 165–67, 187, 191, 196
creation, *ex nihlo*, 50
creation, new, 28–29, 35, 44
creation, six-day, 158–59
creation theology, 156
creation, works of, 52
creation, young earth, 149, 159–62
creator, 5, 22, 45, 53, 65, 74, 99, 121, 156, 159, 166, 173, 183, 188
creator-creature relation, xi, 154
criminal law, 65
Cromartie, Alan, 65–66, 69
cross, 120
Crutcher, Timothy, xii, 125
Cullender, Rose, 66
culture, 57, 104–5, 107–8, 111–12, 145, 147, 149–150, 153–54, 173–74, 186, 196
Cunningham, Andrew, 9, 15, 58, 96, 188
curriculum, Christian, 17

Darwin, Charles, 4, 43, 48, 152, 157–58, 163
Darwinism, 43, 157, 172, 173, 180, 184, 192
Davis, Edward B., 47
Dawkins, Richard, 162
day, 152
De Laplace, Pierre-Simon, 86
Dear, Peter, 11, 15, 58
death, 121, 133, 148, 165, 169
Decety, Jean, 200–201
Deck-Stack, 191, 195
deduction, 21, 125–27

deism, 43, 47–48, 74, 80, 83, 85, 87–88, 90, 96–97, 99, 101, 180, 189–90, 193
deity, 146, 167
Dembski, William A., 23, 173–76, 180–81, 191
demon, 75
demythologization, 146
dendrites, 204
Dennett, Daniel C., 167
Derham, William, 18, 20–21, 34, 37, 187–88
Descartes, Rene, 12, 39, 41, 109, 127
design, 88, 90, 97, 100–101, 103, 192, 195
determinism, 32, 55
devil, 53
dialogue, 1, 16, 24–25, 26–31, 33, 108
dialectic, 10
disease, 167–68
discernment, 75
divination, 114
divine, x–xi, 22, 68, 77, 89, 98, 100, 116, 118, 120–21, 139, 141, 144, 148, 150–52, 166
divine-creature synergism, xi
divine design, 19
divinity, 110
doctrine, Christian, 25, 50
doctrine, religious, 66, 131
dogmatism, 136
Donat, James G., 8
Dunbar, Robin, 209–10
Dunbsr Numbers, 209
Dunning, H. Ray, 139, 153–54
Duny, Amy, 66
Duten, 102
dyad, 204, 209

earth, 19, 34, 89, 104, 108, 117–18, 121, 141, 144, 146, 149, 151, 157–58, 169
earthquake, 44, 52–53, 115, 118
Ebla, 146

ecclesia, 212
ecclesiola, 212
ecclesiology, ix
ecology, ix, 121
ecology, modern, 30
economy, 88–89, 101, 107
economic advantage, 184
Edlin, Jim, 142
Edwards, Jonathan, 38
education, 66
Egeland, B., 205
Egypt, 119–20
Einstein, 126
electricity, 44, 55–56, 89, 186
electrostatic, 56
elements, 19
elementary particles, 108
Elish, Enuma, 146
Elizabeth, Queen, 60
Ellis, George, xi
emblem, 46
empirical detection, 12
empirical verification of hypotheses, 9
empirical theology, 5
empiricism, 39–40, 97, 124, 128, 134–35, 183, 189, 192
En-memgal-Anna of Bad-tibira, 148
energy, 114, 164, 184
English, John Cammel, 7, 38, 40, 54
enlightenment, 11, 25–26, 54, 56, 78, 86, 122, 125, 127
Entelechy, 12
enthusiasm, 62, 70
entrepreneurial social action, 186
environment, 34–35, 105–6, 108–9, 163, 202, 209
epistemic Humility, 26
epistemology, ix–x, 24–25, 39, 97, 123, 127, 134, 143
epistemology, legal, 61, 63, 65–66, 71–72
epistemology, religious, 59, 72, 77, 189
Eriugina, Scotus, 110

eschatology, 31
essence, 116, 128
eternal (eternity), 74, 77–78, 99, 121, 147
ethereal medium, 94
ethics, ix, 26, 62, 76, 136
Eucharist, 115
eugenics, 184
Evangelicalism, 51, 57, 83, 85, 103, 153, 186
evangelistic strategy/motive, 24, 102
Eve, 146–48, 161–62
evidentialism, 23, 136
evidentialist apologetics, 20, 189
evil, 53, 71, 162, 175, 186
evolution, xii, 43, 112, 152, 157–58, 160, 165
evolution, atheistic, 162, 192
evolution, biological, 152,
evolution, convergence, 195
evolution, Darwinian model of, 3
evolution, Darwin theory of, 5
evolution, differential, 184
evolution, mechanism of, 163, 192
evolution, natural, 172
evolution, neo-Darwin theory, 173
evolution, theory of, ix, xii, 143–44, 156, 159, 162–63, 164, 169, 182
evolution, theistic theory of, 152, 159, 192
evolutionary Process/Change, 156–57
eyewitness, 143
existence, xi, 16, 20, 145, 159, 164, 197
Exodus, 119, 143, 145
experience, 24, 27, 32–33, 40, 60, 68–69, 77–78, 82, 100, 104, 125, 127–28, 130–37, 145, 201, 205–6
extracanonical, 74
extra-empirical, 182

Fairnbairn, W. R. D., 205
faith, 17, 54, 56, 59, 72, 74, 76–77, 79, 86, 111, 124–25, 132, 152–56, 180, 187

faith, rational, 37
faith, saving, 71–72
Falk, Darrell R., 144
fallibility, 24–25, 119
Faraday, 183
Father (God), 101
feeling, 135
Felleman, Laura Bartels, xii, 6, 8, 20, 82–83, 96, 188
Ferngren, Gary, 17
fertility (fertilization), 167–68
fetuses, 164
Feyerabend, Paul, 26, 124
Final Cause, 67
finite, 120
fire, 19, 94
fire-fluid-spirit, 89
First Cause, 22, 66
Fisher, Eugene, 149
Forrest, Barnara, 174–75
fossil, 149, 162
flagellum, 177
Flew, Antony, 180
Flietstra, Rebecca J., xii
flood, 146, 148–50, 158, 160
force, external, 12
Ford, David F., 16
foundational, 8
Franklin, Benjamin, 38
freedom, x, 55, 118, 120
freethinkers, 80
French Revolution, 115
Fretheim, Terrence E., 143
friendship, 207
Fundamentalism, 5
Fuller, Steve, 170, 175, 183

Galileo, 13, 85–86, 97, 110, 126, 141
Gascoigne, John, 11–12, 51
geo-centricism, 126, 130
geography, 146
geology, 44, 144, 149
geometry, 10
geometric order, 51

Index

genealogy, 145
general scholium, 13, 15, 18
genes, 164
Genesis, xii, 3, 35, 42, 44–45, 117, 136, 138–39, 142–46, 148–50, 153–55, 160, 166–67
genetics, 144, 148, 158, 162, 203
genus, 128
Gilgamish Epic, 147–48
Gingerich, Owen, 141, 144, 192
Glacken, Clarence, 30
glory, 116, 121
God, 53, 58, 75, 84–85, 86, 90, 93–95, 98, 100–104, 109–10, 113, 119–22, 129, 136, 142, 145–48, 151, 153, 155–56, 159–62, 165–66, 169, 187–91, 195, 197
Godsey, J. D., 119
Goldsmith, Oliver, 38
goodness, 46, 84, 162, 188
Görritz, Brigitte, 114
Görritz, Thomas, 114
gospel, 37, 115
Gould, Stephen, 33
grace, xii, 101, 103, 115–16, 154, 160, 164, 166, 169, 211–12
gradualism, 157–58
grammar, 10
Grant, Edward, 58
Grant, Robert C., 43
gravity, 13–14
Grayling, A. C., 171
Great Mathematician, 190
Greek, 87, 116, 119
Gregersen, Niels Henrik, 1
Gregory, Jeremy, 15
Green, Timothy M., 142
Grider, Kenneth, 139, 154
Gross, Paul, 174–75
Grotius, Hugo, 62

Haarma, Loren, 177
Haas Jr., John W., xii, 7, 43, 57
habitat, 109, 113

Hale, Matthew, 22, 65–67, 70, 84
Hales, Stephen, 37
Hargitt, Charles W., 5
Harrison, Peter, 15, 35
Hartley, David, 31, 33, 39, 41, 55
Harvey, William, 66–68
Hasel, Gerhard, 146
Hasker, William, 195
Haughty, Roger F., 1
Hawkins, Greg, 198–99
Hawthorne, Nathaniel, 104
Hayes, John H., 147
healing, 104, 119, 200
heaven, 10, 28, 45, 73, 76, 82, 100, 104, 117, 152
Heinman, P. M., 49
Heitzenrater, Richard P., 8, 66
helio-centricism, 126, 130
Hendricks, M. Elton, 48
heretics, 80
hermeneutics, 8, 16, 109, 111, 114, 125, 131–32, 150
Herrmann, Robert L., 26
Hervey, James, 46
Hetzel, Peter G., 109
High Church, 41–42, 47–48, 50–51, 57
Higley, J. D., 203
Hills, A. M., 139, 151
Hinddley, J. C., 134
historical-literal interpretation, 138
historiography (historiographer), 9, 23
history, 61, 68, 115, 119, 121, 138, 142, 144–45, 147, 152, 154–55, 159, 169, 178
Hodge, Charles, 152
holiness, 133, 152, 154
Holy Spirit, 73, 101, 139, 141
homeostasis, 168
homosexuality, 115
hope, 76, 116
Horsley, Bishop Samuel, 37

human, x, 29, 32, 97, 101, 106–7, 109–10, 113, 118, 120, 122, 124, 131, 139, 145–46, 148–50, 158–63, 201, 209
human Body, 40
human consciousness, 32
human control, 33
human development, 204
human Flourishing, 207
human knowledge, 25, 40, 44, 49, 59, 82–84, 88, 94–95, 101
human moral, 32
human nature, 32
human observation, 12
human possibility, 96
human race, 86
human reproductive Organs, 19
humankind, 53, 55, 97, 100
humanitarianism, 38
humanity, 24, 29, 110, 112, 146–48, 155
Hume, David, 39
humility theology, 26
hurricane, 94
Hutchens, Robert M., 42
Hutchinson, John, 38, 43, 47, 49
Hutchinsonianism, 49–50
Huyssten, J. Wentzel, 1
Hybel, Bill, 198–99
hymn, x

illumination, 103
imagination, 67
immanentism, 49, 121, 193–94
immaterial, 40, 69, 73, 78
immortality, 147–48
immutability, 5
incarnation, 42, 139, 154
induction, x, 40, 125–27
indwelling, 120
inerrant, 154
infallible, 60, 62, 71, 152, 154–55
infinite, 120
inorganic, 41

inspiration, 139, 144, 150, 153, 155, 158
intelligent being, 15, 29
intelligent design, xiii, 23, 157, 170–97
interactive design, 191–92
invisible, 74–75, 78, 103
ions, 135
Islam, 2, 76
Israel, 119, 138, 145–47, 149–50, 154

Jacob, Margaret, 57
Jackson, Thomas, 38
Jesus Christ, x, 119, 120, 165
Jewish, 74, 76, 111–12
Job, 42, 94
Johnson, Phillip, 174, 178
Johnson, Samuel, 39
Jones, Scott, 127
Josephus, 142
Judaism, 2
judgment, 55, 65, 150
jurisprudence, 60
justice, 32, 73, 148
justification, 76

Kagam, Jerome, 203
Kant, Immanuel, 108, 115
Käsemann, Ernst, 120
Kelly, G. B., 119
kenosis theory/model, xi
Kepler, Johannes, 6, 85, 110, 188
King, Lord Peter, 129
kingdom of God, 77, 118
Kingsley, Charles, 194
Kitcher, Philip, 183
Kitzmiler v, Dover Area School District, 183
Knight, David M., 18
knowledge, 54, 68, 70, 76, 90, 98–101, 111, 107, 124–25, 127–28, 130–31, 135, 184, 190
knowledge, Browne's Scale of, 63–64
knowledge, evident-based, 63

knowledge, faith-based, 78, 80
knowledge, field of, 13
knowledge, mathematical, 60
knowledge, physical, 40
knowledge, practical (*ars*), 10
knowledge, nature of, 17
knowledge, religious, 39
knowledge, sensory-based, 72, 74
knowledge, spiritual matters, 77
knowledge, system of, 88, 123
knowledge, testimony-based, 60, 63–64
Kuhn, Thomas, 27, 123, 129, 139–40
Kusukawa, Sachiko, 17
Kuyper, Abraham, 190

La Voisier, 6
Lakatos, Imre, 13, 27, 123–24, 126, 128
Lamarck, Jean baptiste, 157
Lang, Bernhard, 28
Larkin, Francis, 5
law, 135, 140
law of motion, 51
Law, William, 39
Lee, James W., 4–5
legends, 151
Leibnitz, 38, 191
Lesch, K. P., 203
Liberal Arts, 10
liberty, 32–33, 76
life-giving, 89, 116
life processes, 164
light, 110, 112, 146
Lindberg, David C., 7, 13, 47, 85–86
linguistic, 125
literal interpretation, 158
living beings, 164
living things, 112
living organism, 158, 162
Locke, John, 5, 39–41, 72, 77, 124, 126, 128, 131, 134
Lodahl, Michael, ix, xii,
logic, 10, 128–29, 189

logical positivism, ix
Lord's Supper, 115–16
love, x, 76, 98, 101, 103–4, 156, 162, 166
Lovejoy, Arthur O., 5
Low-Church, 42, 47, 48
Lucretius, 43
Lutheran, 17

machine, 55–56, 89, 92–93, 97, 100, 105, 109, 183
MacIntyre, Alasdair, 199, 206–9
macroevolution, 160
Madden, Deborah, 8
Maddox, Randy L., xii, 8, 24, 28, 35, 82, 185, 187, 211
Madonnia, Raphael Sistine, 107
magic, 114
magisterial, 33
Malebranche, Nicholas, 39, 41
Malony, H. Newton, 56
Malthus, Thomas R., 163, 166
Mansion, Neil A., 196
Marion, Sarah D., xiii
Mary, 165
material world, 53
material, 54, 67, 70, 108, 138, 145, 173
materialism, 43, 55, 73, 173–74
mathematics, 7, 9–11, 62–64, 82–83, 86, 105, 110, 131, 154
Mather, Cotton, 38
matter, 55, 62, 112, 120
Maximus, the Confessor, 110
Maxwell, James, 13
Mayr, Ernst, 157–58
McDannell, Colleen, 28
McMullin, Ernan, 196
mechanical accounts of motion/ nature, 12, 90, 94, 97
mechanical clock/ watchmaker, 82–83, 86, 98, 109
mechanical theism, 23,
mechanism, 192–93
medicine (medical), 8, 55–56, 78, 186

medieval theology, 46
Meeks, M. Douglas, 28
Meltzoff, Andrew, 200–202, 209
memory, 67, 111–12, 205
Mendel, 183
Menninga, Clarence, 143
Merchant, Carolyn, 33
Mercury, Orbit of, 126
Mesopotamian, 141, 145–47, 155
metaphor, 46
metaphysical hypothesis, 14
metaphysics, x, 10, 116–17, 128
meteors, 19
method, hypothesis based, x
method, radio-metric, 149
method, theological, xii, 126
methodology, hypothetico-deductive, 9, 14
Methodism, 4, 43, 56–57, 66, 77, 127, 129–30, 134, 150–51, 211
microcosms, 31, 87
microorganism, 157
Middle East, 2
Miles, Sara J., 54
Miley, John, 139, 151
millennium, 147
Miller, J. Maxwell, 147
Mills, William Harrison, 4
miracles, 68
mission, holistic, 35
modern atheism, 23
modern dilemma, 42
modernity, 16, 26, 139, 140, 142, 153, 170, 174, 193
modernity, post, 16, 139
modernity, pre, 16, 126–27
modernism, 5, 109, 144
molecule, 108
Moltmann, Jürgen, xii, 106–21, 161
money, 34, 184
moon, 141–42
moral, 17, 22, 42, 60, 64, 68, 71, 74, 80, 152, 208
Morgan, Thomas, 20

Morris, Henry M., 143–44, 158–62, 165
Morris, Simon Conway, 195
Morus, Iwan Rhys, 7, 9
Moses, 142, 147, 151
mosaic creation story, 66, 152
mother nature, 108
motor cortex, 201
multicellular bodies/organism, 164, 168
multiplication of species, 157
Murphy, Nancey, xi, 33, 193–94
Murray, Michael, 178–79, 185, 191, 195
music, 10, 87, 92
myth, 122, 145, 147

Nahor, 147
nations, 166
natural atheism, 45
natural creation, 48
natural cause, 66, 177
natural history, 54
natural knowledge, 48, 87, 93
natural law, 13, 17–18, 37, 173
natural light, 49
natural mechanism, 177
natural oddities, 81
natural processes, 172, 93
natural religion, 64–65
natural selection, 157–58, 162–65, 167, 173
natural species, 19
natural systems, 55, 195
natural theology, 17–20, 23, 46, 51, 56, 96, 111, 115, 180, 189
natural world, 10, 17, 27, 30, 33, 38, 43, 46, 58, 74, 82, 176, 181, 185
naturalism, 173–78, 186–87, 191, 193, 196
nature, 10, 84–85, 92, 95–104, 108–9, 111–13, 116–17, 152, 177, 183, 193, 195
nature, academic study of, 10

nature, animated, 45
nature, empirical, 116
nature, exploitation of, 35
nature, harmony of, 30
nature, law of, 51, 179
nature, materialistic account of, 15
nature, necessity of, 21
nature, operation, 85
nature, scientific account of, 44
nature of the universe, 11
nature of spiritual beings, 16
Nauta, L., 15
Needham, 48
neocortex, 210
nerves, 79
neural processes, 202
neurobiology, 33, 200, 205
neurodevelopment, 199
neuron, 201, 209
neuroscience, xiii
New Testament, 87, 15, 166
Newell, Arlo F., 153
Newton, Isaac, 6–7, 9, 11–15, 18, 37, 39–40, 46–50, 52, 82, 85–86, 97, 126, 131, 183
Newtonian (Newtonianism), 41, 49, 84, 95–96, 129, 189
Nieuwentyt, Bernard, 20
night, 111
Noah, 143, 148, 158
Nobis, H. N., 109
nomic regularities, 173, 179
nonbeing, 119
nonmaterial, 54
non-western culture, 174
Norris, John, 39–41
Nouwen, Henri J. M., 166
Nucheotude Bases, 164
Numbers, Ronald L., 7, 47
Nuttal, Geoffrey, 69

O'Connor, Robert, 179
objective, 122, 140
ocean, 94

Oct, Philip W., 41
Old Testament, 42, 115, 145, 148
Olson, Richard G., 18, 39, 57
omnipotence, 159
omnipresence, 38
ontology, 130, 181
Opennheimer, Mark, 180
order, 98, 188
organic, 41, 157
organism, 41, 108, 158, 168, 178
Oriental, 153
Origin of Species, 43
original sin, 42
Orthodox (Orthodoxy), 50, 53
Otto, Marc, xii
Outler, Albert C., 47, 127

Paley, 51
pan-psychic, 12
pantheistism, 49
paradise, 118, 147
Parker, Simon, 145
pathology, 206
Paul, 114, 120
Peirce, Charles Sanders, 184
Pellowe, William C. S., 5–6
Pennock, Robert T., 183
People of God, 153
peoples, 166
perfect being, 29
perfection, 82, 116, 132–33
personal piety, 186
Peter, 165
Peters, 33
Pettit, Norman, 69
phenomena, 19, 87, 93, 107, 177, 179, 189
phenomena, natural, 38, 44
philosophy, 9, 10, 48, 124, 207
philosophy, Christian, 178
philosophy, Latin, 116
philosophy, materialistic, 174
philosophy, mechanistic, 83, 90, 95–97, 102

philosophy, modern, 78
philosophy, moral, 10
philosophy, natural, 3, 10–16, 18–19, 31, 33, 37, 40–41, 43, 47, 49–50, 57, 58–82, 84–87, 89, 92, 95–99, 103, 187–88
philosophy, Newtonian, 49, 95
philosophy of science, post-positivistic, 177
physical matter, 12
physical psychology, 31
physical senses, 54
physical world/universe, 131, 151
physico-theology, 18, 34, 50, 84
physics, 10, 13, 19, 48, 62, 84–87, 95, 130, 193
physics, contemporary particle, 196
physiology, 41, 44, 55, 113, 203
physis, 116
piety, 37, 42
pietistic theology, 57
Pinnock, Clark, 195
Placher, William C., 166
planet, 126, 141, 146
planetary motion, 86–87
Plato (Platonic), 107, 113
Pluche, Noel, 84
Polkinghore, John, xi, 23, 110, 112, 190, 193–96
Polyani, Michael, 123–24, 126, 128
polygenesis, 147
Pope, Alexander, 39
Pope, William Burt, 139, 150–51, 153
Popkin, Richard, 59
Poppe, Kenneth, 172
population, 149, 157, 163, 165
Porter, Roy, 11
power, 46, 95, 108
practice, 153–54
pragmatism, 107
predestination, 132–33
pre-Enlightenment (pre-Modern), 125–26
pre-Fall, 29, 44

prefiguration, 121
pre-history, 138
prevenient (preventing) grace, x–xi, 65, 72–74, 79, 82, 100–101
Priestley, Joseph, 37, 51
Priestly, Writer, 6, 145–46
Prigogine, Ilya, 112
primeval ancestors, 148
primeval history/chaos, 143, 146
Principia Mathematica, 10–13, 15
principle of life, 89, 97
principle of logic, 129
principle of self-motion, 53
principle of sufficient reason, 193
probability, 59
prophecy, 68
Protestant (Protestantism), 17, 61–62, 74, 76, 153
providence, 22, 34, 37, 47, 50–53, 88–89, 100–101, 110, 190
providential governing of nature, 195
providential superintending of universe, 191
psychotherapy, 199, 205
psychology, 199–200, 204
psychosomatism, 109
ptolomaic system, 125–26
Ptolemy, Claudius, 141
Puritan, 46, 71, 85–86
Pythagorean doctrine, 141

Quaker, 134
Quantum Divine Action (QDA), 194
quantum indeterminacy, 195
Quartz, Steven, 202–4, 209

race, 154
Ramsay, Andrew, 51
random genetic mutation, 173
randomness, 195
ratiocination, 74
rationalism, 127
rationalistic Orthodoxy, 57
Ratzsch, Del, 183, 190

Ray, John, 20, 22, 30, 34, 38
reality, 11, 64, 82, 103, 118, 122, 125, 128, 196
reason, 17, 20, 34, 39–40, 42, 48–49, 56–57, 67, 72–73, 80, 92, 93, 100, 105, 108, 111, 117, 127, 130, 134, 191
reasoning, analogical, 64
reasoning, practical, 207
reasoning, religious, 73, 84
reasoning, speculative, 77
reconciliation, 76
redemption, 28, 42, 102, 119–20, 150, 154, 159
reductionism, 183, 193
reductive physicalism, 192
Reformers, 17
Reid, Thomas, 39
Reill, Peter Hanns, 11
relational theology, 194
religion(s), 2, 60–61, 65, 70, 112, 123–24, 137, 170
religious, 9, 14, 64, 151–52, 177, 180, 190
religious faith, 1
religious tradition, 2
Renaissance theology, 46
repentance, 76, 187
reproduction, 163, 168, 173
revelation, 17, 43, 49, 54, 64, 74, 100–101, 109, 111, 113, 123, 150, 178, 196
Revelation, Book of, 166
revelation, natural, 17
rhetoric, 10, 20
Rice, Richard, 195
Ripley, 90
Robertson, John, 51
Rogel, Samuel J., 56
Roman Catholicism, xii
Rosser, Aelred R., 166
Royal Society of London for Improvement of Natural Knowledge, 34, 86–87, 103

RNA, 164
Runyon, Theodore, 124
Rutherforth, Thomas, 78
Russell, Robert J., 194

Sable, P., 205
sacramentalism, 116
Sanders, John, 195
salvation (salvific), x, 18, 27, 61, 76, 78, 119, 132, 153–54, 189
Saran, Nahum M., 147–48
Schleiermacher, Friedrich, 199, 206, 208–9
Schofield, Robert E., 6, 82, 84, 87
Schore, Allen, 205
Schreiner, Susan Elizabeth, 17
science (study of nature), 36, 111, 123, 135, 140, 144, 154, 172, 174
science, atheistic, 159, 162
science, Chinese, 112
science, creation, 143
science, history of, 6
science, Indian, 112
science, medical, 78
science, modern, 7, 33, 35
science, nature (Natural), 16, 33, 180, 185, 190
science, mathematical, 51
science, mechanistic natural, 42
science, Newtonian, 42
science, philosophy of, 9, 27
science, progress of, 37
science, sociology, 9, 183
science of mind, ix
scientia, understanding of reality, 10–11
scientific, creationism, 143, 159
scientific models, 16
scientific Orthodoxy, 184
scientific paradigm/method, 27, 124, 156, 181
scientific racism, 184
scientific reductionism, 108
scientific revolution, 109, 139

scientism, 26, 55
Sebundus, Raimundus, 110
Second Coming, 75
Secondary Causes, 54
Sejnowski, Terrence, 202–4, 209
self-sensation, 63
self-transcendent, 117, 120
sensation, 55
sense-data, 67
Shamash, 146
Shannon, C., 203
Shapin, Steven, 49
Shapiro, Barbara J., 59–62, 65–66, 72, 75
Sheldrake, Rupert, 111
Shem, 147
Siegal, J. M., 205
signs, 111, 113, 115, 119
sin, 133, 166
skepticism, 50, 151
Sloane, Hans Sir, 87
Smith, George, 145
Smolin, Lee, 130
social sciences, ix, 202
social structure of the church, 211
Socinianism, 80
solar system, 85, 130
son (Jesus), 101
soteriology, 154
soul, 17–18, 40, 54–55, 67, 78–79, 83, 89, 91, 109, 113, 117, 120, 131, 152
Southgate, Christopher, 1
sovereign, 32
space, 141, 164
Spalding Gentlemen's Society, 39
Sparks, Kenton L., 145–46
species (Forms), 110
Speiser, E. A., 146
sphere, 125
spirit(s), 55, 75, 82, 120–21, 154
spirituality, 121, 209
spiritual beings, 28, 121
spiritual formation, xiii, 198
 spiritual knowledge, 48

spiritual maturity, 199, 206
spiritual rebirth, 187
spiritual senses, 54, 77, 79–80, 134–35
spiritual transformation, x
spiritual world, 46, 74–75, 77, 79
Sroufe, L. A., 204–5
Stafford, Gilibert W., 153
stars, 112, 141–42, 146
Stengers, Isabella, 112
Stenmark, Mikael, 26
Stephen, Leslie, 2–3, 6, 9
stewardship, 34–35, 63, 66, 68
Stewart, W. Christopher, xiii
Stillingfleet, Edward, 24, 62, 65, 129
Stoeger, William R., 194
Stone, Lawson G., 147
Strawn, Brad, 200
Strong, A. H., 152
substance, 143
Sumarian story, 147–48
sun, 141–42, 146
Suomi, Stephen J., 203
supernatural, 37, 53, 124, 131, 134
superstition, 7
sustainer, 53
Swift, Jonathan, 39
syllogism, 62, 64, 127
symbol, 109
synthesis, 66–67
Syrian Fathers, 110
system of belief, 76

Tanzella-Nitti, Guiseppe, 109
Taylor, Stephen, 17
technology, 33, 108, 174
teleology, 176
telescope, 87
Telford, A. M. John, 56
terrestrial life, 159
testimony, 135
theism, 49, 175, 186, 189, 191, 194, 196–97
Theism, Open, 194–95

theocentrism, 35
theodicy, 29
theogony, 145
theology, traditional, 27
theory, attachment, xiii
theory, dynamic inspiration, 139, 150–51, 153–54
theory, heat kinetic, 182
theory, quantum, 129, 131, 134
theory, hypothetical, 7
theory of learning. 202
theory of mind, 201
theory of motion, 41
theory of natural selection, 162–65
theory of relativity, 126, 129, 131
theory of the universe, Copernican, 139–41
Thompson, Bert, 143–44
Thorsen, Donald, 134
Tilloston, John, 24, 62, 65
time, 141, 149, 157, 184, 190
Toulmin, Stephen, 26
typology, 46
tradition, 27, 49, 118, 121, 127–30, 145, 173
transcendent, 49, 117, 120–21, 179
transfiguration, 68, 110
Trial Scopes, 5
Trinity, 50, 73
Trivers, Robert L., 164
truth(s), ix–x, 32, 40, 46, 55, 62, 64, 67, 73, 75, 124, 131, 134, 141, 151, 191
tsunami, 115, 118

universal, 30, 67, 177
universe, xi, 10, 28, 55, 83, 85, 87, 89, 94–95, 97, 100, 103, 105, 110–11, 119, 121, 130, 140–41, 143–44, 146, 151, 158–60, 166, 173, 178, 189–91, 192–93
universe, sun-centered, 86
universe, nature of, 11
Utilitarianism, 108

Ultimate Being (God), 16
ultimate spiritual beings, 28
ultimate, 27, 108

values, x, 143
Van der Meer, J. M., 182, 191
Van Leeuwen, Henry G., 24, 59–60, 62
Van Till, Howard J., 143–44, 177–79, 196
Vanderjagt, A., 15
Vatican Council, First, 136
Vatican Council, Second, 115
Venus, 126
violence, 108
volcanoes, 44
voluntarism, 49, 76
Von Uexdüll, Jakob, 106, 109
Von Weizsäcker, Carl Friedrich, 112

Wainwright, W., 17
Wallace, Alfred Russell, 163
Wallace Jr., Dewey D., 18
Walsh, John, 17
Walter, Maxine, 33
Walton, John H., 146–47
war, 115
Ward, Seth, 62, 65
water, 19, 93, 141–42
Watkins, Owen C., 69
Watson, 139
Watts, Isaac, 39
wealth, 66
Webster, 85
Wehr, G., 113
Welker, Michael, 118, 208
Wesley, Charles, 31
Wesley, John, *passim*
wesleyan quadrilateral, x, 27, 127, 134
Wesphall, Richard S., 47
Westermann, Claus, 148
Western culture/worldview/society, 1, 117, 153, 172–74
Westfall, Richard S., 85, 141

White, Andrew Dickson, 3, 6, 9, 43
White, S. S., 153
Wilcox, David L., 148
Wilde, C. B., 49
Wiley, H. Orton, 139, 153
Wilkins, John, 60, 62, 65
Williams, Perry, 9, 58, 188
Willow Creek Church, 198, 206, 211
Wilson, Captain, 131
wisdom, 46, 84–85, 89, 95, 99, 110, 187–88
Wolt, Peter, 130
women preachers, 27
Wood, Paul, 23
Wolterstorff, Nicholas, 17, 189
wonder, 88, 98, 99–101, 103
world, 51, 53, 81, 88, 89, 92, 98, 104, 109–10, 114–15, 118, 120, 126, 131, 142, 144, 147, 155, 167, 191, 194
Worldview, 117, 173, 175–76, 180–81, 187, 190, 196
worship, 88, 98, 99–101
Wykstra, Stephen J., 181–82, 190

yin-yang, 117
Young, Davis A., 143–44, 149

Zijlstra, Ton, 210
Zinzendorf, Count, 131
zoo, 87